Pain and Joy

in intimate relationships

By the same author

Lives People Live:
A Textbook of Transactional Analysis
(Wiley 1980)

How To Choose A Mate
(Marion Boyars 1981)

Discover Your Real Self
(Hutchinson 1983)

Okay Parenting
(Judy Piatkus 1991)

Mavis Klein
Pain and Joy
in intimate relationships

Marion Boyars
London · New York

Published in Great Britain and the United States
in 1993 by Marion Boyars Publishers
24 Lacy Road, London SW15 1NL
237 East 39th Street, New York, NY 10016
Distributed in Australia by
Peribo Pty Ltd., Terrey Hills, NSW

© Mavis Klein 1993

All rights reserved.
No part of this publication may be reproduced, stored in a retrieval system or transmitted in any form or by any means, electronic, mechanical, photocopying, recording or otherwise except brief extracts for the purposes of review, without prior written permission of the publishers.

Any paperback edition of this book whether published simultaneously with or subsequent to, the casebound edition is sold subject to the condition that it shall not by way of trade, be lent, resold, hired out or otherwise disposed of without the publishers' consent, in any form of binding or cover other than that in which it was published.

British Library Cataloguing in Publication Data
Klein, Mavis
  Pain and joy in intimate relationships.
  I. Title
158.2

Library of Congress Cataloging in Publication Data
Klein, Mavis
   Pain and joy in intimate relationships/Mavis Klein.
   Includes bibliographical references.
   1. Interpersonal relations. 2. Personality. 3. Intimacy (Psychology) I. Title.
HM132.K467   1992
158'.2--dc20   91-38881

ISBN 0-7145-2943-5 Original paperback

The right of Mavis Klein to be identified as author of this work
has been asserted by her in accordance with the Copyright,
Designs and Patents Act 1988.

Typeset in Baskerville
by Ann Buchan (Typesetters)
Printed by Itchen Printers Limited, Southampton.

Contents

Introduction   9

Being Human

Chapter 1: Human Consciousness   23
    Truth — Good and Evil — Fate and Free-will

Chapter 2: From Birth to Death   36
    Lifelong Issues — Birth to Six Months — Six to Twelve Months — One to Three — Three to Six — Six Years Old — Six to Twelve — Twelve to Sixteen — Sixteen to Twenty-one — Health and Pathology in the Functioning of the Ego States — Critical Ages in Adult Life

Being an Individual

Chapter 3: Life Sentences   84
    Messages and Decisions — Survival and Love — Life as Metaphor and Art — The Genius of the Unconscious — Honour Thy Father and Thy Mother? — The Uses of Pain

Chapter 4: Five Personality Types and Their Compounds   118
    Confirming Our Painful Decisions — Categorizing People — The Miniscript — The Five Personality Types (table) — Permissions of the Five Personality Types (table) — The Basic Decisions People Make (table) — Samenesses and Oppositeness Between the Five Personality Types (table) — Be Perfect — Hurry Up — Please — Try Hard — Be Strong — Some Typical and very Reliable Indicators of the Five Personality Types (table) — The Compounds of Personality

Chapter 5: Life Tasks Transmuting Pain into Joy — Be Perfect — Hurry Up — Please — Try Hard — Be Strong — Assets and Liabilities of the Five Personality Types (table)	171

Being a Couple

Chapter 6: Making Love Being Loving — How We Choose an Intimate Other — Re-forming Ourselves and Our Partners — Keeping Love Alive — Matching Metaphors	193
Chapter 7: The Enemies of Love Fear and Righteousness — Duty — Need — Expediency — Togetherness — Sex — The Five Faces of Righteousness (table)	216
Chapter 8: The Five Personality Types in Intimate Relationships Life and Love as a Game of Cards — Be Perfect — Hurry Up — Please — Try Hard — Be Strong	230
Chapter 9: Fifteen Couplings Pain and Joy in Intimate Relationships — Interpersonal Relationships — Table of Interpersonal Compounds	256
Chapter 10: Till Death Do Us Part? Life as Faction — Revenge is Sweet — Laughter and Forgetting — In Appreciation of Milan Kundera	272

Bibliography	288
Glossary	297
Index of Names	304
Index of Subjects	306

And all that is the lot of human kind
I want to feel within my inner self.

Goethe, *Faust*

Introduction

This book is for people who have high expectations of life and insistently go on asking 'why' about life in general and their own experiences in particular, although not necessarily as desolately as Nietzsche:

> Half of your life is done.
> And it was pain and error through and through.
> Why do you still seek on?
> Precisely this: I seek the reason why!

Reduced to its essence human life is a continuous, desperate bid to deny or to find compensation for the fact that we must die. To this extent we live most authentically and contentedly when we are explicitly fighting for our survival. But with full stomachs and in peace-time, our personal problems serve to evade the unbearable burden of facing our mortality head-on, by giving us 'causes' and 'fights' that, with enough determination, we can win. Struggling and eventually succeeding in overcoming our problems provides us with the necessary illusion that our will to survive can triumph.

All races and cultures throughout history have found in the quest to love and be loved the fantasied panacea against the actuality of death. Love is the ultimate metaphor for the ecstatic moments which people see as the justification for, and use as the rationalization of, the inbuilt need in us all to 'have something worth living for'. Yet in no experience of life is the platitude, 'You get what you pay for', a more certain truth than in love. The game of love is universally and timelessly renowned to be fraught with vulnerability and pain proportional to the joy that is being sought. Freud put it beautifully:

> One procedure . . . holds fast to the original passionate striving for a positive fulfillment of happiness. And perhaps it does, in fact, come nearer to this goal than any other method. I am, of course, speaking of the way of life which makes love the centre of everything, which looks for all satisfaction in loving and being loved. . . The weak side of this technique of living is easy to see; otherwise no human being would have thought of abandoning this path to happiness for any other. It is that we are never so defenceless against suffering as when we love, never so helplessly unhappy as when we have lost our loved object or its love.

In our ever-increasingly affluent Western world the two most popular pre-occupations that express our intense need to feel we are struggling to survive are the fear of ecological disaster and an increased degree of dissatisfaction and insecurity in our intimate relationships. While many books are currently being written and read that deal with commonplace but particular patterns of unhappiness in intimate relationships, it is my ambitious aim in this book to deal comprehensively with all the patterns of pain and joy that exist both within the hearts and minds of individuals and in their interactions with others. My presumption that I can achieve this aim derives from a theory of personality I have developed from fifteen years' experience as a psychotherapist in private practice. Specifically, my theory derives from the theory of 'the miniscript', established in the 1970's by Taibi Kahler; this is grounded in the theory of Transactional Analysis, the brain-child of Eric Berne who achieved fame with his best-seller, *Games People Play*; which, in turn, is grounded in Freudian psychoanalytic theory.

In my theory there are five basic personality types, ten compound types, and fifteen possible pairings of one type with another in interpersonal relationships. The dimensions of my theory were born and developed in my mind inductively; that is out of my noticing items of attitudes, thoughts, feelings and behaviour that seemed contingently to form five distinct clusters; but I have lately come to realize that these five clusters are not merely contingent but necessary manifestations of the irreducible issues in the human ego as I see it. Two of the five ego issues are alternative possible attitudes to life itself; the other three are the possible orientations to love.

In terms of 'provability' my theory, like all psychological theories, stands somewhere between the theories of physical science and Plato's Theory of Forms. It is that kind of theory whose truth or falsity may be assessed in terms of its accuracy when measured against the experience of the reader; it is not testable in terms of precision in measurable exactitude, which is appropriate only to the physical sciences.

Freud elucidated many mechanisms construed by the human mind to protect the ego from the pain of the knowledge of its mortality and all the pains derived from this knowledge: from the most determinedly repressive and primitive defence of denial, in which any price is worth paying for 'not knowing', to the most sophisticated and productive defence of sublimation, in which a maximum amount of available energy is deflected away from the self onto a 'higher purpose'. All of civilization and its constructs — art, philosophy, science, history — are the products of sublimation.

We all live out our lives shiftingly between denial and sublimation. In the name of being 'realistic' most people most of the time prefer the ease of denial with all of its stultification, to the struggle of sublimation with its rare moments of triumphantly achieved 'meaning'. Being 'realistic' is living in the certain, rational outer world, from which we can interact with each other with ease; but the 'reality' of this book is the uncertain, irrational, inner world of shame, doubt, guilt, fear, love and hate, through which we are so often thwarted in our longing to be understood by others.

Contrary to popular misapprehension, 'irrational' and 'illogical' are not synonymous. Indeed the irrational realm of the human mind conducts its affairs with such logical stringency as to put to shame the inconsistencies and contradictions with which our rational, 'reasonable', 'realistic' lives are fraught. The irrational mind does come to different conclusions from the rational mind, but once the superficially implausible assumptions of the irrational mind are discovered and known, its conclusions can be seen to be derived with thoroughly deductive rigor. The assumptions, arguments and conclusions of the irrational mind are the subject-matter of this book.

But before I can begin this book properly there is a confession I want and need to make to the reader: as well as being a psychotherapist, I am an astrologer. I hope, by the evidence in this book of my intelligence and sanity, I may play my part in furthering the acceptance of astrology amongst intelligent people who, at present, thoughtlessly reject it as superstitious hogwash. Also I have made some explicit use of astrology in this book, which needs justifying. So, herewith, I offer readers my intellectual autobiography by which, I hope, I will make myself clear. Those willing to 'suspend their disbelief' are welcome to skip straightaway to Chapter 1.

When I was a psychology undergraduate, amongst the plethora of mirror-drawing, statistics and cat physiology which were anathema to my quest to learn about the human mind, there were two theories I learned that made it all worthwhile. These were the basic Freudian theory of child development, personality and pathology, and the reinforcement theory, operant conditioning, of the experimental psychologist B.F. Skinner. Recalcitrant student that I was, I sought to appease my teachers by my expression of enthusiasm for these two theories of mental functioning whose truths, it seemed to me, happily co-existed side by side, each available for providing appropriate understanding in different contexts. But bearing allegiance to both these theories only increased the irritation of my teachers towards me. These two theories, I was peremptorily informed, were totally incompatible with one another and I had better make up my mind to 'believe in' one or the other, or I would probably fail my exams. The true believers in psychoanalysis dismissed operant conditioning as dangerous, mechanistic, simplistic, dehumanizing, trivial nonsense; while the committed experimentalists went to considerable lengths to persuade me that psychoanalysis was pernicious, unscientific, tautological, mythological rubbish. I got my degree by the skin of my teeth, breathed a sigh of relief, and from then on have happily defined myself as an anti-academic intellectual.

Then, in 1972, I discovered Transactional Analysis, the theory of Eric Berne, which instantly became the third psychological enthusiasm of my life. It was so clear, so precise, so concise, so tangible. I took up its practice as a serious hobby and two years later became a qualified Transactional Analyst and practising psychotherapist, which I have been ever since. Only some time into my training in Transactional Analysis did I suddenly realize that it was the brilliant amalgamation of psychoanalysis and operant conditioning that my unconscious had been patiently waiting to find.

TA is a child of psychoanalysis, and Eric Berne remained throughout his life committed to the central tenets of traditional Freudian theory, although he parted company with psychoanalysis as therapy. TA as a theory of personality may be thought of as a spin-off from TA as therapy, which evolved out of Berne's dissatisfaction with the slowness of psychoanalysis in curing people of their psychic ills. The slowness of psychoanalysis resides in the time it takes for the analyst to facilitate the analysand in penetrating to his or her core pre-verbal reality, knowledge of which, psychoanalysis insists, is the necessary precursor of a satisfactory resolution of the patient's consequential conflicts in the present. Out of his creative struggle to disavow the necessity for the very prolonged process of reaching to the depths of our pre-verbal selves effectively to solve our present problems, Berne realized that the core existential reality of any human being is accessible through the conscious ego, and can be revealed by a skilled psychotherapist in a few hours rather than a few years!

This is so, argued Berne, because the 'realities' of any individual's conscious ego are very closely analogous to his or her original pre-verbal realities. The 'repetition compulsion' ensures that the frames of reference and 'truths' construed consciously by the child roughly speaking in his primary school years (the 'palimpsest') are made by the child selectively perceiving events and facts that accord with his already rigidly determined pre-verbal frames of reference (the 'protocol'). Only in cases of very severe repression, where the usual 'defences' of the ego are absent, is traditional psychoanalysis needed; in all other cases, fully conscious confrontation of and dialogue with the ego states of the palimpsest — Parent, Adult and Child, derivative from the unconscious protocol of Superego, Ego and Id — is all that is needed to relieve a patient of his psychological ills. And so, over the past twenty-five years, it has proven to be.

The concept of the ego states and the delineation of their natures is undoubtedly the central genius of TA theory. But what makes TA more than 'psychoanalysis without the unconscious' is its concept of 'strokes'. Strokes are reinforcement, and a singularly powerful component of TA as theory and therapy is the use it makes of its understanding of 'positive' and 'negative' strokes and their equal potency in reinforcing behaviour. That is, contrary to 'common sense', TA knows that punishment does not work. Punishment merely suppresses undesirable behaviour momentarily while it is being inflicted; in the long run, punishment actually increases the frequency and intensity of the behaviour it seeks to eliminate. This is pure operant conditioning, the learning theory of B.F. Skinner, the proof of whose theory is sufficiently contained in his having used it successfully to teach pigeons to play ping-pong! TA is a genius blend of psychoanalysis and operant conditioning that overcomes the limitations of each of them in their separateness and, as theory, makes sane the previous fragmentation of Psychology into theories which were either precise and meaningless or profoundly true but inoperative. TA is the bastard child of psychoanalysis and operant conditioning. It is both 'hard' and 'soft', diagnostic and prescriptive, subjective and objective, holistic and atomistic.

And so it was that I settled down into being a TA psychotherapist, with a deeply satisfying conceptual frame of reference that gave me the professional confidence of knowing what I was doing and of being able to justify my taking money from people for doing it. Until, in 1978, I had my mind blown again.

One day a man who had been in one of my therapy groups for two years came to a session and said he had just consulted an astrologer and please would I listen to a tape-recording he had made of the consultation. Very sceptically, but indulgently, I agreed and turned it on and listened to it with half an ear while attending also to the late-afternoon cacophany of my children and their demands. Within five minutes I was astounded. The astrologer, Howard Sasportas, with no knowledge of my patient other than his time, place and date of birth, had already said everything — and more — about him that I had discovered over two years of laborious analysis. I consulted the same astrologer for myself and was overwhelmed by the authenticity and depth of what he told me about my character and my life experiences. In the following weeks and months I devoured shelves of books on astrology. I had never before been so excited; everything was changed.

In my excitement I felt I had to share my revelation with everyone around me, including my patients. Those who, from past experience, trusted the efficacy of my understanding and methods tended smilingly to indulge this amusing aberration in me. Others who newly consulted me sometimes expressed anger that they had been misled into thinking they were consulting a competent psychotherapist only to find themselves in the presence of a mumbo-jumboist. I was embarrassed by myself and, notwithstanding that I had to earn my living, I seriously considered that, in all conscience, I could not continue the hypocrisy of practising as a psychotherapist. The horoscope determined everything: the supposed influence of early childhood experiences was a total lie.

However, I could not deny that in my work I was still experiencing daily the tangible and metaphorical consequences of the imprinted experiences of the first few years of our lives; and especially the profoundly formative influence of the Oedipus complex in the years between three and six, which I saw, in practice as well as theory, not only moulds the shape of our individual sexual propensities but is also a crucial determiner of our world views. At the conclusion of the Oedipus stage of our development we each emerge like everybody else in the generality of our experience and different from everybody else according to the unique specificity of our own family circumstances. The eternal triangle of Mother, Father and Child struggling together through the issues of sex, aggression, rivalry, jealousy, blame, identification and responsibility makes us all alike and all different. All this, too, made comprehensive sense and 'worked'. But how could we be comprehensively understood both in terms of the a priori determinism of our natal horoscopes, defined at the moment we take our first breath, and as the consequence of the contingent, fortuitous experiences of our first six years of life? From being a thoughtlessly, thorough-going environmentalist, committed to the view of the new-born brain as a *tabula rasa*, I had crashed headlong into 'nature'.

It would have been easy if all I had to do was acknowledge some specific characteristics in human beings as innate, leaving my assumption that 'all the rest' is conditioned intact. But it seemed I was being forced to choose whether to commit myself to the belief that everything is innately pre-determined or that everything is conditioned in our earliest months and years of life.

The struggle to reconcile these apparently incompatible opposites has led me into many by-ways, some of which have turned into the cul-de-sacs of various timeless philosophical problems. But, mundanely, I am now at ease in using both TA and astrology, side by side, and slipping from one to the other whenever I feel like doing so, because I now understand them to be two languages; and my knowledge of both, rather than one, extends the boundaries of what I am able to think and to say.

Within very broad limits any language is capable of expressing any thought that any human being wishes to utter: we are all one species. However, environmental conditions, both physical and psychological, have created differences in the relative importance and pertinence of various elements in different peoples' experiences of life. And these differences are reflected in the vocabulary of any given culture-language. A centrally important issue will have invoked the creation of minutely discriminating words to match the need to perceive vital distinctions. Thus the Eskimos, I am told, have about twenty words for our one word 'snow'; and the little Yiddish I know enables me, for example, to describe varieties of fools with subtlety and gusto that English cannot match.

The language of astrology has been developed by every known civilization, which bears witness to its capacity to express universal constructs of the human mind that cannot be expressed in any ordinarily spoken lanauage. At core, it is a form of mathematics, an algebra, the 'x's' and 'y's' of which can be used to solve many of the 'arithmetical' problems of life that would otherwise be insoluble. In the ancient world astrology 'understood' much that can now be understood more conveniently and precisely by materialistic science and by such psychological theories as psychoanalysis; but only religions — and probably only the mystical aspects of religions — bid fair to compete with astrology in its ability to satisfy mankind's need to describe and resolve our spiritual needs.

In our Western culture, until the rise of scientific materialism in the seventeenth century, astrology's truth was never questioned because it was completely consistent with every person's acceptance of himself and his life as participating in the cosmos as a whole, in accordance with God's immutable will. However, by the beginning of this century science could apparently account for everything in materialistic terms. The earth was no longer the centre of the universe, man no longer a special species, and indeed was not even able to know the depths of his own mind. Thus God — in man's image — sitting super-powerful on a throne in the sky, was undermined. So too was astrology, which became increasingly marginal and unrespectable.

But in the course of this century the existential consequences of Heisenberg's uncertainty principle, Einstein's theory of relativity and post-Einsteinian cosmologies, full of uncertainties and such nihilistic horrors as Black Holes, have permeated the everyday consciousness of very large numbers of people. Without God to fall back on, we are left trembling at Nothing.

My own view is that we cannot manage without God, or some transcendental alternative, because of our deepest need to believe in a meaning and purpose in the face of pain and death. And I predict that within the next century astrology will become the umbrella under which all the monotheistic religions will be contained and united in a new holism that creates a new blend of materialism and mystery and determinism and choice that we so timelessly crave.

This philosophical aside is only relevant to this book to the extent that astrology has added a religious dimension to my thinking which may be seen by the reader to be a pervasive background to all that I have to say. In a nutshell, it means that I subscribe to the view that 'the bottom line' condition for our achievement of contentment in our lives is our choice to 'go with' and appreciate whatever we are and whatever befalls us out of our belief that there is positive 'meaning' and 'purpose' in everything that is, notwithstanding that it is beyond our limits fully to apprehend it. Astrology has made me specifically aware that to some extent we are able to choose the level — physical, emotional, intellectual or spiritual — on which our necessary experiences will manifest.

Psychologically speaking, TA as language is my 'native' and preferred everyday vernacular, especially my own personality typology, presented in this book. The only point at which it was not possible to express all that I wanted to in TA was when it came to describing the general developmental stages of adult life (Chapter 2), at which point I have 'slipped into' astrology.

Some astrologers believe theirs is a mystical, holistic world, which can only be spoilt by the intrusion of scientific enquiry into its workings; but there are others, like me, who believe astrology is true in a scientific sense as well. I have listed a number of books in the bibliography that may serve to whet the appetites of readers who are presently skeptical, yet open-minded.

For any astrologers amongst my readers, my birth data are: 7.53 p.m. British Summer Time, September 24, 1937, Manchester, England; from which I am sure they will readily understand both the necessity and the fulfillment for me in the writing of this book.

Being Human

Chapter 1
Human Consciousness

Truth rates with God alone, and a little bit with me.
Yiddish proverb

Truth

All truth is created by the human mind. Without our consciousness of anything, it might as well not exist and, in fact, does not exist; from which discomfiting thought we can only be saved by positing the omnipresent, eternal mind of God which Bishop Berkeley went to such lengths to postulate. 'Truth' is the observation of and interpretation of 'facts'. The existence of our sense organs determines that we cannot avoid being constantly bombarded with facts; our physical and psychological survival in the material world and the world of people necessitates our collecting and interpreting clusters of facts into theories, which we call the truth. The number of facts in the universe is infinite; we don't need them all. Once we have experienced and interpreted into 'truth' a sufficient number of facts about matters pertaining to our continued existence in the context of our personal environment, we stop. Thereafter, our minds filter out the data received by our sense organs which are not relevant to or contradict the theories we have formulated. Those facts which subsequently bombard us which are irrelevant to our theories we shrug off as 'noise'; those which are incompatible with our formulated theories we deny — if necessary vehemently — until they 'go away'. In the rare instances where external conditions are so grossly unstable or the individual has some innate incapacity to formulate a minimum number of necessary theories out of his discrete experiences, the outcome is what we call 'insanity'.

By and large we have each formulated all our essential theories about the nature of the material world, our own existence and the nature of our relationships with others by the age of about six. Thereafter, some baroque flourishes may be added to the basic structure of our achieved frames of reference but, to all intents and purposes, our minds are now closed, and nearly every experience we subsequently allow ourselves to have is a recapitulation, literally or metaphorically, of 'evidence' for the truths we have established.

So contrary to the common-sense view, 'happenings' in people's lives are chosen by them. People happen to events in as many ways as events can reinforce established beliefs in people's minds.

> You think me the child of my circumstances:
> I make my circumstances. *Emerson*

But our minds are not completely closed, either individually or collectively, for two reasons.

Firstly, it can happen that facts incompatible with our theories insistently 'will not go away', and we are willy-nilly forced to extend or totally reformulate our theories, however uncomfortable and frightening the process. Once in a while in human history the collective mind is assaulted by an Einstein who challenges the profoundly held 'certainties' of a Newton. Although, at first, we fight tooth and claw to resist the new fact with denial, ridicule, inquisitions and any other weapons we can muster, in due course, when its time has come, an idea will be heard. 'Truth' is adjusted to accommodate it, and it becomes the basis of a new orthodoxy; until the vagaries of a determinism beyond our understanding deem it, too, to have had its day. 'It is the customary fate of new truths to begin as heresies and to end as superstitions' (Huxley).

In the lives of individuals, too, contingencies may sometimes, though rarely, arise from nowhere that force us, partly or wholly, to reformulate our meanings of life. From the testimonies of those individuals whose truths have been resoundingly shattered, forcing them to create new theories to live by, the precipitating experience seems nearly always to be one in which they nearly died in physical actuality or else suffered extreme traumas, such as being forcibly incarcerated or brainwashed so that they nearly died psychologically.

The second condition that keeps our minds from being completely closed is the quest to experience again the excitement of our earliest years, before we had yet decided on the life-preserving truths we would live by, and our survival still depended on the loving watchfulness of our caretakers. In our grown-up lives, the omnipresent, loving care that we normally received from our parents in infancy is no longer available, so the extent to which we can retrieve the irresponsible excitement of a theory-free existence is very severely circumscribed. And some people, who lack confidence in their ability to survive independently because of their inadequate 'existence theories', may actually seek and welcome incarceration in a prison or mental hospital — 'asylums' as they used more aptly to be called — where the constraints on their freedom are a price they are happily willing to pay for being kept safely alive.

Nonetheless, without wanting to die and having taken appropriate safety precautions, we desire to and do from time to time, choose to give ourselves the thrills of unpredictable and somewhat dangerous experiences:

The function of death is to put tension into life. . . . All our pleasurable experiences contain a faint yet terrible element of the condemned man's last breakfast.

Fowles

Most people select body experiences for such excitement: rock climbing, skiing, motor racing, riding the big dipper, etc. Intellectuals may be defined as those who choose 'mind-blowing' experiences, which are speculating on the possible invalidity of what they take for granted as truth in the realm of their favourite subject-matters. The most explicit basic training in adventurousness of the mind is offered by university departments of philosophy. There, eighteen to twenty-one-year olds, emerging into the world away from their families, who have given them basic, solid sets of theories by which to live their lives, may be further educated into realizing that all knowledge and all beliefs are actually tenuous and 'not proven'. By being intellectually shattered they are appropriately divested of smug righteousness associated with their well-adapted belief systems, while emotionally they remain securely attached to their beliefs. However, in young adults who, for whatever reasons, do not have secure and adaptive belief systems, exposure to philosophy may precipitate in them 'a nervous breakdown'. In my psychotherapeutic practice I also come across people who have, out of an unloving family background, construed for themselves a lonely and alienated belief system, masked as philosophical detachment. While becoming academic philosophers or lawyers may be an adaptive outlet for the way they are, if they are ever to form satisfactory superficial or intimate relationships with other people, they have to realize that philosophical detachment can only be authentic after a subjective attachment to 'relative' beliefs is established and lived by.

By and large, both physically and mentally, we venture only a short way from our places of safety and on very strong and tethered ropes; but without some risk we could not have the excitement we crave, so every now and again an irreparable injury to a person's body consequent on a physical adventure permanently changes his physical life. And every now and again an irreparable injury to a person's mind consequent on a mental adventure permanently changes his mental life, and out of which he may even write a book!

Thus 'truth' is forever a tentative 'as if' for as long as it works, both in the collective and the individual mind. Our truths are like balloons which contain the facts we breathe into them until they are stretched to their limit and burst. As each balloon bursts we start to blow up another, for we need our minimum number to clutch to avoid being sucked into the annihilating vortex of the ultimate Black Hole.

The separate balloons in our particular clutch exist compatibly but unrelatedly to each other, one or other being 'best' for the particular purpose of a given moment. Accordingly, there is, for example, no such thing as the correct definition of the table in front of me. It can equally validly and comprehensively be defined in terms of its physical properties, its chemical composition, its functional qualities, its colour, its shape, etc. Thus the more balloons we have the greater our versatility in our responses to the 'facts' of life.

And yet we long for one huge, unburstable balloon which will contain us and all our small balloons, but which will also exclude all Black Holes. Some people find this balloon and call it God; others are still seeking it in a mathematical formula they call Unifying Field Theory.

Good and Evil

As we are born, the first separated 'facts' we apprehend are our bodily experiences of contentment versus pain. We like contentment; we don't like pain. In due course, this basic dichotomy gets refined by further differentiation, and we become able to calibrate and name our experiences as different degrees and kinds of contentment and pain. We continuously struggle to maintain contentment and eliminate pain from our lives but we never succeed for long. So the first truth we seek in our lives is that which makes sense of these two facts, contentment and pain. Contentment becomes 'good' and pain becomes 'bad'. This basic dichotomy of good versus bad in the human psyche is the core concept in the psychoanalytic theory of Melanie Klein, who argues that from earliest infancy a baby projects this truth onto her mother, who is perceived by her as being divided into 'a good breast' and 'a bad breast'. (See Segal 289)

Soon we come to realize that our attempts to eliminate pain from our lives are essentially and repeatedly doomed to failure, and this realization becomes another fact that needs to be made sense of in terms of theory. That is, we require a meta-theory that explains to us how the pain we continuously experience is necessary. Even, and often especially, when we are most contented, the pain of our knowledge of our mortality continues to haunt us. 'Everybody wants to make pain interesting. . . It's impossible just to suffer pain, you have to suffer its meaning' (Roth). So the second essential theory we formulate invariably construes 'good' and 'evil' forces that permeate the universe. The unavoidable corollary to this truth is that, inasmuch as we ourselves are part and parcel of the universe, the good and evil forces of the universe must also be in us. Thus, irrespective of the variability of 'truths' espoused by different individuals and different cultures, no individual and no culture can manage life without the concepts of 'good and evil', 'blame and guilt', 'reward and punishment'. These concepts are the necessary foundation for all our individual and collective meanings-of-life.

> One thing only do I know for certain and that is that man's judgements of value follow directly his wishes for happiness.
> *Freud*

To the extent that we seek to evade the necessity to accept responsibility — badness and blameworthiness as well as goodness and praiseworthiness — in ourselves, we invent 'good luck' and 'bad luck'; by which concepts we acknowledge the necessary existence of 'good' and 'bad' in the universe while at the same time dissociating them from goodness and badness in ourselves: in effect we dissociate ourselves from the universe! In truth, the only authentic use of the world 'luck' is in reference to matters like just catching or just missing a bus. In only a few of such events the good and the bad luck cancel out to zero.

There may, of course, be no meaning of life; the universe may be ultimately chaotic. Espousing this possibility as a 'certainty' eliminates the need to make sense of pain. Pain becomes merely one of the contingent facts of life and no more explicable or inexplicable than any other. Everything is simply the way it is and neither good nor bad; so we are wasting our time asking why. '. . . There are no sins in the metaphysical sense but, in the same sense, neither are there any virtues' (Nietzsche). Non-reflective playing out of our lives in keeping with the biological propellants of our constitution is all. This is the way of life for other species. '. . . The animal kingdom manages its learning without anything that can really be called punishment' (Wren-Lewis); paradoxically, this is also the position of the mystic, whose achieved attitude is of joyously interpreting everything we experience as 'for no reason', just the way it has to be. The way of the mystic is called 'transcendental'; but the same way, when we refer to other species is not. This is so because mystics have transcended their fear of death and other, derivative, ego fears; animals don't have a conscious fear of death to transcend.

Our human life begins without any awareness of the separateness of ourselves from the universe. But from when we first say 'I' we become more and more consciously differentiated from everybody else: we develop our individualities, our egos. Our ego's self-esteem, by rights, should grow and grow until, fully assured of our individual worth, we begin to transcend our egos and, ideally, come full circle to oneness with the universe again, as achieved by the mystic.

The task of developing our egos is essentially the task of struggling through our fears which are manifest as our hang-ups. In the final analysis all our fears may be reduced to our fear of death. Knowledge of our mortality is the central pain of life and is universal, although each of us, in accordance with the individual differences between people, has specific fears and associated pains that we struggle to overcome. The struggle for a well-developed ego, which gives a sense of our own importance through our achievements, is a manifestation of our doomed-to-fail quest for immortality. As Freud taught us, each human being in his Id believes he is omnipotent, supremely attractive and immortal. Out of this universal trilogy in the Id, each person in his Ego has to come to terms with the opposite realities of his helplessness, ageing and death.

Yet the universal quest for 'meaning' in our lives bears witness to the fact that we never fully come to terms with the ultimate meaninglessness that death makes of all our mundane ego concerns. Some of us deny death by a belief in some form of eternal continuation of life; others seek a symbolic continuation of their lives after physical death by being remembered for their works or deeds; and most of us find some comfort in the knowledge of the survival of some of our genes in our children, grandchildren and further descendents. Mary Douglas, in her brilliant book *Purity and Danger*, cites a tribe who have even managed to 'prove' that nobody has to die. When members of this tribe are clearly close to death they choose to commit suicide, so those who survive them can go on believing in their freedom to be immortal if they so desire. The constructions of the human mind to reconcile desire with reality are apparently limitless! But one way or another the happinesses that are available to us in our limited lives are contingent on us living life as if it has meaning, even if it doesn't.

Thus the courageous confrontation and growth of our egos

is the principal task of our lives, for as long as it takes. The mystical position of detachment, which may well be the ideal goal for all of us, cannot be achieved pre-emptively. Nobody has yet transcended his or her ego without having an ego to transcend. And whatever categories and concepts our minds may prompt us to impose on the universe, one formulation is absolutely necessary, irrespective of culture or individuality, the something that rationalizes and justifies pain. And that something has to be 'good and evil' with its derivative moral constructs which polarize blame and responsibility, righteousness and guilt.

Fate and Free-will

'The problem of free-will' has always been available for the pleasure of mental masochists. It cannot be solved, only dis-solved. Like the matter of whether or not there is an overall meaning/purpose in our lives, the logic of the matter of 'free-will' is that, by definition, we cannot ever know. The existence or non-existence of 'meaning' and 'fate' are concepts that refer to a 'higher' state of consciousness than our own. By definition, the human brain is only capable of comprehending that which is less complex than itself; and, by definition, our concept of 'fate' refers to a 'meaning' more complex than we can apprehend, emanating as it does from a source whose power is greater than our own. So we can only solve the problem pragmatically, by living at the highest level of free-will available to us while accepting, from the evidence, that there are bound to be times in our lives when a higher consciousness than we are capable of mocks our lower level morality and conscious purposes. It is simply pragmatically the case that we live our lives most satisfactorily to ourselves when we behave as if our free-will is paramount.

As an unknown rabbi succinctly put it, 'We've got to believe in free-will, we've got no choice.'

However, notwithstanding that we may never know the nature of the ultimate level of purpose/meaning/free-will that determines all things (since it retreats from us in an infinite regress), it seems to be the case that we do get glimpses of the 'next level above us', at which level mundanely experienced incompatible opposites are contained in a higher unity. 'The knowledge of opposites is one' (Aristotle). Sometimes our glimpses of a higher realm are contained in an experience of serene knowledge that 'everthing is as it has to be'; such an experience is often the unexpected outcome of a long battle we have fought with an issue of 'good' and 'evil' in our mundane lives. Whether it be an event or a state of being, such moments in our lives fill us with a sense of wonder, are very memorable to us and have the power permanently to enhance our overall sense of well-being.

There is one aspect of our mundane existences in which a higher-level fatedness is very apparent, and that is in the matter of the determinism of our genetic constitutions. We all accept the immutable limits imposed on our lives by genetics, both in our definition of ourselves as the same as all other members of the species *homo sapiens* and in the summation of idiosyncratic characteristics by which we define ourselves as unique. In nearly everybody, the birth of a baby invokes a wondrous awe that pays homage to the inscrutable combination of 'chance' and 'necessity' immediately obvious in that new human being. His mother's eyes, his grandfather's forehead: Who or What ordained and Why, that it would not be his grandfather's eyes and his mother's forehead? Yet we also know in advance when, within usually narrow limits, he will get his teeth, reach puberty, go grey, lose his teeth, and die, just like all the rest of us.

What we understand and act on implicitly, whether or not we make this understanding fully articulate, is that the wondrous joy we experience at a birth is in the as yet totally unactualized potential contained in that new human being.

How great a number of genetically-determined characteristics there are to be realized beyond the shape of his eyes and his forehead! What will his inheritance enable him to do and to be? What will he want to do and to be? What can he and we do, as his potential unfolds, to fulfil rather than frustrate his desires within the bounds of the general assets and liabilities of his nature that were determined at the moment of his conception?

In asking these questions we discover that free-will is contained in the responses we choose to make to our fate.

> What we are equipped with is innate *propensities* that require environmental input for their realization. Thus, what we need to look for is a *combination* of the innate predispositions and the range of environments compatible with them. *Fox*

There are three broad categories of response to our fate: impotent, angry frustration; placid, unambitious acceptance; and creative struggle. These correspond to being five feet tall and wanting only to be an Olympic high jumper; having a beautiful voice and being content to sing only for oneself and the pleasure of a few friends; and in whatever realm of our being or doing, stretching ourselves to the very limits of our capacity or endurance to reconcile desire with 'reality' in achieving the nearly, but not quite, 'impossible'.

> Whatever limits we call Fate. . . But Fate has its Lord; limitation its limit. . . For though Fate is immense, so is Power, which is the other fact in the dual world, immense. If Fate follows and limits Power, Power attends and antagonizes Fate. . . To hazard the contradiction — freedom is necessary. . .
> If you believe in Fate to your harm, believe in it at least for your good. For if Fate is so prevailing, man is also part of it, and can confront fate with fate. *Emerson*

The third option, creative struggle, alone gives 'meaning' and 'purpose' to our lives, and can prevail from the largest to the smallest moments in our lives, from Michelangelo painting the ceiling of the Sistine Chapel to someone adding a cup of water to a pot of soup to cater for an unexpected guest. For each of us, the largest 'nearly impossible' is a private, deep-seated dream contained within the 'story of our life' and seen through the lens of our unique reality. It needs to be brought to the surface and articulated before the creative struggle for its fulfillment can begin.

> From the 'divine blessing' I will excerpt only this one significant passage: 'May every man meet again those images he once beheld as a child in the shimmering dream of the future'. This is an affirmation that childhood fantasies strive for fulfillment; the images are not lost, but come again in ripe manhood and should be fulfilled.
> *Jung*

Thus our freedom exists in our responses to what fate offers us. Our responses are our choices, and these have consequences. We cannot avoid making choices. Passivity is the self-delusion of 'no choice'; but, of course, it is a choice and like all others has consequences. Every moment of choice is the cause of the inexorable train of events that follows in its wake, to the natural conclusion of a 'happening' in our lives. 'The things that happen to a person are as characteristic of him as his deeds' (Peck). When a conclusion is painful we are loath to remember the moment of choice that determined it, although repression can never be complete, and often the knowledge that we have chosen a path to pain is manifest as an obsessive fear of that pain, too late, and a conscious struggle to avoid it. 'We choose our joys and sorrows long before we experience them' (Gibran). We actually do know, in our hearts, that we have made the choices which have led to their inevitable conclusions.

> Freedom is the content.
> Necessity is the form.
>
> *Jung*

In our most intense moments we are reduced to knowing, in all its simplicity, that we get exactly what we set out to get and so, what we deserve. 'Destiny is simply what we desire coming up to us in the disguise of what we deserve' (Barker). Why and how we often choose to get pain instead of joy is the central substance of this book.

Chapter 2

From Birth to Death

> They strive after happiness, they want to become happy and to remain so . . . on the one hand, at an absence of pain and unpleasure and, on the other, at the experiencing of strong feelings of pleasure. . . What we call happiness in the strictest sense comes from the (preferably sudden) satisfaction of needs which have been dammed up to a high degree, and it is from its nature only possible as an episodic phenomenon. When any situation that is desired by the pleasure principle is prolonged it only produces a feeling of mild contentment. We are so made that we can derive intense enjoyment only from a contrast and very little from a state of things.
> *Freud*

Lifelong Issues

The basis of all of our lives is that we are utterly self-seeking; yet we cannot fulfil our selfish wants without the help of others; so we are forced to pay homage to the fact that all the others are self-seeking too, and to give them some of what they want in order for them to be willing to give us some of what we want. Balancing 'giving' and 'taking' is the central preoccupation of all relationships. The experience of satisfaction in any particular relationship is largely based on the subjective perception that we have got this balance just right.

The quest for the just right balance also applies to the biological fact that we are homeostatic organisms, inescapably swinging between 'arousal' and 'quiescence' for as long as we are alive. Factually, this is all we actually do; but the human mind has at its disposal thousands of words, which it applies descriptively to the basic dichotomy of arousal and quiescence, and so creates for itself a large range of qualitatively discrete experiences. Our reaction to anything we experience is the product of arousal and evaluation. We are taught by our parents and other caretakers how to evaluate arousal by means of context: arousal when we haven't eaten for five hours becomes 'hungry'; when we haven't slept for sixteen hours, 'tired'; in response to a potentially life-threatening stimulus, 'frightened'; in anticipation of the fulfillment of desire, 'excited'; to the total blocking of desire, 'frustrated'; to the unexpected blocking of desire towards which we are already moving, 'disappointed'.

Pleasure is contained in the transitional moment of quiescence consequent on the fulfillment of desire, before the memory of the desire has quite faded and before the movement that is called being alive propels us into the chase after another desire. The intensity of any moment of pleasure is directly proportional to the intensity of desire that preceded it, as is the intensity of pain that may also be the conclusion of the chase, because no fulfillment of desire is guaranteed before it actually happens. We are inescapably bound to the essential biological reality that every degree of attained pleasure is the not-inevitable reward for our having risked an equal degree of pain.

The prototype for nirvana is the contentment of an infant at its mother's breast, which is the reward for the absoluteness of its pain preceding the fulfillment of that desire. The grown-up equivalent is in the ecstasy of sexual orgasm with a partner whom we passionately desire. Sexual desire and its fulfillment is the most sought after experience because the arousal before the fulfillment is also intensely pleasurable due to the unique cooperation in this experience of the sympathetic and para-sympathetic nervous systems, which sets sexual desire apart from all other arousal and, in the right context, may be evaluated as the condition in life whose ecstasy rivals the fear of death in its intensity.

In the beginning, it may be inferred, our first cry on being born is the expression of our first experience of painful, unfulfilled desire. We have emerged from the condition of having all our needs met without having to do anything; now we have to breathe and cry. We have no concept of ourselves or of anyone else: the universe and ourselves are one. The only distinctions we make are of total satisfaction, in which case we are either feeding or asleep, or of total pain, in which case the universe consists wholly of our screaming desire for food or the elimination of bodily pain.

The life cycle of the human being naturally progresses from birth to death, from unknowing one-ness with the universe, to individuation, to knowing one-ness with the universe again. The difference between a newborn baby and a wise old person, who has ideally attained a degree of mystical transcendence over his desires and fears, is in understanding. Between the end-points of being a newborn baby and a serene mystic lies the vast territory of the ego and its demands for the achievement and maintenance of our self-esteem, the fulfillment of our changing desires and the overcoming of our individualistic fears. In the rest of this chapter, and in Chapters 3 and 4, I will be describing the growth and general nature of the ego and its defences.

Inasmuch as I want the reader to reach the substance promised in this book's title as quickly as possible, I will be presenting a fairly condensed outline of the concepts pertaining to the ego which are necessary to make sense of my theory of inter-personal relationships. I hope that the Glossary (pp. 297) will aid the reader's digestion of the unavoidable theoretical terminology.

In order to serve the ego's needs, we need to develop the means of growing and maintaining our self-esteem within the constraints imposed on us by physical reality and by other people. To these ends we are innately endowed with two lifelong motives: to get 'strokes' and to make sense of the world and of other people.

A stroke is any acknowledgement of us by another. When we are babies our need for strokes is quite literal. The loving skin to skin contact that parents give their babies is as vital to their survival as food. And this is no exaggeration. During the 1940's the psychologist Renée Spitz, investigating the high death rate among babies in a particular orphanage, discovered that all the babies were kept clean and well-fed and had no discernible physical disease. Yet many lost weight and seemed simply to 'waste away', sometimes to the point of death. Spitz identified the one vital element that was lacking in these babies' lives: an abundance of close physical contact in a loving and intimate relationship with one other person, who is usually but not necessarily, the baby's mother. Most parents instinctively give their babies all the tender loving physical stroking that is so vital to their well-being, and most babies grow and thrive. A contented baby held lovingly in its mother's arms is the epitome of bliss, to which state we all long to return.

This nirvana can no longer be had once infancy is past. The closest we get to it again is in loving sexual intimacy. But even this is not enough. Our stroke needs are continuous and imperative throughout our lives, and even people passionately in love cannot fulfil all of each other's stroke needs. We find our solution to this dilemma by learning to value as strokes symbolic substitutes for the literal skin to skin contact that we continue to crave but can no longer have, except rarely. Thus we give and receive strokes through talking to each other, expressing in words: affection, appreciation, admiration, gratitude, sympathy, pleasure in each other's company. We also 'say it with flowers' and in many other symbolic gestures; and we grant these gestures power to make us feel as contented, or nearly, as if we were being physically stroked.

Thus our stroke hunger is, to a greater or lesser extent, sated whenever another person does or says anything to us that acknowledges our existence. Any intentional body contact is a stroke, but so too are a frown, a smile, a telephone call, a criticism, an invitation, a thank-you note. Strokes vary in their value from the most nourishing and highly-prized, 'I love you', to the very slightly valued nod of recognition from a passing acquaintance.

Strokes that make us feel good about ourselves are called positive strokes. But our need for strokes is so great that any stroke is better than none. We would rather receive a negative stroke — an angry word, a put down, or a hostile glance — than be ignored, that is receive no stroke at all. Every parent and teacher is familiar with the child who, being unable to get any positive strokes for being 'good', at least makes sure of getting some negative strokes for being 'bad'. Grown-ups may be more subtle about it than children but are actually no different.

Whether positive or negative, strokes may be unconditional or conditional.

Possibly the only truly unconditional positive strokes are those given by a loving mother towards her children. These strokes effectively say, 'I love you because you are you, irrespective of anything you do to please or displease me'. Unconditional positive strokes are not available in healthy, loving sexual relationships; those people who implicitly demand them usually end up alone.

Unconditional negative strokes effectively say, 'You are unworthy of love, irrespective of anything you might do to please or displease me'. The consequences of a child receiving unconditional negative strokes from his or her parents are inevitably tragic for the rest of that child's life.

The overwhelming majority of strokes on offer in the world are conditional. Their prototypes are also found in mother–child transactions, such as, 'You can watch television if you're good and tidy up your toys' (positive), or 'Do that once more and I'll wallop you' (negative).

Positive strokes make us feel good about ourselves, negative strokes make us feel bad about ourselves. All strokes reinforce the behaviour they are given for. Punishment (negative stroke) does not work in its avowed aim of eliminating undesirable behaviour; it only seems to work because the undesirable behaviour is temporarily suppressed while the punishment is being inflicted. It is demonstrably proven that future expressions of that undesirable behaviour will be more rather than less frequent consequent on punishment.

The inefficacy of punishment in eliminating undesired behaviour has been indisputably demonstrated in the results of the experimental work of the psychologist B.F. Skinner, the far-reaching implications of which are dishearteningly little appreciated in the relevant professions. It needs to be asked of those who, for example, still advocate corporal punishment in schools and support inhumanity with phoney pragmatism, 'How can it be that if hitting children works, the same children receive the same punishment time and time again for the same offences?' In fact, again irrefutably demonstrated by Skinner, the only way undesired behaviour can be extinguished is by consistently ignoring it, that is giving it no strokes of any kind, by which means slowly but surely, the frequency of its manifestation will decrease to zero. It is a sad irony that emotionally as well as economically the rich tend to get richer and the poor to get poorer. Receiving positive strokes induces the recipient to give positive strokes which, in turn, encourages others to give him or her more positive strokes. . . Unfortunately, exactly the same applies to negative strokes. The nastiest people are almost always those who feel nastiest towards themselves as well as others. Breaking into the vicious cycle of negative strokes, usually begun in childhood, is a very difficult task and probably the chief task of all kinds of psychotherapy.

While the getting of strokes is our primary lifelong psychological motive, we have another fundamental motive necessary for maintaining our independent viability in the world, and that is to make sense of our experiences. Making sense of our experiences is making confident decisions for ourselves about the nature of physical and psychological reality, through which we make life predictable, and on the basis of which we may confidently interact with the material world and with other people. If strokes are our food, our decisions are our digestive system.

A newborn baby in its earliest days of being alive almost certainly has only the single inchoate experience of the world as a buzzing, whirring confusion. The only distinctions it can make are those of overall satisfaction or of overall pain. It and the universe are one.

But step by step, to the delight and awesome wonder of most parents, the baby begins to know things. By about a month he can focus his eyes and a single object can be seen by him as separate from the totality of everything else in his field of vision. By about six months of age he clearly demonstrates that he knows the difference between 'self' and 'not self'; he can reach for and hold and drop an object and cry for it when it is out of his reach. From this time onward his knowledge of the physical realities of life increases by leaps and bounds. He learns that if his body comes into too rapid or forceful contact with an object 'it hurts'. He learns that hot things hurt, too. He learns that 'what goes up must come down'. He learns that some things are heavy and some things light, and that some things too heavy to lift can be moved by horizontal force. He learns that objects vary in their fragility. Until, by about the age of four, his practical knowledge of the laws of physics is virtually complete.

Alongside all the knowledge he gains in these few years about physical reality he acquires an equivalent amount of knowledge of psychological reality. At about six weeks of age he knows that human faces bring him pleasure, and he proves he knows this with a stroke-inducing smile. By about two months he knows his mother's face as distinctive amongst all faces in promising the most strokes of all, and by about seven months he probably responds to the absence of his mother with terror. He is beginning to experience what stroke deprivation means. By about nine months he knows cunning ways to get attention, that is strokes, if they are not forthcoming, for example, by banging his spoon on his high-chair tray when his mother is paying attention to someone other than himself, and in so doing he is himself giving strokes. Until, by about six years of age, from his experiences of family life, he knows all the essentials of psychological reality: the meaning of strokes and how to get them.

The abundance of knowledge that we all have to have minimally to survive as independent entities in the world of things and people necessitates some structures in the mind to contain and categorize our impressions and decisions. These structures develop contemporaneously with the acquisition of new kinds of information which need to be distinguished from each other.

The three broad compartments of our minds which contain all our impressions and decisions are called in Transactional Analysis our ego states. The Child ego state is our feeling self, the Adult ego state is our thinking self and the Parent ego state is our evaluating self. These ego states are separate, independent entities in the totality of our being; we do not have one 'real self' but three selves, and all the difficulties we ever have in 'making up our minds' derive from this fact. Sometimes, in consideration of a given matter, our ego states all agree with each other, and we make up our minds easily and quickly. But at least as often as not our Parent, Adult and Child ego states battle with each other and we have to work hard to make peace between them or else to choose to pay heed to one and discount the desires and opinions of the others. We are constitutionally 'inconsistent'.

The concept of ego states is the central genius of Transactional Analysis (TA) providing us as it does with a radically new framework within which to experience ourselves. The separateness of the ego states furnishes us with permission to experience ourselves as necessarily inconsistent, which although a simple thing in itself, I have seen provide considerable relief from suffering for many anguished people. 'Contradiction is not a sign of falsity, nor the lack of contradiction a sign of truth' (Pascal).

While observation suggests that people are innately endowed with varying amounts of energy, it is assumed in Psychoanalysis and TA that for any individual his or her endowment of psychic energy remains constant throughout life and, in approximately the first six years of life, the basic reservoir of energy gets distributed amongst the ego states in the course of their development. Out of what is inferred to be a combination of innate predisposition and the variable stroking that a child's emerging ego states receive, the end result is that individuals vary in the proportions of their total energy invested in their separate ego states. By and large, everybody has enough energy in each of their ego states to cope with the normal demands of living, as well as some deviation from the perfectly balanced 'norm' of all ego states being equally energized. Out of this variability, people can readily be observed to have different temperaments, consonant with their general preferences for being in one ego state rather than another. The unbalance of ego states in an individual represents his or her inherent aptitudes and liabilities. Analogously, two people with markedly different distributions of energy in their ego states may experience themselves as positively complementary or negatively incompatible.

Birth to Six Months — The Natural Child

In the beginning we have only our Natural Child ego state, designated C_1. The Natural Child is biologically given and is universally demanding, completely self-centred, spontaneous, honest and uninhibited. Strokes given to the Natural

Child ego state reinforce the capacity of the individual spontaneously to express his or her emotional desires. Particular expressions of the Natural Child, such as joy and exuberance, that are reinforced by positive stroking will find enhanced pleasurable expression throughout the life of the individual. These stroke-enhanced attributes of the Natural Child are called permissions.

The only sense the Natural Child makes of the world is expressed in its instinctual fears of loud noises and of its body lacking support, that is, being dropped. It is completely unaware of its own selfhood, let alone the selfhood of other people; so it is completely incapable of 'giving'. Thus the survival of a newborn baby depends on the impulsive willingness, contained in the maternal instinct, to give it unconditional positive strokes.

Six to Twelve Months — The Little Professor

In the second half of the first year of life part of the energy of the Natural Child becomes differentiated in another ego state called the Little Professor, designated A_1. The Little Professor is the precursor of the thinking Adult ego state, but it is still a part of the Child ego state and is therefore as much a feeling as a thinking state. It is a manifestation of the drive to explore the environment, and its emergence is biologically programmed as it is in other species. More than anything else it grants the infant the capacity for 'psyching things out'. On its own, the Little Professor (A_1), is probably recognized as simple cunning but developed hand-in-hand, later, with the purely objective Adult (A_2), it is potentially the most rewarding and valuable ego state throughout life, granting intuition, hypotheses, insight and the basis of all forms of creativity. Particular expressions of the Little Professor such as curiosity and play that are reinforced by positive stroking will find enhanced pleasurable expression throughout the life of the individual. The stroke-enhanced attributes of the Little Professor are also called permissions. Between six and twelve months the energy of the psyche is distributed as:

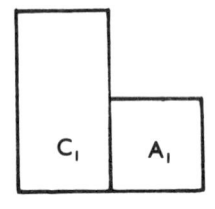

Figure (i)   Six to Twelve Months
(Although 'the energy of the psyche' is qualitatively real, it is not possible to measure it as a physical entity. Thus this block diagram and the ones that follow should be read as broadly descriptive rather than precise quantitative delineations of the distribution of energy between the ego states.)

The child now knows he is a separate being from his mother and is poignantly aware of his dependence on her for his survival. He now experiences his first ego fear, that his mother will abandon him, manifest as 'separation anxiety', which reaches its peak at about eight months. To make his fear of abandonment tolerable, towards the end of the first year the child learns to enjoy playing 'peek-a-boo'; he pretends his mother has left him but makes her come back, at his bidding, when he takes his hands away from his eyes. The tension of his fear is dissolved in the ensuing laughter. This game continues to be played by human beings throughout their lives in the thrills they get from pretend life-threatening experiences, such as riding the big-dipper.

One to Three — The Adapted Child and the Adult

In the interests of the child's safety and socialization and the preservation of the parents' sanity it becomes necessary, from about one year of age, to inhibit and constrain some manifestations of the Natural Child and the Little Professor with a large number of 'Don'ts', which are punitive negative strokes. These strokes are given in the interest of necessary expediency, because a child of this age does not have the knowledge (Adult) or the care and consideration for himself or others (Parent) that would enable him voluntarily, for example, not to tear his parents' books up, not to scream for what he wants and not to jump off a sixth floor balcony. So at this stage parents are bound to inculcate fear of retribution into their child, with sufficient power that the child internalizes their punitive wrath into his own mind. A smack or an angry look on the part of a parent accompanied by 'Don't touch the stove', 'Don't pull the cat's tail', 'Don't scream', 'Don't pick your nose', 'Don't take. . .', 'Don't hurt. . .', quickly become a part of the child's own mind, after which he automatically responds to these prohibitions even when his parents are not around. If he disobeys a prohibition, he no longer needs Mother or Father to smack him or give him an angry look; he gives himself a negative stroke in the form of a bad feeling. The ego state that develops at this time to contain the prohibitions is called the Adapted Child, designated P_1. It is the precursor of the true morality of the Parent ego state (P_2), which emerges between three and six years of age, during the Oedipal stage of development.

The Adapted Child is that part of ourselves which automatically makes us feel bad about ourselves in response to any impulse in our Natural Child or Little Professor for which we have been given negative strokes at this stage in our development. The problem is that, as already pointed out, negative strokes actually reinforce the impulses they are given for every bit as much as positive strokes. The imprinted anticipatory fear of retribution in our Adapted

Child may be great enough to forever inhibit the actual behavioural manifestation of those impulses to which our parents gave us a punitive 'Don't'; but the impulses themselves, together with the fear surrounding them, will be large and powerful components of our self-consciousness throughout our lives. And if and whenever we do defy the 'Don'ts' of our Adapted Child, we will feel very bad about ourselves.

The fearful inhibiting 'Don'ts' that constitute our Adapted Child are called injunctions. Some of them, such as the fears of crossing the road before looking both ways or of damaging other people's property remain, throughout our lives, as useful to the preservation of our own safety and to our social acceptability as they were when first imposed. Many of our injunctions, though, serve no positive purposes at all; they were imposed on us merely through the laziness of our parents, who chose expediency over more effortful and positive ways of protecting and socializing us; or else as the transmission to us by our parents of their own hang-ups.

The injunctions imposed on us by our parents' hang-ups are often transmitted covertly and non-verbally and thus more powerfully, because actions speak louder than words. A young child who is frequently pushed away when he tries to clamber onto his father's knee probably receives the injunction, 'Don't be close' and is always likely to have difficulty in forming intimate relationships. An embarrassed look as the usual response of a mother whose child says, 'I hate my brother', is likely to be received as 'Don't express bad feelings', and she is likely to be rigidly polite and inauthentic in her emotional expressiveness for the rest of her life. An angry look repeatedly given to a child whenever he praises himself for something he has done well, is understood by the child to mean, 'Don't succeed', and he is likely chronically to judge himself a failure irrespective of his actual accomplishments. And disgusted looks given to a child when he accidentally soils his pants most likely means, 'Don't feel good about yourself'; this child will grow up to be a perfectionist who chronically feels guilty about his own behaviour and is chronically critical of other people as well.

While it is probably the case that only parents who are unusually and scrupulously introspective, seek self-consciously to avoid passing on their hang-ups to their children, all normally loving parents instinctively make an effort more often to protect and socialize their children by positive rather than negative strokes. Many — but perhaps too few! — parents realize that, for example, 'Mummy is cross with you when you don't eat up all your dinner' will as surely create a grown-up woman who does not eat up all her dinner — and feels bad about herself for this — as, 'What a good girl eating up all your dinner' will create a grown-up woman who licks her platter clean — and feels good about herself for so doing.

Between the ages of one and three, alongside the crucially significant development of the Adapted Child, the Adult ego state is also emerging and growing. The Adult ego state expresses objectively acquired knowledge and skills. It does not itself contain or express feelings, but positive strokes given to the Adult are 'passed on' to the Child who feels good about them. Thus positive strokes to the Adult not only reinforce the child's impulses for knowledge and competence, but make the child feel good about himself or herself when expressing these impulses. Thus a well-stroked Adult ego state enhances an individual's ability to feel good about him or herself in activities that do not necessitate interactions with other people. This 'self-sufficiency' is, of course, of the utmost value when for any reason throughout life intimate others are not available to give us strokes. Between one and three years of age the emerging Adult is manifest largely in practical skills such as: feeding oneself, building a tower of blocks, blowing one's nose, pouring water from one container to another and, above all else, in the acquisition of language.

The child is now aware that his parents' (and others') loving approval of him is by no means unconditional. He knows that he must be 'good' to get the loving strokes he wants. But he does not yet have a moral code by which to justify his 'good' behaviour; despite any apparently 'caring'

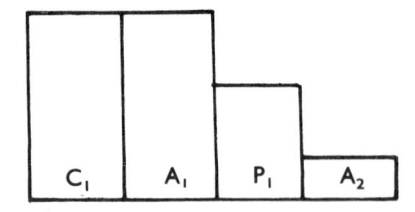

Figure (ii)   The distribution of the energy of the psyche between one and three.

or 'sharing' behaviour he may display or words he may utter, these are actually only mechanically imitative of his parents. His ego is threatened by the fear of retribution, the defence against which is obedience.

Three to Six — The Parent

Between the ages of three and six every girl falls in love with her father, wants to get rid of her mother in order to possess him, and has to come to terms with the realities that she can neither possess her father nor get rid of her mother. She is forced to compromise her desires and, ideally, she reconciles herself to her frustration by deciding, 'When I grow up I am going to be a lady like Mummy and marry a man like Daddy'.

Between the ages of three and six every boy falls in love with his mother, wants to get rid of his father in order to possess her, and has to come to terms with the realities that he can neither possess his mother nor get rid of his father. He is forced to compromise his desires and, ideally, he reconciles himself to his frustration by deciding, 'When I grow up I am going to be a man like Daddy and marry a lady like Mummy'.

Accordingly, at this stage of the child's development,

parents must express the best possible compromise between 'stroking-up' the child's sexual self-esteem while denying it the specific gratification it presently seeks. The boy wants to feel his mother loves him more than she loves his father; the girl wants to feel that her father loves her more than he loves her mother. It is imperative that the child be defeated in this aim. The child experiencing him or herself to be victorious in this battle is one of the greatest tragedies that can occur with respect to his or her subsequent lifelong ability to form satisfying relationships with the opposite sex and, indeed, to establish and maintain a satisfying self-image and satisfying attitudes to the world and life in general. The conduct and outcome of the Oedipal battle, played out by Mother, Father and Child are overwhelmingly the most deterministic events in the formation of our individuality and our relationship propensities and needs for the rest of our lives. 'If you take a person's adult life — his love, his work, his hobbies, his ambitions — they all point back to the Oedipus complex' (Malcolm). For essentially healthy functioning throughout our lives, the Oedipal battle must be lost by the child.

On the other hand, the subsequent healthy sexual self-esteem of the child also depends on the receipt of positive strokes from the opposite-sexed parent to his or her crypto-sexual overtures. A girl profoundly needs her father, at this stage, to express admiration for her looks and her clothes and to pay homage to her sweetness and her charm; and a boy profoundly needs his mother, at this stage, to express admiration for his attempts to impress her with his strength and bravery and power. Thus, when Daddy comes home from work and his daughter rushes to kiss him before Mummy can, a loving mother understandingly allows this to happen, and a loving father plays with his daughter for a while before firmly telling her that it is time for them to stop playing because he wants to talk to and cuddle Mummy. And when Daddy comes home from work, a loving mother insistently pushes her son away from her, telling him she wants to be with Daddy now that he has come home but that after dinner Daddy will play with him. This stereotype is, of course, no longer the overwhelmingly normative situation in our society. Nevertheless, even when various family circumstances appropriately qualify how best to fulfil the child's needs to relate to each of his or her parents, the general principles I have described still hold true.

From this prototypical scenario it is evident that girls' and boys' experiences of the Oedipal stage are not usually symmetrical. Both girls and boys need to be granted some gratification of their possessive attachment to their opposite-sexed parent, while at the same time being somewhat coercively propelled into relinquishing that possessiveness in favour of modelling themselves, by identification, on the attributes of their same-sexed parent. But both boys and girls typically spend much more time with their mothers than with their fathers, so a boy's possessive attachment to his mother is likely to be greater than a girl's possessive attachment to her father. In the ordinary course of events, a boy has to struggle harder to free himself from his mother and attain his sexual autonomy than a girl has to struggle to free herself from her father and attain her sexual autonomy. This, I believe, accounts for, to a considerable extent, the comparative 'immaturity' of men compared to women in matters pertaining to love in grown-up life. On average men, having been dependently bound to their mother's apron strings — and indeed born out of their mother's bodies — when grown-up defend themselves, as far and as long as possible, against being sucked into —literally and/or metaphorically! — a recapitulation of the humiliating dependency they felt towards their mothers. In spite of popular mythology to the contrary, men resist love more than women do because they are less able than women happily to combine love with self-sufficient autonomy.

The ego state that emerges between three and six years of age to accommodate and express all the precepts and understanding that are the outcome of the Oedipal battle is called the Parent, designated P_2. The Parent contains and expresses morality and is comprised of 'nurturing' and 'controlling' components which, fundamentally, serve both to nourish and to curb the libidinous impulses (aggressive and sexual) of our Natural Child and our Little Professor in the light of appropriate recognition of both our own and others' desires. Derivatively, the nurturing and controlling components of our Parent ego state also serve us as arbiters of our own and others' righteousness in non-sexual as well as sexual matters in life. Our Parent ego state tells us when to feel guilty and when to blame others. The non-sexual moral precepts of our Parent ego state are attained through the strokes given by our parents at this time to behaviour that expresses sharing and caring towards other people and appropriate self-discipline that maintains our own general well-being.

By and large, our Parent constrains us from expressing the same self-destructive and socially maladaptive impulses as our already established Adapted Child does. But now we know the 'reasons' for these constraints and so we are enabled to feel good about ourselves, to give ourselves positive strokes for our righteous acts as well as feel bad about ourselves and give ourselves negative strokes for our transgressions.

However, there are in all of us some precepts 'stroked into' our Parent ego state by our parents that are in direct contradiction to injunctions they previously 'stroked into' our Adapted Child. Consider, for example, the father who explicitly exhorts his three-to-six-year-old child to, 'Be sober', but himself does, and in the recollection of the child always has, come home drunk every other night. Or the mother who explicitly argues to her three-to-six-year-old child the supreme value of marriage as the path to happiness, but herself has constant unhappy quarrels with her husband to which her child is witness. The first child has 'Be sober' in his or her Parent and 'Don't be sober' in his or her Adapted Child; the second child has 'Be happily married' in his or her Parent and 'Don't be happily married' in his or her Adapted Child. The conflicts contained in such pairs of messages given by parents will always be of central importance in the child's outlook and experience for the whole of his or her life.

'Tell me to what you pay attention and I will tell you what you are' (Ortega y Gasset). The Adapted Child message, being imprinted earlier and with the added power of being non-verbally transmitted will always hold greater sway than the contrary Parent messages, no matter how vociferously the Parent messages are given. The Adapted Child messages that are thus given us, inviting us to various kinds of misery in life, are the evils perpetrated on us by our parents.

As well as enabling us to give ourselves positive strokes for our 'good' behaviour, the maturity we attain through our acquisition of an explicit general moral code adds flexibility to our behavioural repertoire. A two-year old, for example, may never eat chocolate after 7 p.m. without feeling bad about himself, in accordance with an injunction in his Adapted Child; a six-year old, understanding the general principle that sugar causes tooth decay which must be protected against by tooth-brushing, may quite self-righteously choose to eat some chocolate after 7 p.m. so long as he cleans his teeth straight afterwards, even though he also cleaned them just before. A two-year old may imitatively 'share' some chocolate with her dolly — and then 'eat it for her'; but a six-year old is capable of truly sharing a bar of chocolate with a friend. And a six-year old is, in principle, capable of understanding such concepts as 'a white lie' where a smaller 'good' is sacrificed to a larger one. Particular expressions of the Parent such as honesty and tolerance that are reinforced by positive stroking will find enhanced pleasurably righteous expression throughout the life of the individual. The stroke-enhanced attributes of the Parent are called counter-injunctions. During this stage, alongside the emerging Parent, the Adult continues its now rapid development in the acquisition of knowledge and skills that prepare the child for school.

The child now knows that 'giving' as well as 'taking' is inevitably demanded of him if he is to receive the loving strokes he wants from others. From now on, he or she is implicitly aware that tenderness and aggression have to be balanced in the expression of our desire for intimacy with

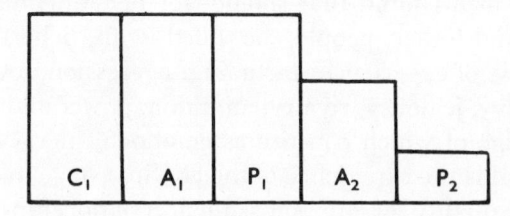

Figure (iii)   The distribution of the energy of the psyche between three and six.

others. Undissolved symbiotic attachment to our opposite-sexed parent will incline us to too much tenderness, that is, to an underdeveloped ability to express lusty sexual desire and eroticism; undissolved symbiotic attachment to our same-sexed parent will incline us to too much aggression in our subsequent sexual relationships, that is an underdeveloped ability to love ourselves and, therefore, others.

> If the tender component related to longing is cut off, the look will be hard and even hostile. . . If the aggressive component is weak, the look will be appealing, but it will fail to touch the other person. Both components are needed for good eye contact.   *Lowen*

The ego of a boy is now threatened by the fear of castration; the ego of a girl is now threatened by the fear of being undesirable. The defence against these fears is compromise between one's own desires and the desires of others.

From the evidence of children brought up in orphanages or communes or in the absence of one of their parents, it would seem that the Oedipus complex is, at least partly, biologically precipitated into the experience of three-to-six-year-old children, irrespective of external reality. And even if its experience is, to some extent, dependent on the external reality of the nuclear family setting, any child in our culture who is enabled to 'bypass' the Oedipal battle is inevitably severely handicapped throughout his or her life by the lacunae in his mind that should, for his adjustment to the world and other people, be filled with beliefs about a multitude of experiences including: aggression, love, blame, guilt, envy, jealousy, rivalry, ambition, power and revenge – knowledge of which constitutes emotional literacy. Indeed, so crucial is the experience of the Oedipal stage in determining the quality of our subsequent relationships and our attitudes to nearly everything else as well, that the implications of any contingent deviation from the norm of the eternal triangle of mother, father and child are likely to be overwhelmingly significant to the child for the rest of his or her life. This is so true that when somebody consults me as a psychotherapist and quickly reveals some obviously anomalous condition of his or her Oedipal stage of development, such as the absence by death or separation of one parent, I enquire no further before fully elucidating the near-certain implications of that fact as the most dominant motif of that individual's life.

Six Years Old

There is a special charm evident in a six-year-old child due to the achieved existence of all his or her ego states and the harmonious distribution of energy between them.

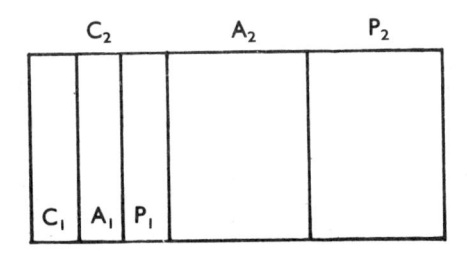

Figure (iv)   The structure of the mind at six years old

The Natural Child, the Little Professor and the Adapted Child together constitute the totality of the Child ego state, which is the personality of the individual; the Parent ego state is his character. The total ego may now be drawn as it conventionally is in Transactional Analysis as:

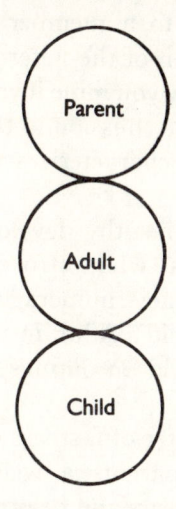

Figure (v)   The Ego States

The structures of the ego are all now functionally existent and we are equipped for authentic relationships. However, the achieved balance of the ego states in the six-year old is transitory; there are three more stages of development to be experienced before our functional capacity for loving sexual intimacy is fully honed.

Six to Twelve — Latency

Recoiling bruised from his or her rejection in love, the child now seeks compensation in control over external reality through the acquisition of knowledge and competence, and through growing identification with the ways of being and doing of his or her same-sexed parent and same-sexed peers. The pain of love is defended against with a 'yuk' attitude towards the opposite sex. A particularly unwelcome punishment that teachers may impose on children at this age is making them sit next to a member of the opposite sex; although the suppression of the heterosexual impulse is far from complete, 'I'll show you mine if you show me yours' is a popular and frequent intermission in the aggressive hostility between the sexes that characterizes this stage of development.

Much of the child's healthy development is now in the hands of his teachers who 'stroke up' the culturally demanded skills of literacy, numeracy and sociability. Parents 'stroke up' their child's Adult in their own individualistic ways, taking the child on outings, arranging swimming and music lessons, etc.

The dominating matter-of-factness of this stage of development provides for parents a welcome calm after the intensity of the earlier years and before the storm of puberty. Now children are less vulnerable than they previously were or than they will be subsequently to traumatic events that may befall them. So this is the time to teach them the facts of sex and generally to grant them knowledge of emotionally charged aspects of reality, which they are able to take in as Adult information while their Child and Parent remain more or less callously indifferent. This is the time, if needs be, when the separation or divorce of parents is likely to produce the least damaging long-term effects on the child.

But turning away from the quest for painful sexual love in favour of autonomous control of the external environment exacts its fearful price, too. The quest for omnipotence is poignantly linked to the awareness of our mortality, and the six-to-twelve-year-old child realistically knows about death in general and that he, too, must one day die. His fear of death may be a closely-guarded secret, observable only in the many obsessive-compulsive rituals and magical rites he surrounds himself with in his fearful bid to 'stop bad things

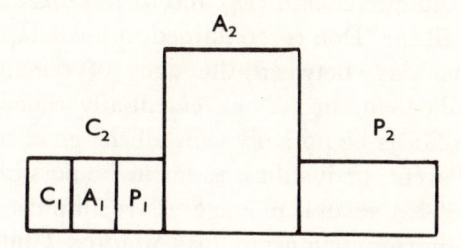

Figure (vi) The distribution of energy among the ego states between six and twelve.

happening'. More defiantly, he is likely to revel in war games, horror stories and violent films, the more gruesome the better; although girls are more inclined — possibly because of their anatomy — to prefer psychological to physical viciousness.

But these defences are, for many children, only partly successful against the fear of death, which is the greatest threat to the ego. Cynicism and depression are more often experienced during this stage of development than is commonly appreciated.

Twelve to Sixteen — Puberty

At puberty the child is suddenly overwhelmed by a biologically determined surge of sexual-aggressive energy into the Natural Child (C_1) and manifestly demands its fulfillment as if in infancy again. But he is not an infant and he cannot escape the established realities of his Adapted Child (P_1), his Adult (A_2) and his Parent (P_2). Much as he might wish, he cannot escape into the naivety of infancy, but nor are his Adult and Parent powerful enough to contain the insistent demands of his libido. What he does to help himself is to revert to his Adapted Child (P_1) and turn it upside-down. In response to all the 'Don'ts' contained in his Adapted Child, to which he was, between the ages of one and three, essentially obedient, he is now essentially rebellious. Discounting, as far as he possibly can, all the good sense of his Adult and Parent, he justifies, as far as he possibly can, the expression of his sexual and aggressive impulses with the obverse of the injunctions in his Adapted Child. All his previously accepted inhibitions imposed on him by the 'Don'ts' in his Adapted Child now become 'Do's'. He behaves rudely, inconsiderately and often with scant regard for his own safety and well-being. He is much less trustworthy, less reliable and less sensible than he was when he was ten. He treats his parents with disdain and contempt and anger as the gaolers he perceives them to be.

Loving parents know that all this is the natural and healthy way for the child to be at this stage of his or her development; that their task is to walk the tightrope of tolerating just so much and no more; and they are at least glad of the obvious 'normality' of their child. Indeed, any parents who, in comparing notes with other parents of pubescent children, smugly insist that their children are 'no trouble at all', are actually revealing that their children are seriously pathologically repressed. Sooner or later the children of these parents will be beset with incapacitating psychological handicaps in their grown-up lives, and the faults of the parents in causing this will probably come home to roost.

One very vivid instance of parents being appropriately punished was brought to me in my psychotherapeutic practice about a year ago. A couple in their seventies consulted me, overwhelmed with sorrow and despair that their forty-year-old son and only child, since his marriage five years ago, had virtually cut himself off from them and, 'because of his wife', refused to allow them to visit or be visited by their one and only grandchild. The mother told me how incomprehensible it was to her that her son, who was now treating her with such hatefulness, had been 'an angel' throughout his childhood and adolescence, while all her friends' children caused their parents so much heartache! The many other details these parents revealed to me made it abundantly clear that the son was now being the pubescent he had not been at the appropriate time. The son, rather unwillingly, agreed to come and see me once, and I did my best, gently and clearly, to explain to him and his parents what was happening between them. None of the parties took kindly to my interpretation, each insisting on the absurdity of 'thirty years ago' being a cause of the present situation, for which they each had their own much more plausible, and to them 'realistic', explanations concerning present transactional difficulties between them. They rejected my help on the basis I offered it to them, so I don't know whether this belated pubescence was successfully worked through and transcended or remained stalemated in the profound unhappiness of parents and son alike.

Since the child now utterly disregards their approval, the parents of an adolescent have to struggle to find sanctions that they can effectively impose on him. Often the granting and witholding of money which the child now explicitly wants and needs, is the only power parents maintain over their child at this time, and they use it to manipulate the child into minimal acquiescence to their demands. Appeals to the child's 'better nature' are a waste of time; he has virtually no 'better nature' now.

To a large extent puberty is a recapitulation and honing of the one-to-three-year-old stage of development. At that pre-Oedipal stage obedience was, by and large, a small price for the child to pay for the maintenance of the love of his parents, who overwhelmingly provided him with his greatest interpersonal gratifications. Now, post-Oedipally and with his newly acquired and overwhelmingly powerful genital sexual impulses, his parents no longer fulfil his most imperative needs. So, at this time, it is as if he regrets having 'given', in his obedience, to the wrong people, and he seeks to correct this 'mistake' by rebellion against them. Not until he has proudly and happily established a secure sexual relationship

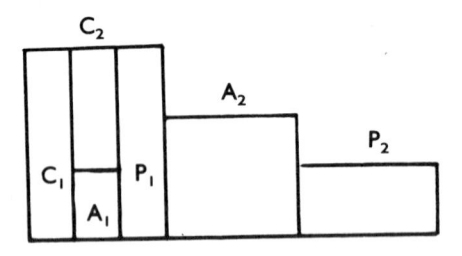

Figure (vii) Distribution of energy in the psyche at twelve to sixteen

for himself will his parents cease to be the threat to his autonomy and sexual gratification that they now seem to him to be. Then, ideally, his relationship to them will revert to its pre-Oedipal quality of non-sexual mutual love they all once knew. For the time being, the child must struggle through his confusion, while his parents poignantly accept the present necessity for things to be as they are.

Transitionally, in our culture, before the child is mature enough emotionally for him or her to be encouraged to express his full genital sexuality, he or she finds a temporary salve to his self-esteem through exaggerated identification with his same-sexed peer group. This is comparatively easy for him, because it is a natural extension of the same-sexed friendships he became competent at during latency, although this may now precipitate some homosexual impulses which may be expressed physically, but often only emotionally, especially in girls.

Sixteen to Twenty-one — Adolescence

By this stage the Adult (A_2) has normally received some potent stroking through educational attainment, and energy is now more harmoniously distributed between the total Child (C_2) and the Adult (A_2) than it has been since the age of six, but the Parent (P_2) still needs its full share of energy for the sweet harmony of the six year-old to be restored. The distribution of the energy of the psyche now looks like:

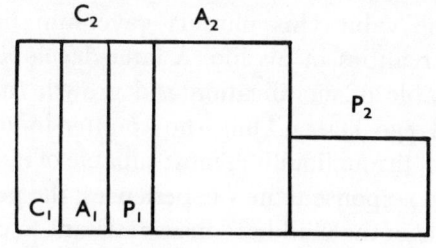

Figure (viii) Sixteen to Twenty-one

Although in many respects things are 'getting better' in the family, and the child is exhibiting a modicum of good manners and some absorbing educational or other interests of which the parents basically approve, emotionally the child is still very much at odds with his or her parents. The Oedipal battle is now being replayed and, just as between twelve and sixteen the Adapted Child was functionally completed through being expressed as disobedience, now the Parent ego state is made functionally complete by the child rejecting the love of his or her opposite-sexed parent and angrily competing with his or her same-sexed parent for sexual potency and desirability. Wise and loving parents, secure in their own sexual and other self-esteem, collude with their child in these aims. Incestuous impulses are felt and must be fought against by both parents and child. An opposite-sexed parent needs insistently not to talk about sexual matters to the child and to appreciate and welcome, rather than 'feel hurt' by, the child's expression of revulsion towards intimate contact between them; a same-sexed parent needs constantly to express admiration for the child's accomplishments and his attractiveness and to play down his or her own accomplishments and attractiveness.

However, in general moral matters, the child still needs his parents' loving control for the attainment of a well-enough developed Parent ego state so that he can go out into the world armed with a convinced set of beliefs and values that will stand him in good stead until, as an adult established in the larger world, he may safely and assuredly modify the values his parents gave him in the light of changing realities in his life. A later-developed ego state is more capable of modification and growth than an earlier-developed ego state. Thus the counter-injunctions of the Parent are, throughout life, most capable of modification and increase in response to new experiences; the permissions and injunctions of the Child are most resistant to change.

At this stage the child knows that he still needs his parents to help him achieve this final stage in the functional maturation of his ego states. But because of his struggle against incestuous desire for his opposite-sexed parent and his rivalry with his same-sexed parent, which prompt him to keep a comfortable distance from both of them, he is resentful of his continuing need of them and so has to camouflage this need. With his now well-developed Adult, he initiates arguments with his parents, launching a two-pronged attack on their Adult and Parent ego states with consummate debating skill and sophistry. Covertly, he is begging them confidently to lay down the law from their Parent ego states so that he may firmly introject their values and achieve their confidence in himself. The last thing he really wants is for them to crumple under his attacks, although manifestly this seems to be his aim. The essential transaction between an adolescent and his or her parents is as diagrammed on page 65, the dashed line representing the covert plea of the child.

At first, most parents are inclined to fall into the adolescent's trap by responding to his Adult attacks on their beliefs

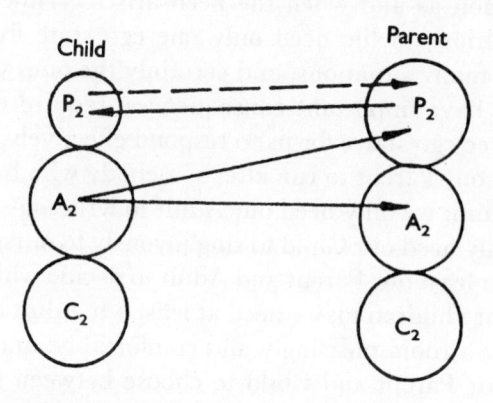

Figure (ix) The Game Adolescents Play

and principles with their own Adult reasoning, and the child often 'wins' the argument. But, in due course, parents realize what is going on and accept this final essential responsibility of child rearing, which is insistently to assert the validity of their own beliefs and to discount the relevance of any Adult 'facts' to the contrary. Internally, the child is profoundly grateful, but is unlikely to show it, and will certainly not explicitly express thanks to his parents for it until he is confidently established in adult life and has probably become a good and loving parent himself.

The harmonious distribution of energy into all the ego states, previously only manifest transiently in the charming six-year old, is restored; and grown-up life can begin.

Health and Pathology in the Functioning of the Ego States

Functionally, the healthy adult is one who has all his or her ego states well developed and well differentiated from one another, and is also able to bring them into effective collaboration as and when the need arises. While the simplest situations in life need only one ego state for healthy handling, many situations, and certainly the ones where our responses have important consequences, require the use of two or three ego states for us to respond effectively. Thus we only need our Parent to run after somebody who has left her purse behind; we only need our Adult to write out a cheque; and we only need our Child to sing joyously to ourselves. But we need at least our Parent and Adult to decide which school to send our children to; we need at least our Adult and Child to arrange a room pleasingly and comfortably; and we need at least our Parent and Child to choose between some new clothes or a holiday.

The Parent and Adult between them form judgements; the Parent and Child form compromises; and the Adult and Child find creative alternatives. And in all really important matters in our lives we usually need the harmonious cooperation of all of our ego states for the outcome of our decisions to be satisfactory. It is probably for this reason that traditional education, from the ancient Greeks to our present day, emphasizes the importance of physical games, which are an excellent medium for training the effective collaboration of all three ego states. When a boy is playing football, his Parent is obeying the rules, his Adult skills and competence are being exercised, and his Child is having a marvellous time!

Functional pathology is evident when an individual either does not have access to a particular ego state when its use is appropriately called for, or when the attempted collaboration of two ego states results in an unsatisfactory outcome.

The commonest form of functional pathology occurs when two ego states pull in opposite directions and the individual is locked in an impasse. For example, the Socialist principles in a parent's Parent ego state, which are against the purchase of privilege, may be matched against the equally powerful Adult reality that the only state schools he could send his children to are unsatisfactory, and he is beset by indecisiveness about whether or not to send his children to a fee-paying school. The Child of a woman very unhappily married to a brutal man, who will not willingly separate from her, may long to flee with her three children, but this Child impulse is matched by the equally powerful Adult reality that she has no money of her own and no means she can see of earning enough to support herself and her children, and she is overwhelmed by despair. And the Child of an unhappily married man may long to dissolve his marriage and find another love, but this impulse is matched by his equally powerful Parent conscience concerning the effect on his children if he leaves them, and he is locked in conflict.

Many briefly experienced impasses are a normal part of daily living and, as such, are in no way pathological. Normally, one or other of the battling ego states gives way a little, and indecisiveness dissolves into a judgement, despair into the discovery of alternatives and conflict into compromise. Only when a particular impasse experienced by an individual becomes a chronic 'bee in his bonnet' is it appropriate to consider it pathological.

At a deeper level pathology occurs, chronically or transiently, when two battling ego states, instead of facing each other in honest battle, seek a pseudo-resolution of their differences by contamination, for which a high price is paid. The individual deludes himself that he is satisfying both ego states, but neither ego state is actually satisfied and, moreover, an excessive amount of energy becomes bound in the contamination, restricting the individual's response options to relevant situations in life. 'Symptoms are compromises between impulse-expression and defence against it. That is why they are so resistant. They are sustained from both sides.' (Freud). For example, a man who has a Parent belief, 'Astrology is bunk', has just been to a dinner party where a fellow guest spontaneously and correctly named the Sun signs of all five other guests, who were strangers to her. Unwilling to modify his Parent to accommodate this Adult reality, he says, 'That doesn't impress me. It was just a fluke.' Parent-Adult contaminations are prejudice.

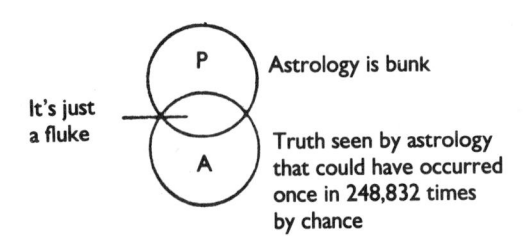

Figure (x) Prejudice

A girl in love (Child) with a man who in reality (Adult) is barely aware of her existence, may say to herself, 'He must be in love with me or he couldn't have ignored me the way he did.' Adult-Child contaminations are delusion. Somebody

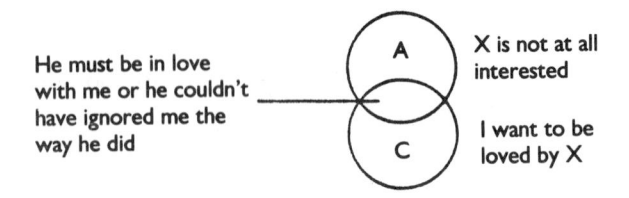

Figure (xi) Delusion

who wants some expensive clothes they see in a shop (Child), but whose Parent says it is an unjustifiable extravagance, may write out a cheque for them and ask the shop to deliver them to their home, only to have the shop telephone later to say they can't deliver them until another cheque is sent as the one written has next year's date on it. Parent-Child contaminations are confusion.

There is an even more radical resolution for the problem of an impasse between ego states than contamination, and that is exclusion. By relegating the attitudes or percepts of one or two ego states to unconsciousness, impasses are denied by evasion. This clearly leads to a greatly impoverished life.

```
Paying for what I want        P      Buying expensive
with an invalid                      clothes is unjustifiable
cheque enables me to                 extravagance
have it and not have
it at the same time           C      I want some expensive clothes
```

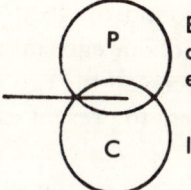

Figure (xii)   Confusion

The *uncaring* person is one whose Parent is largely exluded, leaving him or her without the necessary generalized precepts to behave responsibly or in a caring way towards himself or others.

The *turbulent person* is one whose Adult is largely excluded, leaving him or her in a chronic condition of emotional highs and lows.

The *joyless person* is one whose Child is largely excluded, leaving him or her without the capacity to express joy, sorrow, spontaneity, or insight.

The effective exclusion of two ego states from most of an individual's daily life is clearly the most impoverishing defence of all against awareness of impasses.

The *harsh or smothering person* is found in the stereotype of the preacher who is all Parent and, metaphorically, refuses to take his dog-collar off, even in bed, rather than bring Adult reality to terms with his Child fantasies. The smothering version is exemplified in the archetypal Jewish mother of *Portnoy's Complaint*.

The *cold person* is observed in the stereotype of the utterly boring scientist, who insists on using his Adult exclusively to avoid facing his unresolved Parent-Child conflicts.

The *infantile person* is found in the stereotype of the woman who impulsively lives the whole of her life according to her Child whims of the moment, rather than testing her usually harsh, Parent against Adult reality and extracting some useful generalizations from the dialogue.

Functional pathology derives from substantial amounts of psychic energy being bound or 'fixated' around particular contents of one or other of our ego states, which prevents the free-flow of energy between all the ego states that are needed for healthy responsiveness to present experiences of life.

> The important thing is to allow your energy, which after all is your healing life force, to flow without obstruction.
> *Ray*

According to psychoanalytic theory, 'fixations' at a particular stage in childhood development have four possible causes:
1) excessive gratification, too much stroking, which makes the ego reluctant to progress to its next stage of development;
2) stroke deprivation, which prompts the ego to cling to that stage in a bid to get appropriate gratification, before moving on;
3) swings between excessive gratification and deprivation;
4) gratification, strokes, and anxiety being received concurrently as, for example, in sexual caresses a parent may give a child.

No human parent can possibly walk all these tightropes without sometimes slipping, so we are all, to a greater or lesser extent, functionally sick.

Cure of functional pathology consists of bringing the excluded or contaminated ego states into the open confrontation of the impasse they have been avoiding and, through experiencing the impasse squarely, the individual is enabled to resolve it healthily into a judgement, a compromise, or the discovery of creative alternatives. This process involves inducing in the patient the anxiety he or she has been avoiding by his exclusion or contamination, which makes comprehensible the therapeutic platitude, 'You've got to get worse before you can get better.'

Exclusions represent profound pathology, which can usually only be cured by prolonged psychotherapy. Contaminations are less profound and can more quickly be cured by the device of breaking up the contamination by use of the other, non-involved ego state. Thus, the man prejudiced against astrology may be enabled to face his Parent-Adult impasse by confronting him with the Child question, 'How did you feel when that woman guessed all those people's sun signs?' The girl in love with the man who doesn't at all care for her may be helped with the Parent remark, 'He's not worthy of you. Why bother? There are plenty more fish in the sea'; and the person confused about whether or not to buy some expensive new clothes may be helped by the intervention of an Adult remark, such as, 'If you actually have enough money to buy it, do; if not, don't.'

Critical Ages in Adult Life

From the traditional psychoanalytic point of view, as well as from the evidence of ethology and commonsense observation, the earlier in life any learning or influence occurs the more likely is it to be permanent and the greater will be its effect on the personality and character of an individual for the whole of his or her life. This simple generalization is qualified by clear-cut ethological evidence that there are critical ages in the development of all species; these ages are optimal for the learning of specific skills. This generalization in turn is qualified by the rule that the higher up the evolutionary scale a species is, the longer it takes for its young to develop to self-sufficient maturity, and the greater flexibility all members of the species display in their capacity to learn specific new skills other than at optimal ages in their early development. The eighteen or so years it takes a human being to develop to full self-sufficiency is by far the longest developmental time for any species, associated with which is human beings' enormously flexible capacity to learn new skills throughout their lives.

However, despite our obvious superiority as a species in respect of our learning capacity, we too are ultimately bound to our biological limits. Like all other species, it is generally true for human beings that their ability to learn new skills easily and well diminishes with age; and, as described earlier in this chapter, there are clearly defined emergent stages from birth to adolescence that are the most natural and, therefore, optimal times for the acquisition of the specific cognitive and emotional skills required of a competently functioning adult human being.

The psychoanalytic model of human development together with its many derivative theories, including TA, has been so successful as a description and explication of human psychological development that it has been absorbed into the collective consciousness of all contemporary Western cultures. Psychoanalytic theory is at least partly 'known' by even those people who have never heard of it. Yet as a theory of human development Psychoanalysis explicitly assumes that the abidingly influential causative experiences of psychological development are virtually over by the age of about six and absolutely over by the completion of adolescence. This assumption belies the reality that there are further universal emergent phases throughout adult life that overlie individual differences, notwithstanding that these phases are inevitably weaker in their formative power than the universal stages of development in childhood. So new 'fixations' can occur in adult life when an individual evades the transitional challenges of new grown-up stages of development. The widely accepted 'mid-life crisis' is a particularly challenging transition in adult life, and those who resistantly avoid the growth demanded of them at this time will thereafter be observably more 'neurotic', that is 'stuck', at a grown-up stage of development inappropriate to their chronological age.

Some homage is paid to adult stages of development by a few post-Freudian theorists, most notably Erik Erikson in his book *Childhood and Society*; and the enormous popularity of Gail Sheehy's *Passages — Predictable Crises of Adult Life* bears witness to people's appetite for a comprehensive delineation of the universal stages of adult life comparable in detail and depth to the psychoanalytic theory of child development. In adult life, as in childhood, our age continues to be fairly accurately definable in terms of the anatomy and physiology of our bodies; and in adult life, as in childhood, our age can be fairly accurately defined in terms of the current quality of our psychological experiences, even though the externally observable events associated with a given psychological experience may vary widely from one individual to another.

I have found the deepest and most comprehensive explication of the psychological stages of development in adult life in astrological terms, which I now present. For those readers who are curious to know more than is contained in my brief outline I recommend Marc Robertson's *Critical Ages in Adult Life*.

Astrology defines with profundity the critical ages in adult life in terms of the precisely predictable ages at which all human beings will experience crises, which may be known by subjective experience or external 'happenings' but usually by both. The pattern of the unfolding of our individuality can be discerned by a multitude of techniques that may be applied to our unique natal horoscopes; the unfolding of our humanity is discernible in the single astrological factor of the 'major transits' of the outer planets to the same planets' positions in our natal horoscopes. These 'transits' occur at approximately the same ages for everybody.

The 'outer planets' are usually taken to mean Saturn, Uranus, Neptune and Pluto. Saturn takes approximately twenty-nine years to orbit the Sun, Uranus eighty-four years, Neptune one hundred and sixty-eight years and Pluto two hundred and forty-five years. When an individual is about twenty-nine years old, Saturn will be in the same position in the zodiac as it was when he or she was born; this transit is a 'conjunction' of Saturn to Saturn in the natal horoscope, which is reflected in a powerful 'identity crisis'. While the transit by conjunction is the most powerful, other angles formed by Saturn to its position in the natal horoscope are also felt keenly. The 'major' angles are the conjunction (0°), the 'sextile' (60°), the 'square' (90°), the 'trine' (120°) and the 'opposition' (180°), which are respectively experienced in the first twenty-nine years of life at approximately shortly after birth and twenty-nine, five and twenty-four, seven and twenty-one, ten and nineteen, and fourteen-and-a-half-years old. Each 'aspect' has its own characteristic 'flavour', which will qualify the basic Saturnine energy that is the essence of the transit. In the normal human life-span, a complete Saturn to Saturn cycle will be experienced two or three times at approximately twenty-nine, fifty-eight and eighty-four years of age.

For an individual who lives to be eighty-four, a complete Uranus cycle will also be experienced. Obviously nobody lives long enough to experience a complete Neptune or Pluto cycle. Nevertheless, Neptune can form a sextile, a square, a trine and an opposition to its natal position in a normal life-span; and these transits are experienced very powerfully in an individual's life.

As I have already mentioned, healthy development through the stages of adult life requires that the challenges of transitional crises be faced squarely. Suppressing, as far as possible, full consciousness of the necessary fears and pains that accompany some transits produces 'fixations', just as in childhood. However, to a considerable extent, our comparative helplessness in childhood may justify us in considering ourselves to have been victims of our parents' ineptitude or evil; in adult life there is no evading our full responsibility for the way we handle our transits. Indeed, many of the 'difficult' transits of adult life may productively be used to liberate the energy bound in our childhood fixations.

Twenty-one to Twenty-two

Saturn square Saturn and Uranus square Uranus. Now the young adult steps out into grown-up life and makes his or her first autonomous choice: to 'do his own thing', sow his wild oats and live for present impulse; or to work hard to establish himself securely within the conventional structures of society. While the choice may not be a complete either-or, by and large one of these alternatives is chosen and the other put aside.

Twenty-four to Twenty-five

Saturn sextile Saturn. A time of equilibrium and balance. Conscious goals are paramount.

Twenty-eight to Thirty

Saturn conjunction Saturn, Uranus trine Uranus and Neptune sextile Neptune. A time of reckoning and one of the most significant turning points in life. True adulthood begins now as the individual realizes the world is not his oyster, but rather that his life is severely circumscribed by his abilities, his childhood conditioning and the consequences of the choices he has already made. Depression is common at this time, accompanied by a feeling of 'My life is nearly half over and I've accomplished nothing!' In truth, the life of the autonomous ego is just beginning. Those who rebelled against staid conventionality at twenty-one now urgently want to 'settle down'; those who created conventional structures in their lives may feel desperate to escape from the prisons they feel they have locked themselves in. Childhood is over; adulthood begins with the realization that only we can make our dreams come true by what we are willing to do for ourselves.

Thirty-four

Saturn sextile Saturn. As at twenty-four to twenty-five, a time of equilibrium and balance as conscious goals are pursued.

Thirty-five to Thirty-six

Saturn square Saturn. Between the crucial awareness associated with the first Saturn return and the mid-thirties, most young adults are progressively and diligently pursuing their ego goals. But at thirty-five to thirty-six, stumbling blocks are encountered and/or a sense of boredom and stagnation sets in. Early ambitions for affluence and prestige may be well on their way to fulfillment, but the price now seems high. Life seems full of duty and responsibility.

Thirty-eight to Forty-four

Saturn opposition Saturn, Uranus opposition Uranus, Neptune square Neptune and, for recent generations, Pluto square Pluto. Between thirty-eight and forty-four life crises crowd in on one another, and the individual may wonder if he will ever again be free of depression, self-doubt, onerous burdens and obligations, nervous instability, confusion about anything and everything, painful confrontations and forced catharses of his deepest hang-ups. This is a time of reckoning for wrong choices made, and past ego goals are now seen as illusory in terms of their hoped-for satisfactions. But concurrently there is excitement, albeit unstable and somewhat frightening, for this is also a time of revelation, when the mind is opened up to new possibilities and, for the first time, the 'other side' of some coin we have been trading with all our lives is seen. It was at this time in my life that I discovered astrology, and my previous core intellectual beliefs were 'turned upside-down'. Long-buried ambitions, often dating back to the dreams of glory we had for ourselves at our first Saturn opposition when we were fourteen or fifteen, may re-surface and seek fulfillment. At first, in response to the excitement of this time, the individual may kick over the traces, in whatever area of his life his new awareness pertains to, and the 'opposite' values of the past may be totally discarded. However, gradually, the new and the old are recognized as two sides of one coin and they become integrated at a higher level where they are no longer incompatible.

Forty-seven

Saturn trine Saturn. A period of steady and responsible work within the established structures of the individual's life, giving satisfaction and a sense of security.

Forty-nine to Fifty-one

Saturn square Saturn and Chiron conjunction Chiron. Chiron is a small planet, only discovered in 1977, between Saturn and Uranus. It takes approximately fifty years to orbit the sun. Its symbolic meaning is already confidently established as that of 'the wounded healer' and it tends to be prominent in the natal horoscopes of people who experienced particularly painful childhoods. The speed of its orbit is very erratic, so there are no universally applicable ages at which it forms aspects to its natal position. However, it always forms a conjunction to its natal position at about age fifty. The individual has no option now but to admit he is middle-aged, and there is a last surge of ambitious energy directed to the fulfillment of our ego goals 'before it is too late'. 'At 49, one hefts the dice in the hand as the last throw beckons, and cares a little less whether they might be loaded.' (Coren) Concurrently, especially for those people who are conscious of bearing deep scars from their childhood wounds, there is a dissolution of fears lived with up until now, and a serene self-acceptance emerges.

Fifty-four

Saturn sextile Saturn. Ego challenges that were met at forty-nine to fifty-one are now integrated as achieved structures in life, and opportunities open up for new patterns of living. For many people this is associated with the last of their children leaving home.

Fifty-six to Sixty

Saturn conjunction Saturn, Uranus trine Uranus and Neptune trine Neptune. This time is in many ways a recapitulation of the 'identity crisis' of twenty-eight to thirty. We are again forced to face our limitations and we again feel 'time is running out'. As twenty-eight to thirty brought awareness of the limitations of our abilities and our childhood conditioning as a preliminary to autonomously pursuing our ego goals, fifty-six to sixty brings awareness of how far we have fulfilled our worldly ambitions, and recognition that the era of ego development is essentially over. Now we should have, and appropriately want, more time to enjoy contemplative pursuits, general relaxation and the enjoyment of life for its own sake. While we may not be able from now on to gain much more power in the external world, this is compensated for by our realization that we now care more for self-approval than for the strokes that are on offer in the world at large. We are looking forward to progressive changes in our lives arising from our diminished need for striving, and we are becoming more idealistic and serene.

Sixty-three

Saturn square Saturn and Uranus square Uranus. We are nearly old and, especially for men, there is a mixture of excitement and fear at the prospect of retirement. The anthropologist, Margaret Mead, said, 'When men retire they die; when women retire they go on cooking.' New and absorbing activities must be found to structure the post-retirement years.

Seventy

Saturn opposition Saturn and Uranus sextile Uranus. At seventy, everybody is aware that their three-score-years-and-ten are up, and continued life is a bonus. Now is the time when we need to put our worldly affairs in order, in readiness for death. But at the same time there is also a sense that our duties are finished and, with whatever life is left to us, we are entitled to 'do our own thing', out of which a seventy-year old may develop a new enthusiasm or activity or new friendships, untrammelled by any 'oughts'.

Eighty-four

Saturn conjunction Saturn, Uranus conjunction Uranus and Neptune opposition Neptune. Now the whole of our lives can be surveyed with wisdom and detachment. With a total sense of selfhood, we withdraw from mundane concerns into a serene, mystical transcendence of the ego and all its fears and strivings. Now is a good time to die.

At every moment of our lives our overall response to our situation and to other people is informed by three contexts: the unchanging attributes of our humanity described in Chapter 1; our present stage of development in life described in this chapter; and our individuality which is the core subject matter of the rest of this book. The relative influence of each of these contexts on a given moment may vary although, broadly speaking, our 'stage of development' tends to predominate in childhood, our individuality in our middle years, and, ideally, as we grow old, the spirituality associated with coming to terms with our humanity, especially the issues of pain and death.

In my practice as a psychotherapist I am mainly concerned with helping people to get their egos into good shape; that is enabling young and middle-aged adults to understand and develop their individualities to their full potential. However, as well as bearing in mind and referring people to the specific issues associated with their present stage of development in life, I continually bear in mind and refer people to the broader issues of their humanity such as pain and death, good versus evil, the conflicting quests for excitement and security and the overall quest for meaning in our lives.

My preferred language for delineating the issues of individuality in people's lives is Transactional Analysis out of which, over fifteen years of practice, I have developed the typology that is the basis of this book. Secondarily, in my psychotherapeutic practice, I refer to people's individual horoscopes and the transits to their horoscopes that facilitate them in understanding the particular kinds of issues that have beset them at particular times in the past and that are besetting them now; as well as preparing them to make best use of the transits that will occur to their horoscopes in the next year or so. While it is not relevant in this book for me to describe in detail the uses of astrology in psychotherapeutic practice, I highly recommend Robert Hand's *Planets in Transit* and *Modern Transits* by Lois Rodden; two books that offer comprehensive interpretations of the possible major transits to individual horoscopes and interpretations of the transits that universally occur to all of us at particular ages, which I have outlined in this chapter. Occasionally, I will refer to relevant astrological transits that are highly pertinent to crises in the lives of people I am describing, but the rest of this book is centrally a delineation of my original theory of 'five personality types', derived from Transactional Analysis, its parent theory Psychoanalysis and my own experience and understanding.

Being an Individual

Chapter 3

Life Sentences

Every new mind is a new classification. *Emerson*

Messages and Decisions

We got strokes, positive and negative, from our parents for what they told us, overtly and covertly, to do and not to do, to be and not to be. These are the 'messages' we received from them. Obedience to our parents' messages got us strokes from them and, because these messages were delivered to us in our earliest months and years of life when imprinting holds sway, we continue to believe throughout our lives that obedience to these messages constitutes the surest ways to get our stroke needs met. We find it very difficult to believe in a stroke offered to us for something we are or do outside the range of what our parents stroked us for. And we expect, and usually manage to get, the strokes, positive and negative, for our ways of being and doing that our parents stroked us for. 'People happen to events' (Rudhyar). Universally, we all seek strokes all the time; what kinds of being and doing we seek strokes for are our individual 'stroke currencies'.

Consider, for example, a girl who as a young child was stroked by her father for her lovely curly auburn hair. She will continue to seek strokes from men for her curly auburn hair for the rest of her life, and she is likely to get them. How? Probably by two means. First, having acquired the belief that her hair is lovely she will, consciously or otherwise, make and keep her hair objectively lovely, in order to maintain congruity between her beliefs and reality. Secondly, again consciously or otherwise, she will not notice men who do not, pretty quickly, remark on her lovely hair.

> Everything we see, even in the physical world, involves a non-seeing of something else. We know that perception, whether visual or cerebral, involves the filtering out of thousands of competing stimuli to retain that which has 'meaning'.
> *Blair*

Conversely, perhaps the girl with the lovely auburn hair is also, objectively, very intelligent but was not stroked in childhood for her intelligence. If and when she is given a stroke for her intelligence during the rest of her life, she will find it difficult to believe in the genuineness of this stroke and is unlikely to feel nourished by it. Thus, ironically, we want to be told the same nice things about ourselves over and over again, even though we 'know' them to be true; and we are not really interested in being told nice things about ourselves that we haven't heard before. 'We hear and apprehend only what we already half know' (Thoreau).

Sadly, we also seek, repeatedly and chronically, the negative strokes our parents gave us and by the same means. However, we are generally less conscious of the means whereby we repeatedly and chronically seek the pain of negative strokes, because we all agree that pleasure is 'good' and pain is 'bad', and it 'doesn't make sense' to seek pain. Nonetheless we do and in exactly the same ways as we seek out our positive strokes; that is by being or doing that which objectively solicits negative strokes from others, and by not noticing people who don't give these strokes to us.

For every individual, some strokes are more valuable than others. The strokes we value most are our 'target strokes'. We each have positive and negative target strokes, the things we like most and least about ourselves. When we are given our positive target stroke we feel great pleasure; when we are given our negative target stroke we feel great pain. Some common positive target strokes are for looks, intelligence, generosity and sympathy; some common negative target strokes are for stupidity, selfishness, meanness and untrustworthiness.

We, often mistakenly, tend to assume that other people's target strokes are the same as our own; so an individual's target strokes may be quite reliably inferred from the positive and negative strokes he or she tends to give others. Thus, 'What a kind woman' is likely to be said by a woman whose own positive target stroke is her kindness; 'What a mean bastard' is likely to be said by someone whose own negative target stroke is meanness. 'A man always describes himself unconsciously whenever he describes anyone else' (Shaw).

Hence there is nothing more conducive to increasing the overall pleasure in a relationship between any two people than each consciously knowing the other's positive and negative target strokes and giving the former in abundance and scrupulously avoiding giving the latter. But there is poignancy in this, too. If one person, sensitively and with love and despite repeated and escalating provocations, refuses to give another his or her target negative stroke, the one who is denied his or her target negative stroke will appreciate the other less rather than more for this denial. It is usually only with hindsight, often several years on, that we may sadly reminisce how we failed to recognize the rare love that was offered us by those who refused to give us our negative target strokes. Thus it so often comes about that alliances between people are formed out of their mutual willingness to give each other their target negative, as well as positive, strokes: to cause each other repeatedly to experience their deepest pains.

> We are all the invention of each other . . . The hatred required to begin to heal the wound . . . The question asked by those still struggling to separate from mothers, fathers, or both, or from the stream of mothers and fathers projected onto sexual partners, and, that is, 'Is this my fiction?' . . . The burden isn't either/or, consciously choosing from possibilities equally difficult and regrettable — it's and/and/and/and as well. Life is and. . .
> Roth

We all need strokes as much and as continuously as we all need food. Strokes are our psychological food, and any strokes are acceptable when we are starving; otherwise we prefer to gorge on some strokes and to reject some as unpalatable. Psychologically as well as physically, we all like some 'junk foods' that are bad for us. Some people get by nearly exclusively on junk.

It is difficult but not impossible to expand the range of the positive strokes that nourish us beyond those that our parents gave us; and it is difficult but not impossible to stop seeking the negative strokes our parents gave us. Giving up one source of strokes, like giving up say, sugar, may be difficult at first but doesn't make us starve; olives, when we first taste them, may seem very unpalatable but a little practice may make them 'delicious'.

While the messages our parents gave us taught us how to fulfil our stroke needs, in order for us to be viable, independent entities in the world at large, we need also to be able to make coherent 'sense' of all the messages we received. Otherwise, we would experience ourselves, the world and other people as an inchoate jangle of unpredictable stimuli, by virtue of which we would be as helpless and utterly dependent on others as when we were new-born babies. We need to interpret the messages we receive, so that we may confidently predict the outcome of our actions on the physical world and on other people, and thus feel more or less safe in knowing what to expect.

> Among the laws of the universe there seems to be a sort of cosmic Bill of Rights which guarantees that all of us, no matter how low, no matter how bright or dull, can take part in causing lawful things to happen through the firmness of our desire, belief, and expectancy.
> *Silva and Miele*

The deepest level 'senses' we make of our messages are our 'decisions', which are the theories about life that we formulated, when very young, out of all the messages we received to all our ego states. Our lives are dedicated to repeatedly reaffirming these theories. Strokes are our food; our decisions are our digestive systems.

In infancy and early childhood our decisions are made by our Little Professor (A_1), which consolidates and reconciles all the messages received by itself and by the Natural Child (C_1), and the Adapted Child (P_1). Later on, between the ages of about six and twelve, the Adult (A_2) consolidates and reconciles all the messages received by itself and by the whole Child ego state (C_2) and the Parent (P_2), after which our picture of the world is complete.

Amongst our decisions by which we basically define the way things are, there is usually at least one that defines the course of our life and what we will become and how. 'If we wish to know about a man, we ask 'What is his story — his real inmost story? . . . A man needs such a narrative, a continuous inner narrative, to maintain his identity, his self.' (Sachs) Our decisions about becoming are often more conscious in childhood, up to the age of about fourteen, than subsequently, when they tend often to get overlaid by the pragmatic, contingent demands of our maturation into independent and self-sufficient adulthood. Often we are actually unconsciously pursuing our decisions about the course of our lives beneath the chimera of our mundane concerns and, in the transitional existential crisis period between thirty-eight and forty-four, especially when Uranus by transit opposes its natal place, our life plan may re-emerge into full consciousness. Then we may feel an 'Aha!' of satisfaction that things are actually going as planned; or else, if we realize we are seriously off-course, we determinedly drop the irrelevancies and begin to pursue our destiny with determined conviction.

The totality of our messages and decisions, which uniquely defines each of us as seeking certain strokes, having a certain picture of the world and a certain life-plan, is our 'script'.

The contingent samenesses and variations in the scripts of individuals are limited by their species identity, gender identity, cultural identity, family identity and individual identity. Natural Child strokes, especially for sex and love, are universally sought in accordance with our being human and of a given gender; Parent strokes are mostly defined by culture and family; and Adult and Adapted Child strokes mostly by family and individuality. Decisions about physical reality are mostly accepted ready-made from parents and teachers; decisions about psychological reality and the course of our lives are mostly made by the individual himself and may vary from the most banal to the most bizarre.

In principle, no decisions are 'better' or 'worse' than any others. All 'reality' and 'truth' are created by the human mind, and each individual is 'entitled' to construe reality and truth in whatsoever way he or she chooses. Pragmatically, however, it makes a difference whether an individual's decisions make it mostly easy or difficult, mostly pleasurable or painful, for him to get his stroke needs met in his interactions with the material world and with other people. By this criterion, the more commonplace our decisions the easier we find it to fulfil our scripts. But it is also the case that out of the social frustrations we may experience by virtue of our unusual decisions, we may be energized to resolve our isolation in an act of creation. For want of an easily obtainable response from another human being, we make, in a projective, creative act, an 'other' with whom we can communicate effortlessly. With too much commonplaceness, there is not enough stimulus to wonder why; with too much peculiarity, we lack the minimum degree of communality with others necessary for them to listen to us at all.

Whatever decisions we have made, they are right for us. Asking 'whether it is better to be a happy little pig or a mournful philosopher' is an illegitimate question.

By and large, at least within a given culture, our decisions about physical reality are like nearly everybody else's. By and large, our decisions about psychological reality are unlike nearly everybody else's.

In the name of sanity, the vast majority of parents teach their children the 'correct' decisions about the nature of physical reality. All sane adults, at least in the cultures we are familiar with in the Western world, are committed to the decisions that what goes up must come down, because gravity makes it so; that plants need water and sunshine to grow; that germs cause many diseases and are 'catching'; that yellow and blue make green . . . and hundreds of other certainties that parents willingly communicate to satisfy the continuous need to know what, where, how and why of the young child. So by the time the child first ventures forth from the private world of his family into the larger world of others, even as a three-year old in nursery school, he is already well equipped with a huge range of decisions about the nature of physical reality that he can safely share with and have confirmed by the identical decisions of his teachers and playmates.

The effect of each certainty offered in such good faith by an adult and received so willingly by a child is always, no matter how beneficial to the child's needs, an act of closing his mind. I remember feeling some poignancy when one of my daughters, then aged four, asked me, 'Why are all the big aeroplanes at the airport and all the little ones in the sky?' I was bound by sanity to reply, 'The ones in the sky are big, really. They only look little because they are a long way away', thus closing her mind to all other metaphysical possibilities, such as an equally self-consistent and pragmatically applicable theory in which near, big things are 'really' little and small and distant objects look the 'right' size. Nevertheless, the fact that some manifestly sane people grow up to be sceptical philosophers or theoretical physicists, who still find themselves capable of naive open-mindedness about the nature of reality, offers some reassurance that the human mind remains capable of contorting itself to accommodate, at will, the usually mutually incompatible categories of closed-minded certainty and open-minded doubt.

As grown-ups we differ from each other in our perceptions of the physical world to the extent that we each have our own propensities to highlight some, and gloss over other, aspects of reality. Thus an artist may tend to see 'nothing but' colours and shapes, a banker will focus on the economic aspects of reality, and a naturalist may find city streets 'empty'. Nevertheless, we all have been taught to interpret the physical world in ways that all sane people call 'correct'.

What we are each taught about psychological reality is hugely variable, based as that teaching is on the explicit, verbal and implicit, non-verbal messages that were the substance of our early family lives. Some families are generally amiable, some sad, some angry and quarrelsome, some loving, some quiet, some noisy, some organized, some chaotic, some changeable. Thus one child becomes the man whose greatest happiness is his close and loving family life, his greatest difficulty being his constant worry about money. Another becomes renowned in his field of work and feels immensely rewarded by the honours heaped on him but constantly does battle with his inclination to alcoholism. One woman is constantly appreciated for her femininity and beauty but feels inferior for never having completed her secondary schooling, while another is profoundly positively stroked as a mother but miserable as a wife.

Thus, for the joy and the pain in our lives, what is relevant to one person is irrelevant to another.

> No law can be sacred to me but that of my nature. Good and bad are but names very readily transferable to that or this; the only right is what is after my constitution; the only wrong what is against it.
> *Emerson*

Wealth versus poverty, health versus illness, fame versus anonymity, faith versus doubt, intelligence versus stupidity, beauty versus ugliness and security versus adventure are some of the commoner dimensions to be found in people's core decisions. Discovering the life sentences contained in an individual's core decisions is revealing the nature of that person at the profoundest level.

Just as we maintain a lifelong propensity to seek our strokes through obedience to the messages we received in early childhood, so we maintain a lifelong propensity to re-experience and confirm the 'correctness' of our decisions. With just a little introspection, most of us are aware of a satisfaction that we experience each time we throw a ball in the air and it falls down, thus re-affirming that the law of gravity is true; and few adults have not, at some time, spontaneously done such experiments as placing a glass over a lighted candle and experiencing the satisfaction of the candle going out 'when all the oxygen is used up'. So it is with our psychological decisions; we spend our lives repeatedly performing experiments between ourselves and other people that are designed to re-affirm the certainty of the truths of our decisions. 'If a man has character, he also has his typical experience which always recurs' (Nietzsche). We set up the environments of our lives and our relationships so that our psychological experiments will have the best chance of success; and on those occasions when they fail, we discount the significance of our failures as 'flukes' and forget them as soon as possible.

Our different decisions mean that there may be totally different meanings attached to the same overt actions or attitudes displayed by different people. A man may limp, for example, for reasons as various in significance as his having a curvature of the spine, having one leg shorter than the other, having pins and needles in his leg or having suffered a stroke. The symptom itself tells us nothing of the meaning, although many practitioners in the physical and psychological health professions, as well as lay people, treat people as if a particular symptom has a definite and singular meaning. Any therapeutic successes such practitioners have are fortuitous. Our propensity to presume that when people share our psychological 'symptoms' the meanings of those symptoms are the same in them as they are in us, is false. 'One man's paradigm is another man's untruth' (Cohen).

Most people are at least slightly aware of cultural relativity and question the relevance of some of their assumptions when they are in a foreign country; a few pay lip service to individual differences within a culture; but very few indeed are aware of and act on the need to discover whether the people they meet in everyday life really do share their own deepest presumptions.

> People only look alike when you can't be bothered to look at them too closely. . . The longer I live, the more convinced I become that one of the greatest honours we can confer on other people is to see them as they are.
> *Naipaul*

Survival and Love

The meanings we give to our lives by way of our decisions boil down to the issues of survival and love: between birth and three years of age we make our decisions about survival; between three and six we make our decisions about love; between six and twelve we integrate our decisions about survival and love; and between twelve and twenty-one we polish up all these decisions.

During the period from twelve to twenty-one, when we essentially recapitulate the developmental stages one-to-three and three-to-six, parents are given an opportunity to modify the messages they gave their children at those earlier stages. There is in adolescence still some, albeit little, scope for changes in the child's basic script, and loving parents, if they are willing to put in a considerable amount of effort, may change or at least mitigate some of the more painful messages they have given their children, and children may mitigate some of their more painful decisions.

It is every child's birthright to be given unconditional and constant loving attention for the first year of his or her life; and to be given the utterly reliable and, at least nearly, constant presence of his or her primary caretaker for the next two years. These two conditions are necessary for the child to feel assured of his basic survival and to decide that life is worth living. But it is virtually impossible for a mother to be able to fulfil the condition of being an absolute and constant loving presence for her child every minute of every day for those first three years, even though most do their utmost to meet this ideal. The further the deviation from this ideal the more will the child fear for his survival and the more will he be inclined to the other possible primary decision, that life is not worth living.

That life is a precious gift and unquestionably worth living is the basic assumption of all religions; and all religions teach the accumulated wisdom of mankind concerning how to live most satisfyingly in the knowledge of our mortality. On the basis of this assumption religions teach us how to be 'good'; rejection of this premise means that no goodness is possible. The assumption that life is worth living can lead to goodness; the assumption that life is not worth living may lead to evil. (I think it interesting that 'evil' is 'live' spelled backwards.)

To the extent that virtually none of us can have experienced the absolute unbroken loving presence of our principal caretakers in our first three years of life, necessary for our absolute existential security, there is some evil in all of us. But, ironically, it is 'good enough' rather than 'perfect' parents who love their children best because 'flawed' parents provide an appropriate screen for their children to project blame for their pains; and without this means children have no choice but to blame themselves and find themselves 'evil'. Observationally, some of the most frightened and unhappy grown-ups are so by virtue of having been imbued with the idea of their parents' unassailable 'perfection'. To the extent that most of us were overwhelmingly loved and stayed with by our mothers and other loving caretakers in our first three years of life, and experienced only rare and slight interruptions to this constancy, there is more goodness in most people than there is evil, and most people see more goodness than evil in the world. In those children who, by virtue of unavoidable contingencies and/or the evil in their parents, were subject to marked inconstancy of love in their first three years of life, there is more evil than goodness, and they see more evil than goodness in the world.

Valuing life, which implies fearing death, and fearing life, which implies desiring death, is the basic existential dichotomy in us all; and variations in the proportions of the two poles of this dimension in our decisions about survival represent the most fundamental differences between individuals.

The universal polarities that derive from the fundamental dichotomy of life and fear of death versus death and fear of life are:
> seeking order versus seeking chaos;
> seeking safety versus seeking risk;
> seeking certainty versus seeking excitement.

All human beings, consciously or otherwise, are constantly seeking an optimal equilibrium in substantially balancing the pleasures and pains of order and chaos, safety and risk, certainty and excitement.

Most people establish a fairly stable *modus vivendi* for themselves at a point on the continuum between total love of life and total fear of life; this point represents their deepest decision concerning survival. But, having established that position as our truest way of being, we are still beset by a further balancing act, which is not permanently stable but must be constantly reassessed in response to ever-changing stimuli that force us to make a continuous stream of choices throughout our lives. We constantly have to find optimum balances between thought and effort and between time and money.

Thought and effort are deeply associated with valuing life and fearing death; *time and money* are deeply associated with fearing life and desiring death. The more we value life the more thought and effort are intrinsic to our consciousness and ways of living; the more we fear life the more time and money are intrinsic to our consciousness and ways of living. But thought and effort and time and money are, to a greater or lesser extent, intrinsic to the conscious attitude of us all.

When we veer towards the love of life we must constantly weigh, balance and choose a particular compromise between thought and effort. How much effort is it worth saving by how much thought — to plan this chapter before I begin to write it? To measure up the space before banging in the walls? To weigh the ingredients before baking the cake? To hold back from any action until a degree of ease can assuredly be planned into it?

When we veer towards the fear of life we must constantly weigh and balance and choose a particular compromise between time and money. How much money is it worth saving time to walk instead of getting a taxi or a bus? To save on my grocery shopping by going to a distant supermarket rather than the corner shop? To spend time in order to save money or spend money in order to save time?

In balancing thought against effort we achieve a degree of organization; in balancing time against money we achieve a degree of efficiency. In balancing organization and efficiency we achieve a degree of balance between our love of life and our fear of it.

Having established our position on the dimensions of fear and death versus fear of life, we need then to establish our position concerning love. As previously outlined, in loving relationships the ideal outcome of the Oedipal stage of development for a girl is the decision, 'When I grow up I am going to be a lady just like Mummy and marry a man just like Daddy'; and for a boy, 'When I grow up I am going to be a man just like Daddy and marry a lady just like Mummy'.

As for every stage of human development, it is not possible for the ideal conditions leading to the ideal outcome to be obtained fully and constantly in the experience of the child, so the ideal decision about love is inevitably contaminated by a greater or lesser degree of pain in all of us.

The idiosyncratic, and ultimately unique, contingencies pertaining to the child's experience of his or her relationships to each of his or her parents in the Oedipal stage of development makes for a limitless number of precisely worded decisions about loving relationships that the child may make. Nevertheless, all our decisions about love are variations on three basic themes:
1) when the opposite-sexed parent indulges the child to the extent that the child feels basically favoured over his or her same-sexed parent by his or her opposite-sexed parent, then the child decides, 'I am entitled to anything I want, so I form relationships based on manipulation and covert control'.
2) when the same-sexed parent expresses aggressive, competitive hostility towards the child, then the child decides, 'I am inferior, so I form relationships based on submission and humiliation'.
3) when the child feels redundant to the self-sufficient symbiotic relationship between his or her parents, then the child decides, 'I am unloveworthy, so I form relationships based on my willingness to fulfil others' needs because that is the only reason anybody would want to be with me'.

There is no one decision that is more or less 'selfish' than either of the others. They are all forms of self-righteousness (see Chapter 7) that we formulated for ourselves in response to and in defence against the particular pains we experienced in our family lives between the ages of three and six. As for the two broad categories of decisions we made before the age of three, all of us have some of each of these three Oedipal decisions in our make-up. The differences between people reside in the relative strengths of each of the five broad existential decisions that are all in the make-up of all of us.

The three painful relationship themes are mixed and matched in countless ways in everybody's decisions about love, even though usually one or other of these themes is obviously dominant in the core decision about love made by any particular individual.

Inasmuch as our life experiences are cumulative, our decisions about love are bound to be influenced by our prior decisions about survival. For the majority, who have basically decided, 'Life is worth living', their decisions about love contain an image of the ecstasy of overcoming the fear of death in the surrender to *le petit mort* of orgasmic sexual love. For the minority who have basically decided, 'Life is not worth living', their decisions about love contain an image of unconditional eternal indulgence of their every wish, given them by another, which alone will enable them to find life a basically joyful experience rather than a basically painful endurance that can be relieved only by death.

A delightful way of eliciting people's core decisions about life and love is via the party game of asking people to: 1) name their favourite animal or creature and give a few adjectives to describe it; 2) name their second favourite animal or creature and give a few adjectives to describe it; 3) give a few adjectives to describe the sun; 4) give a few adjectives to describe the sea. The first animal or creature is the person's self-image; the second is the image of his or her ideal partner; the description of the sun is his or her image of home, often referring to childhood family life; and the description of the sea is his or her image of sex. While these revelations are enormous fun for everyone they are also often amazingly precise metaphorical statements of a person's deepest meanings. I recall the hilarity produced by this game at a party I was at, where one man's favourite animal was a cat and his second favourite a budgerigar; and an avowed bi-sexual man described the sea as 'variable'.

Life as Metaphor and Art

We are singular amongst species in our knowledge of our mortality, and for which knowledge we are determined to find consolation and compensation. We seek this consolation and compensation in our quest for meaning in our lives.

Religions offer general meanings that are applicable to everybody. Atheists and agnostics may reject any doctrinaire general meaning of life associated with a Will higher than our own; but everybody has some general meaning they give to life, even if it be as cynically reductionist as 'Every man for himself'.

Each human being also has his own personal meanings by which he seeks to make his individual life significant. Each human being creates myths in which he or she is the hero or heroine. That is, all human beings make decisions about the progressive 'becoming' of their lives as well as decisions about their ways of 'being' in the world. Our personal meanings of life include what we will actively do to unfold our potential and fulfil our dreams, as well as what kinds of attitudes and responses we will have to what other people do to us. Our 'being' decisions refer to survival and love; our 'becoming' decisions refer to achievement and love.

The pursuit of our quest for individual significance propels us into a mythical projection of life as a process towards a golden, perfected future. 'We must select the illusion which appeals to our temperament and embrace it with passion, if we want to be happy' (Connolly). Consciously or unconsciously, crudely or with refinement, we are all artists, creating and re-creating the picture that will coherently tell the triumphant story of our lives. This view of life was portrayed with genius by Dennis Potter in his television drama, *The Singing Detective*. We want our picture to be perfectly finished before we die. Thus everything that happens to us objectively is either experienced as significant by virtue of its symbolic, metaphorical relevance to the ongoing story of our lives, or else is rejected as 'noise'. Our metaphors mediate between our consciousness and external reality. 'A large part of self-understanding is the search for appropriate metaphors that make sense of our lives' (Lakoff and Johnson). Each person's pursuit of the fulfillment of his own myths is his truth; everything else is, for him, irrelevant and, therefore, of no intrinsic interest.

> If you bring off adequate preservation of your own personal myth, nothing much else in life matters. It is not what happens to people that is significant, but what they think happens to them. *Powell*

Man is a symbolic animal and, though only few may articulate this fact, everybody lives it.

The existence of any attribute of a thing or person necessarily implies an opposite attribute that also exists. There is no 'up' without 'down', no 'good' without 'evil', no sound of a left hand clapping. 'Our mission is to recognize contraries for what they are: first of all, as contraries, but then as opposite poles of a unity' (Hesse). Thus the wish to progress towards the fulfillment of our triumphant dreams implies the fear that we may progress towards the fulfillment of our coexisting tragic nightmares. At any time in our lives, in our work and in our intimate relationships we are making our dreams or our nightmares, or both, come true.

Access to our myths is through childhood memory. In childhood, unconstrained by all the sophistication of grown-up 'realism', we unashamedly allowed ourselves to be fully conscious of and free and open to express our dreams of fulfillment. In response to the wry question adults so often ask of children, 'What are you going to be when you grow up?', the answer we gave usually referred to our dream of achievement in the world at large.

Our dreams of love are subtler and, even in childhood, were tainted by shame that prevented us from fully admitting them to ourselves or others. Our shame of our dream of love was proportional to the degree of deviation of that dream from the ideal: 'When I grow up I am going to be a lady/man just like Mummy/Daddy and marry a man/lady just like Daddy/Mummy'. Deviation of our dream of love from the ideal represents the fact that we did not feel fully loved by our parents and did not fully love them in return. And we knew, even in childhood, that grown-ups demanded that we only believe and only utter the acceptable 'truth' that we and our parents loved each other wholeheartedly. 'Of the myriad lies that people often tell themselves, two of the most common, potent and destructive are "We really love our children" and "Our parents really loved us" ' (Peck). Except in the rare instances where the child actually experiences the relationships of his parents to each other and to himself as being very close to the ideal, all children indoctrinate themselves with the untruth based on the false propriety imposed on them, by virtue of which they are bound to live their nightmares as well as their dreams in their grown-up intimate relationships. 'Lying is both a cause and a manifestation of evil' (Peck).

In the matter of people living out their dreams and nightmares, I refer to a person's subjective experience of himself and his life, which may totally lack correspondence to the objective reality. Thus a man I know who is, by any objective criteria, eminently successful in his profession — he is a likely candidate for a Nobel Prize — is more riddled with feelings of inferiority and self-deprecation, in both his working life and in his intimate relationships, than nearly anyone else I know. If anything, there may be an inverse relationship between his objective success and his subjective feelings of inferiority: his desperate bid to bypass awareness of his unresolved rivalry with his father has both kept him enveloped in his feelings of inferiority and driven him relentlessly to compensate for this in his career successes, which will never be 'enough' while he goes on denying the truth of his 'unfinished business' with his father. 'The whole present may become poisoned *by that which we will not remember*' (Collin).

Revivifying and fully articulating our childhood dreams of

achievement and love not only gives us the confidence of knowing where we are going — 'Once one is clear about the "why" of one's life, one can let its How? take care of itself' (Nietzsche) — but also gives us the intrinsic satisfaction of perceiving ourselves as creative artists. For knowing our dreams enables us to incorporate our memories into them. Without this facility our memories are dissociated and fragmented meaningless episodes, which recur with seeming fatality — 'Those who cannot remember the past are condemned to repeat it' (Santayana) — until we imbue them with significance. When significance is added, we can be glad and proud of our remembered pains as well as our joys; all of which can then be experienced as parts of the artistic plan of our lives, of which we are the directors. The past is constantly available to us for re-remembering and reinterpreting for the purpose of unfolding and refining our lives as a work of art.

The Genius of the Unconscious

In intimate relationships, most people live out a mixture of their dreams and nightmares, reflecting the half-consciousness most of us have of what we are doing. Our propensity to half-consciousness derives from a Parent-Child contamination — that is confusion — concerning what we want and what we deserve. This, in turn, derives from an unresolved conflict between our deep Child knowledge of the evil or bad messages our parents gave to our Adapted Childs and the contradictory Parent message that virtually all parents utter to their children; 'Of course we love you more than anything in the world'.

Now if our parents truly love us more than anything in the world, in our subsequent relationships with others we instinctively choose a partner very like our opposite-sexed parent and, in our relationship with that partner, we behave very like our same-sexed parent. We love and are loved wholeheartedly and live happily ever after.

Probably the majority of parents don't love each other or their children wholeheartedly, and the pain in the Child ego states of the children know this. But the Parent ego states of the children have been told that their parents did love each other and them wholeheartedly. So the vast majority of us settle for a Parent-Child contamination something like, 'I know I feel pain, which I wouldn't feel if my parents loved me wholeheartedly. But they said and say that they did and do love me wholeheartedly, so perhaps the fault is in me and the pain I feel is appropriate punishment for my badness. On the other hand, I'm not aware of having been bad to my parents, so perhaps my pain is their fault. I suppose the fairest solution to this insoluble problem is to treat myself as somewhat innocent and somewhat guilty and give myself my just deserts in a relationship that contains both joy and pain.' As Eco put it, 'The fundamental questions of philosophy (like that of psychoanalysis) is the same as the question of the detective novel: who is guilty?'

The extent of pain we experience in the formation and maintenance of our intimate relationships will always be proportional to the amount of unlovingness our parents expressed towards us. The kind of pain we experience in our relationships will reflect the idiosyncratic contingencies of our individual experiences of the Oedipal stage of our development.

But it 'doesn't make sense' at the conscious, 'realistic' level of our being to say we are looking for pain as well as joy. So in response to the deepest anguish felt in unhappy intimate relationships, nearly everybody feels bound to give plausible, socially acceptable explanations for why they embarked on the relationship in the first place, most of which amount to the eminently untrue, 'I didn't know then that he/she was/would become. . .'

In truth, we know everything about another person that is relevant to our personal myths almost instantaneously, say within about the first ten minutes of our first meeting. How we can know so much so quickly is an open question, although I suspect it reflects the intense focusing of our unconscious minds on anything that comes into view that is relevant to our lifelong obsessive concern to play out our myths. To this extent we are all geniuses.

Why we don't know consciously as well as unconsciously all that is relevant to us in another person at first sight probably has a two-fold explanation. Whereas our unconscious minds can know another person holistically in a moment, our conscious minds are not capable of processing instantaneously to full articulation the hundreds or even thousands of 'bits' of information communicated to us by the presence of another human being. Secondly, we don't want to be conscious of the pain as well as the joy that is promised. 'It is easy to confuse hope with probability' (Levi). Retrospectively we often realize that we were, in fact, all but fully aware of the pain in store for us at the first meeting, but swept that awareness under the carpet as quickly as possible, so as not to hesitate in continuing the exciting pursuit of the dreams and nightmares of our scripts.

In general, in response to the dilemma of not knowing whether to blame ourselves or our parents for our intrinsic script pains, we have three basic options: 1) open but statically unresolved Child-Parent conflict, from which position people usually avoid all intimacy; 2) the pseudo-resolution of the contamination of Child and Parent in confusion, which is the position of most people and from which they compulsively form intimate relationships containing both pain and joy, in accordance with their personal myths; and 3) the most mature option of a consciously achieved resolution of the original conflict into compromise, from which position a partner is chosen for the fulfillment of the individual's largest desire or need, but with the full knowledge and acceptance of those characteristics in the partner which will not satisfy the individual's subsidiary desires or needs. 'We are faced with the paradox that to be truly "objective" we must first be aware of ourselves' (Blair).

A few examples from life will elucidate the kinds of choices people make.

A man reared from birth by loving, adoptive parents was never told anything about his natural mother. He was very curious, and tentatively questioned his adoptive mother, who seemed hurt by his interest in the matter. His curiosity became obsessive, and he went so far as to approach the relevant social services and found out that his mother was still alive. For the past fifteen years he has hovered on the brink of finding his natural mother but is held back by the fear that she might reject him, and also that he would be disloyal to his adoptive mother. He has been married and divorced three times. The repeated pattern is that he falls in love and marries the woman he loves, but after he is married he falls in love with an unattainable other woman, and his marriage deteriorates to dissolution.

A girl grew up in the consciousness of her immediate family being the envious 'poor relations' in a very rich extended family. Her parents were very unhappily married and her mother confided jealously in her daughter, telling her that her father loved his sister more than he loved her, his wife. When this daughter grew up she fell in love with and married a millionaire who, from the beginning of their relationship, treated her sadistically and abandoned her every weekend to visit and stay with his mother and sister.

A girl's parents were divorced when she was a baby, she never knew her father and was brought up exclusively by her mother. As a child, she fantasized her father as a gallant, handsome soldier with a beautiful body. As a woman, she has had innumerable exciting one-night stands or very brief affairs with handsome men, none older than thirty. She is fifty and has never been married.

A girl's father was an avowed intellectual snob and an autocratic tyrant to his family. When she grew up she went to university and got a degree, then fell in love with an uneducated immigrant labourer who is kind and gentle. They are very happily married, and she fulfils her own educated interests through reading and the company of like-minded female friends. Naively, it might be asked why she couldn't have chosen a man who was kind and gentle and educated. She couldn't because, in her myth, 'educated' and 'brutal' are indivisibly entwined as one construct, whose opposite is the equally indivisible 'uneducated-and-kind-and-gentle'. Such is the stringent logic of our irrational mind.

> The past can never be cancelled, though it may be utilised... Choice is the assertion of freedom over necessity by which it converts necessity to its own use and thus frees itself from it. *Radhakrishnan*

Honour Thy Father and Thy Mother?

The relationship between parents and children is asymmetrical: children are entitled to be loved by their parents; parents are not entitled to be loved by their children.

Pain is inescapable in life. This fact necessitates 'good' and 'evil' to rationalize and justify it. All relationships between people are tensely and uncertainly bound by the fact that each of us is innately self-seeking and yet dependent on others, who are also self-seeking, to fulfil our needs and desires. 'Giving' and 'taking' is thus the core dimension in all relationships, the balance of which is rationalized and justified by the necessary constructs of 'reward and punishment' and 'blame and guilt'.

In an ideally loving family, between the ages of one and three, a child becomes aware that he or she is sometimes deemed 'bad' and is, therefore, punished by his or her omniscient, omnipotent, entirely 'good' parents. Between the ages of three and six, the child learns the general meaning of his badness as being his wanting too much from and giving too little to his still omniscient, omnipotent, entirely good parents.

Between twelve and twenty-one, the child turns the tables on his parents. From twelve to sixteen, he treats them as they treated him between one and three, arbitrarily deeming them bad and punishing them in accordance with his definition of himself as omniscient, omnipotent, and entirely good. From sixteen to twenty-one, he refuses to give his opposite-sexed parent the intimacy that parent asks of him and disdainfully denies his same-sexed parent the friendship that parent asks of him, in accordance with his perception that his parents give him too little to justify him giving them what they want.

Thus the child's concepts of 'good and bad', 'blame and guilt', 'reward and punishment' are made complete through having lived each of the poles of these dimensions that are essential to all relationships between people. Now he is ready to face the world as an emotionally autonomous being, seeking to be good but knowing he is also capable of being bad, and even evil; ready confidently to 'give' and to 'take' in accordance with his general concept of morality and the particular moral precepts that he has most emphatically been taught.

Parents prevent their children from achieving this ideal in two ways: by blocking the child's healthy functioning through one or more stages of his or her development — most often repressing his pubescent and adolescent rebellion against them by their unloving refusal to meet the challenges of this stage of parenthood — and by imposing bad and/or evil messages on the child.

Some parents who are unwilling to face the full responsibility of parenthood, with supreme self-righteousness, pay to have their pubescent and adolescent children's natural and essential rebelliousness determinedly suppressed in the 'best' schools they can afford. Some parents even go so far as to avoid their children altogether by sending them to boarding school. The result is, inevitably, that these children become emotionally severely crippled adults. Sad to say, such treatment of children in Britain is still widely considered to be meritorious and a privilege for the child; and the mutilated victims are still a majority amongst those who have institutional power in this country.

Any child who is unwilling appropriately to hate the wrongs imposed on him by his parents and to blame them for these wrongs thereby incapacitates himself to love the good they did him and appreciate them for this good. There is no good without evil, no guilt without blame, no love without hate.

Operationally, not having blamed his parents, the child grows up with confusion about blame and responsibility, and is incapable of being a fully responsible or, therefore, a fully loving parent himself. However much he may deny it to himself and others he actually hates his parents for their denial of his full adulthood. This hatred may be expressed directly by cutting himself off from his parents emotionally and/or physically and rarely communicating with them from the moment he is grown-up; or, indirectly, in excessive, guilty dutifulness towards them which compensates for the deep hatred he feels for them. Either way the parents are aware of the absence of the genuine, warm, spontaneous affection they long for from their grown-up children. They get, as all parents get from their children, exactly what they deserve: 'Beware of the man who does not return your blow: he neither forgives you nor allows you to forgive yourself' (Shaw).

By virtue of the bad or evil messages a child receives from his parents he is bound, compulsively, to look for and get negative strokes from 'the world' and from other people by the means his parents taught him, until and unless he is wholeheartedly willing to judge those messages bad or evil and disavow them. I limit my definition of evil here to those messages parents may give their children which effectively say, 'Don't exist' or 'Life is not worth living'. For any such disavowal of parental messages the child has to be willing to accept the price of a diminishment of his parents' love for him; that is, a withdrawal of 'sympathetic' strokes they would give him were he willing to have the resentful, angry, fearful, etc. attitudes they have towards life. Nobody wants anybody else to be happier than they themselves are, and parents especially want, in the depths of their Child ego states, to have their own negative experiences of life reiterated in the lives of their children, no matter how much their Parent ego states want the opposite. When the children reiterate the painful experiences of the parents, the parents' negative attitudes are vindicated by thus being confirmed as 'true'; when the children refuse to reiterate the pains of their parents' lives, the 'necessity' of the parents' negative attitudes to life is held up to the light and seen as actually chosen by the parents. Parents hate their children for doing this to them.

The love of parents for their children is unique. Nobody else in the world will ever be willing to give us the so nearly unconditional love our parents did and usually do for as long as they live. To the extent that they are unloving towards us, our Child deeply yearns to rectify this and, I believe, no child ever entirely loses hope that one day his or her parents will love him or her unequivocally and wholeheartedly. The more unloving the parents the more the child feels the void inside himself where that most essential love should be, and the more he hopes and yearns to fill that void with love. He will never get it from anybody else because only parents can give it; and he will probably never get it from his parents, although it is possible and sometimes happens that parents disavow the negative messages they gave their children, apologize, and love them wholeheartedly thereafter. This is the total cure for the child, and the parents thereby earn the wholehearted love of their child for them for the rest of their lives, which is the ideal concluding resolution of the relationship between a child and his or her parents and which some achieve.

Out of their continuing longing to gain the wholehearted love of their parents, most people are very resistant to blaming their parents or disavowing or disobeying any of their most painful parental injunctions; for the children know and fear that disobeying any of their parental messages would have the consequence of diminishing their parents' love of them, and they have too little of this as it is. Notwithstanding that love given to us conditional on our lives being unhappy in some way is rationally not worth having, the vast majority of people prefer to hang on to their parents' love and their own pain. They look for the wholehearted love they didn't get from their parents from someone else but, of course, however unconsciously, they transfer their expectation of love-contingent-on-unhappiness onto other intimate relationships they form. 'Comfort is the one thing you cannot get by looking for it. If you look for truth, you may find comfort in the end: if you look for comfort you will not get either comfort or truth — only soft soap and wishful thinking to begin with and, in the end, despair' (Lewis).

People's justifications for their resistance to blaming their parents and disobeying their injunctions are almost always, first, 'Honour thy father and thy mother', and second, 'Our parents couldn't help it by virtue of their own unhappy childhood experiences'. Both these justifications are specious.

Even in this secular age 'Honour thy father and thy mother' is a commandment which seems, to nearly everyone, shockingly sinful to break. Its continuing high status is probably due to the indoctrination of children by their parents that they do love them wholeheartedly, and it is expedient for the child to call on this commandment to justify his fear of receiving less love from his parents than he presently does. 'Danger . . . the mother of morality' (Nietzsche). Few people seem to know — or be willing to remember! — that this commandment is promptly followed in the bible by '*I* am the Lord thy God' and an unequivocal statement that when a parent's instructions contradict God's instructions our duty is to obey God. God instructs us to love life and be happy; nowhere does He instruct us, as parents so often do, to not be happy, not feel good about ourselves, not feel worthy of love, not be authentic or not fulfil our potential. And, most certainly of all, He instructs us never to find life not worth living.

The other excuse that most people make for resisting blaming their parents and disobeying their injunctions is 'compassion'. Parents are very fond of letting their children know how much they suffered in their childhoods, by implication excusing themselves for all their negative attitudes to life. The children are thus persuaded to excuse their parents' malevolence towards them on the grounds of 'diminished responsibility'. Furthermore, to the extent that the child sees his parents' negativity to be a direct consequence of 'circumstances outside their control' and he sees the 'circumstances' of his own childhood as so much better than his parents', he is loath to make his parents jealous of him by becoming happier than they are, because he believes he has 'unfair advantages' over them.

Now this argument is valid if the child decides that he, too, is essentially determined by 'circumstances outside his control', and thus has no option but to accept the negative attitudes imposed on him and transmit them to his own children, the effects on whom will not be his responsibility. That is, 'I can't help being the way I am, because circumstances made me so, my parents couldn't help their negativity because of their childhoods . . . and so on, back to Adam and Eve. This is a logically coherent view that essentially negates all blame and responsibility. It is psychologically incoherent because the human condition demands necessarily the concepts of good and evil, blame and responsibility, reward and punishment, through which I do accept responsibility for the harm I do others and I do blame others for the harm they do me. (See Chapter 1) The only logically and psychologically coherent sense that can be made of parent-child relationships is — my parents are responsible for the good and evil they imposed on me, and I am responsible for the good and evil I impose on my children.

When the Child ego state in us has fully felt and acknowledged the pains imposed on it by our parents and has exorcised that pain by transmuting it into righteous anger-against them, when we have successfully disobeyed our most painful injunctions and made ourselves happy, then and only then, can we authentically feel Parent-ego-state compassion and Adult-ego-state understanding for the pains they, our parents, feel in their Child ego states.

> To be free is nothing; to become free is very heaven.
> *Fichte*

Until we know and feel and exorcise the pains in our Child ego state, any avowed compassion for or understanding of our parents is hypocritically false and a wily mask for hate. 'Oh, while you live, tell the truth and shame the devil' (Shakespeare). We owe our parents nothing; we owe our children everything; and the greatest gift any parent can bestow on his or her children is his or her own happiness.

The Uses of Pain

Without evil there can be no good; without blame there can be no responsibility; without pain there can be no joy. Joy is contained in the release from pain. Good is contained in our acknowledgement of evil. 'The great epochs of our life are the occasions when we gain the courage to rebaptize our evil qualities as our best qualities' (Nietzsche).

My emphasis on pain does not reflect any necessary greater proportion of it in our lives than joy. Joy in being alive is given us both biologically and in the positive strokes our parents gave us which reinforce our Parent-ego-state counter-injunctions, in the Adult pleasures we get from thinking and exercising our skills, and especially in the permissions in our Natural Childs and Little Professors. Pain requires all the emphasis I am giving it because we 'don't believe in it'. We take our repeated joys for granted because we believe life ought always to be pleasurable.

In order to exorcise our pains we need to know them for what they are and admit the reality that, however unconsciously, we purposely and compulsively seek to recapitulate them over and over again. The 'repetition compulsion' serves both to get us the strokes our parents taught us to look for, through their messages to us, and to confirm our own decisions which provide us with our existential security. We need to know our unconscious irrationality in order to deal with it consciously and rationally.

Until and unless we make our pains conscious, we merely go on repeating them by becoming unconscious at the point of no return; and so our actions lead to the pains that are the price we pay for maintaining our irresponsibility for what happens to us. 'It is impossible for a man to be cheated by anyone but himself' (Emerson). And, as we grow older and cannot but notice the essential sameness of our experiences leading to our chronic pains; we resignedly impute it all to 'what other people always do to us' and so obey our injunctions, or to 'the way the world is' and so unimaginatively adhere to our painful decisions.

> Whatever they may think and say about their 'egoism', the great majority nonetheless do nothing for their ego their whole life long. What they do is done for the phantom of their ego, which has formed itself in the heads of those around them and has been communicated to them.
> *Nietzsche*

The alternative, through consciousness, is willfully to disobey some of our injunctions and use the pains contained within our decisions imaginatively to further the 'happy endings' of our personal myths. 'It is the business of mythology proper, and of the fairy tale, to reveal the specific dangers and techniques of the dark interior from tragedy to comedy' (Campbell).

Concerning the painful messages our parents gave us, we can choose to disobey them and pay the price of renouncing the strokes that we have so far got from our parents and others for obeying them. As we willfully disavow our quest for pain, we become sadly aware of how many of our relationships are fundamentally based on the mutual give and take of our respective target negative strokes. As we stop inviting our chosen negative strokes and demonstrate our unwillingness to take them when offered, friends drop away, unless our relationships with them also contain the essential give and take of positive strokes. But despite the ensuing loneliness we impose on ourselves, so far I have never met anyone who, once aware of the negative-stroke basis of a friendship, is willing to resume it: as we gain autonomy, we no longer believe that 'any stroke is better than none'. However, in due course and with conscious effort, we can redress our 'stroke-balance' by seeking more strokes from our positive messages by means of forming new friendships and developing new interests.

But our script decisions are essentially immutable. Our deepest existential security and sanity depends on them as much as it depends on gravity continuing to make a ball we throw in the air fall to the ground rather than fly off into space. To disavow a script decision, while not absolutely impossible, is radical surgery of the soul and, in its rare occurrences, usually demands a physical or psychological near-death experience to precipitate it. For those people who live by a large 'Life is not worth living' decision, they have no option but to go through whatever it takes to disavow this decision if they are ever to experience life as other than overwhelmingly painful. But for most people, overcoming the pains contained in our decisions consists of imaginatively living by them but in such a way that pain is transmuted into pleasure; that is, continuing to obey 'the letter of the law', while transforming the maladaptive and painful expressions of the law into adaptive and joyful expressions.

I know three children in a family who all had imposed on them by their parents the gratuitous script decision, 'You'll end up in court.' One became a thief, another a drug addict, and the third a lawyer. While some decisions are obviously much more readily expressed happily than others, there are no decisions that cannot imaginatively be made to bestow pleasure as well as pain on the user. One of the most horrible script decisions I have ever encountered was contained in the mind of a desperately self-destructive drug addict who was living by 'Life is waiting for death'; but even he was able to feel and express some real pleasure that he obtained through his part-time job in a morgue!

The pairs of opposites in our idiosyncratic messages and decisions that most powerfully polarize pain and joy in our lives are obsessively interesting to us. We are constantly driven energetically to pursue joy and avoid pain and progress the story of our lives by means of both. 'Your personal history serves as a foundation for all your capabilities and your limitations ' (Bandler and Grinder). The more intense and focused our personal obsessions are the more obviously 'hung-up' we are and/or the more obviously talented. I saw on television the remarkable performance of a twelve-year old autistic child, taken to New York who, having viewed the Manhattan skyline for a few minutes, reproduced it in a drawing with exactitude down to the tiniest detail. With less realistic verisimilitude, a talented artist might do the same thing. Both would be exhibiting an unsurpassed focusing of attention on that which is intensely interesting to them, by virtue of its relevance to their deepest meanings.

> Our innate gifts are paired with innate flaws. Strong will tends to stubborness, high intelligence to arrogance, and originality of mind to dogmatism. Thus, some very gifted men manage to be very foolish ones. The little wisdom we possess we have gained by ridding our inborn gifts of their flawed companions.
> *Strausz-Hupé*

Pain requires meaning and significance to justify it. While we are experiencing pain, intrinsically it 'doesn't make sense', so unless we have faith that meaning is contained in it, even though we don't presently know that meaning, we will translate our 'senseless' feeling into a bitter and nihilistic attitude to life itself. 'Suffering is not to be glorified; it is to be used' (Rudhyar). Thus faith that there is wisdom greater than our own in God, or the-powers-that-be, is needed for us to interpret our pains as having a presently unknown purpose that is furthering our long-term happiness. We confirm this 'truth' when we retrospectively interpret our past pains as having brought us knowledge, without which we would not be able to experience our present joys and achieved sense of meaning of our lives.

The denial of the necessity for pain is the fundamental lie that human beings tell. Denial of the truths of the past, and blindness and deafness to the truths of the present, for the purpose of avoiding present pain is bound to be paid for now and in the future. The unconscious mind knows the truth all along and, one way or another, will be heard. Our expedient, pre-emptive attempts to bypass our necessary pains may momentarily succeed but will always be punished in the future.

> Pain must never be taken philosophically: otherwise it isn't pain, we haven't been opened up. . . One element of maturity is the realization that we don't get away with anything.
>
> *Prather*

Our courage in facing present pain full-frontally will always be rewarded in future.

Courage is the only irreducible virtue. Hamlet was one level removed from the truth; in the beginning was cowardice, conscience is its justification. 'Three quarters of the evil done in the world happens out of timidity' (Nietzsche). Most people have the cowardice of their convictions.

Your quivering neurotic never has anything happen to him in reality except what he causes to happen in the fears and bogies of his own mind. He invents terrors so frightful that his whole life is an effort to escape from their danger; thus he avoids all positions, emotional and material, in which he might be harmed. The great sudden things, tragic or ecstatic, are reserved for the disciplined, the controlled, whose spiritual stature 'attracts hard events as height does lightning' and attracts also triumph and ecstasy unknown to the fearful and evasive. The back is fitted to the burden, the spirit to the experience it attracts. *Lewi*

The past is made to serve the future, evil is transmuted into good, and pain is transmuted into joy when we voluntarily look our personal truths straight in the eye and fight bravely for our place in heaven.

Chapter 4

Five Personality Types and their Compounds

There is, continued my father, a certain mien and motion of the body and all its parts, both in acting and speaking, which augers a man well within. . . There are a thousand unnoticed openings, continued my father, which let a penetrating eye at once into a man's soul; and I maintain it, added he, that a man of sense does not lay down his hat in coming into a room, or take it up in going out of it, but something escapes, which discovers him.
Sterne

It is only shallow people
who do not judge by appearances.
Wilde

Confirming Our Painful Decisions

Throughout our lives we seek a mixture of pleasure and pain. The fulfillment of our Parent values and experiences of our permissions are pleasure. The experience of being in our Adult is, technically, emotionally neutral, although the opinions of our scripts and counterscripts about the Adult may influence us to interpret the process of thinking as pleasurable or painful. The experiences of our Adapted Child are the expression of our script decisions: some of our script decisions are pleasurable and some are painful.

Our only necessary pains are the physical ones in our Natural Child that tell us all is not well with our bodies, and remind us of the only inescapable pain, our knowledge that we must one day die.

Our unnecessary pains are our obedience to the hurtful injunctions in our Adapted Child, which constitute our hang-ups and are basically responsible for all the unhappiness in our lives.

We continuously devise ways and means to reiterate and recapitulate our earliest imprinted messages and decisions, both pleasurable and painful; but, in accordance with the basic human precept that pain 'doesn't make sense', we are ashamed when we seek it and so feel bound to hide these quests from ourselves and others. In the name of Parent morality we justify the 'truth' and 'necessity' of our obedience to our painful messages; in the name of Adult objectivity we rationalize the 'truth' and 'necessity' of our adherence to our painful decisions.

Our Adapted Child is evident, either in pure form or as a contaminating influence on the expressions of our other ego states, in virtually all that we think, feel and do in our conscious waking lives. The Adapted Child is full of fear. Its fears are the fears we felt when we were very young and utterly vulnerable and helpless. Then, in response to our caretakers' angry 'Don'ts', we were rightfully terrified for our very survival should they withdraw their loving care of us.

Now, in accordance with the repetition compulsion, we interact with other people as if they made the same demands on us and had the same power over us as our parents did when we were very young. And many people maintain their fearful feelings towards their actual parents for the whole of their lives.

> Fear is produced by the memory of defeat — whether this memory is strictly personal in nature or is based on subconscious memory of previous collective defeats.
> *Rudhyar*

We repeat both the pains and the joys of the patterns of our childhoods. We repeat our joys simply; we repeat our pains complicatedly because of our need to believe that we seek joy only.

Playing 'games' with other people — the dynamics of which were made known to millions of people through Eric Berne's best-selling book *Games People Play* — is the chief means by which we each repeatedly re-experience and reaffirm the pains of our Adapted Child. Games are a set series of ulterior, covert transactions with a well-defined, painful psychological payoff for each of the players. The meaningful, ulterior, covert transactions are camouflaged by the 'innocent' transactions that take place between the players at the overt level of communication.

People adopt roles when they play games, and all the 'moves' people make in playing a game are from one of the three possible roles: Persecutor, Rescuer or Victim. Each individual tends to start a game from his or her typical stance, switching roles few or many times in the course of the game but always ending up in the role which is congruent with their painful existential position, the affirmation of which he or she is seeking in playing the game.

' "Why Don't You?" "Yes, But. . ." ', is probably the most commonly played game of all and elucidates well the dynamics of games. Typically, A (Victim) asks B (Rescuer) for advice. B offers several suggestions, each of which is rejected by A with a 'Yes, but...'. Eventually, B realizes that A is not going to accept any of his suggestions, and becomes angry and accusing (Persecutor) towards A (still Victim). A then switches to the Persecutor role, accuses B of not being a real friend after all and slams the phone down on B (Victim). At this point, A may well reaffirm a script decision that 'Everybody wants to dominate me' and B that 'No matter how much I do for people, I'm never appreciated'.

The two broad categories of final payoff available from playing any game are 'Kick Me' or 'Now I've Got You, You Son-of-a-Bitch', reflecting the two broad categories of painful decisions in people's scripts. Kick Me players end up as Victims but typically start their games in the Rescuer role; 'Now I've Got You, You Son-of-a-Bitch' players end up as Persecutors but typically start their games in the Victim role. People pick others to play the hand complementary to their own with unerring precision.

Categorizing People

Categorizing is the primary function of the brain in making sense of anything and everything. Human vanity is piqued by this fact because it reduces the significance of the exceptional characteristics of ourselves, in which most people take such pride. But, outside our essentially narcissistic frame of reference, the two most interesting observations that can be made about people are always their differences and their samenesses. Male or female is the first, and most wide-ranging, categorization of any person that we all immediately make. 'It's a girl' or 'It's a boy' is the first observation ever made about any human being, and a very large number of other dichotomous characterizations by which we describe people, concepts and the inanimate world can readily be seen to be closely derived from the basic category of gender.

Some categorizations, of people and ideas and things, are discrete, and some are sub-sets of wider categorizations we have already made. Which discrete categories we apply and how far we go in refining any of our categorizations by sub-categories depends on the context in which the person, idea or thing is being described. 'Men' is sufficient in the context of public lavatories; 'Female, 5 ft. 6 ins., aged 22, 38–24–36' is sufficient for a beauty contest; and 'Intelligent, moderate, socialist' may be sufficient for a trade union election. So it goes on, to the limiting case of a beloved other whom we wish to describe, and thus 'know', down to the tiniest freckle of his or her physical and psychological being.

In the context of psychology, a sufficient description of a person requires categorization of him or her in terms of a defined number of ways in which individuals express the motivations common to all human beings. A good-enough theory of personality will justify the categories it uses as being comprehensive in relation to its assumptions about human nature; and it will also offer some rationalizations of why individuals differ from each other.

In my experience, the knowledge of a person that can be derived from his or her horoscope is incomparably deeper and more comprehensive than the knowledge that can be obtained from any other source. But the language of the horoscope is abstract and symbolic and the quality of any interpretation of it is so dependent on the intuition, artistry and psychological understanding of the interpreter that it is very difficult indeed to objectify the information. Even the most skilled astrologers can ultimately only suggest the ways in which the configurations and aspects of a horoscope are likely to manifest in the character, motivation and life experiences of the person it describes. In spite of the common misconception to the contrary, astrologers are continually aware of free-will combining with the formal determinism of the horoscope to make for a virtually limitless number of manifest possibilities. By analogy with our genetic make-up — and many astrologers, including myself, believe the horoscope is a map of our genetic inheritance — who can say that a tall and athletic man will choose to use these characteristics to be a basketball player or a high-jumper, a nightclub bouncer, a mugger or a policeman . . . or not bother to use these attributes at all? But once we know he is a basketball player we can readily see the characteristics that enabled him to become one.

Categorizing ourselves and others psychologically by means of theories that are appropriately deep and comprehensive enlarges our awareness of the samenesses and differences between people, adding a dimension of objective understanding to our emotional reactions to events and to other people. In judging others, 'the more like us they are the more accurate our assessment is likely to be' (Nicholson), and unless we categorize people psychologically we implicitly take all of our own characteristics to be the human norm, and we discount the validity of all the characteristics of other people except those which are also our own. Categorizing ourselves and others psychologically facilitates us in bringing out the most and the best rather than the worst and the least in ourselves and others. And understanding the dynamic meaning of our own 'type' in relation to the known 'type' of another individual enables us to please that individual with finesse, if we so desire, and most effectively defend our vulnerabilities against the assaults of that individual, if the need arises. Categorizing people psychologically enlarges our humanity and increases our tolerance of ourselves as well as others; for the price of forgoing some of our narcissistic allegiance to our intrinsic uniqueness, we gain a corresponding diminishment of shame for our shortcomings, which we can now accept as 'only human'.

> Heaven knows we need *never* be ashamed of our fears, for they are rain upon the blinding dust of earth, overlying our hard hearts. *Dickens*

The Miniscript

The 'miniscript' is the brainchild of Taibi Kahler who, in 1974, proposed that all 'games', however apparently various, follow a single sequential pattern leading to the affirmation of a painful decision; and that, however idiosyncratic the 'payoff', there are five and only five ways of entering into a game, namely via one or other of the pseudo-Parent 'Drivers': Be Perfect, Hurry Up, Please, Try Hard and Be Strong. These Drivers are the socially sanctioned devices that enable us to disguise our quests for pain. They are approved short-cuts to reaffirming our most painful decisions.

The miniscript is defined as a sequence of behaviours, occurring in seconds or minutes, which reinforces early decisions. Although, in practice, the miniscript process usually deploys transactions with others, it is possible to proceed through the whole process entirely within one's own head. The general process of the miniscript is as diagrammed below.

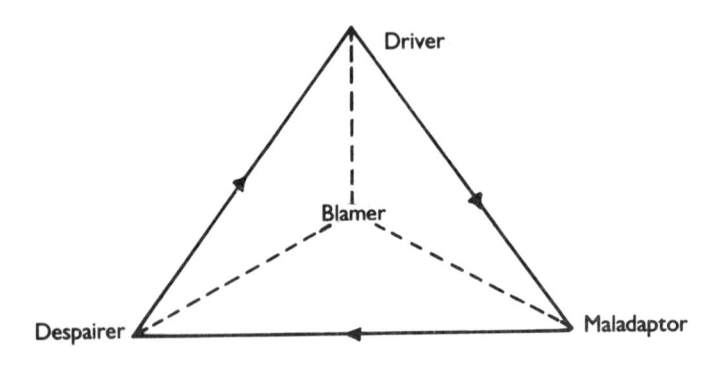

Figure (xiii) 'The miniscript'

We enter into the miniscript process at the Driver position, at which point we delude ourselves that we are doing something good for ourselves, whereas we are actually embarking on the irreversible path to the Despairer position: this is a 'payoff' in which we re-experience one of the painful decisions in our scripts. Between the Driver and the Despairer, we will go through the Maladaptor, which is a 'racket' involving one of our favourite bad feelings such as guilt, anger, frustration, fear of failure. The Blamer position is an 'optional extra' in the process, a spiteful 'I'll show you!', also called the 'antiscript', which provides the individual with the transient delusion of avoiding his or her painful payoff, but inevitably leads him to it, albeit by a devious route.

While the experiences we have in the Maladaptor, Blamer and Despairer positions of the miniscript may be idiosyncratic to our personal scripts, the way into these is only by means of one of the five Drivers, which Kahler discovered are the only five ways in which we all embark on the process towards re-affirming our most painful decisions.

The qualities of the Drivers are, as Kahler describes them, very much in keeping with the names he ascribes to them. Be Perfect represents the pseudo-virtue of perfectionism; Hurry Up represents the pseudo-virtue of restless busy-ness; Please represents the pseudo-virtue of social propriety and niceness; Try Hard represents the pseudo-virtue of repeating efforts that have led to failure; and Be Strong represents the pseudo-virtue of keeping 'a stiff upper lip' and not showing one's emotional vulnerability. Because they are so subtly camouflaged as Parent-ego-state virtues, we all tend to defend these Adapted Child invitations to misery as if they really were virtues, especially the ones that are most prominent in our own Adapted Child! An example of each of the miniscripts in action will elucidate their pervasive occurrence in everyday life.

Be Perfect: I am painting a wall with meticulous care (Driver). When I have finished, I notice an imperfectly covered spot, feel guilty (Maladaptor), keep the spot carefully in focus as I approach it wielding the paintbrush (Driver) but fail to see the tin of paint on the floor and trip over it spilling the paint (Blamer). Then I weep at the 'worthlessness' of all I have done (Despairer).

Hurry Up: I have invitations to three parties on New Year's Eve. I accept them all (Driver). I get to the first very early and leave just as things are warming up (Maladaptor) to go on to the second party (Driver). Soon after I arrive at the second party the hostess serves supper, but I refuse, thinking I'll want to eat at the third party (Blamer). I feel left out while everybody else is eating (Despairer). I go on to the third party (Driver) where most of the drink and all of the food are gone (Maladaptor), and everybody is paired off (Despairer).

Please: I am visiting a friend and she asks me if I would like a cup of tea or coffee. I say, 'That would be very nice' (Driver). She says, 'Which would you prefer, tea or coffee?' I say, 'I don't mind' (Maladaptor). She says, 'It's all the same, a teabag or instant coffee.' I say, 'Please yourself!' (Blamer). She makes tea, I would have preferred coffee (Despairer).

Try Hard: My local church is having a fête and a beautiful baby competition. I think my baby is the most beautiful baby in the world and I'm sure she'll win (Driver) but afraid she won't (Maladaptor). I decide to enter her, but when I get there and see all the other babies my fear of my baby not winning increases (Maladaptor). I don't enter her (Blamer), but compare my baby with the winner and think mine much more beautiful. (Blamer evades awareness of Despairer payoff of failure.)

Be Strong: I have just missed the bus, but it has stopped just ahead of the bus stop at the traffic lights where I am standing. It is a bus with a door that the driver opens and shuts. I want to get on the bus, but believe I have no right to ask (Driver) and I fear the driver would refuse to open the door for me (Maladaptor). I walk away, believing the driver purposely ignored me because I am not attractive (Despairer).

The self cannot but express itself and, with knowledge of the deep meaning and involuntary symptomatic expressions of these meanings, a tiny gesture or a single word can often be sufficient to infer, with great reliability, the nature of the core of the Adapted Child of an individual.

Out of my use of the concept of Kahler's miniscript process in my therapeutic practice, I began to notice that, despite the Maladaptor, Blamer and Despairer experiences being idiosyncratic to any individual, in practice they are all particular versions of general experiences linked to the five Drivers. The typical Maladaptors, Blamers and Despairer I discovered to be associated with each of the five Drivers are tabulated below.

THE FIVE PERSONALITY TYPES

Driver	Typical Maladaptor	Typical Blamer	Typical Despairer
1. Be Perfect	guilt, worry	makes a total mess of things	'I am worthless/ shameful'
2. Hurry Up	panic, can't think, tiredness	lateness, immobility	'I am crazy/ an outsider', 'Life is futile'
3. Please	feeling misunderstood, embarrassed	resentment, willful lack of consideration for others	'Nobody lets me be myself'
4. Try Hard	fear of failure, envy	sour grapes ('I could be the greatest if I could be bothered')	'I am a failure/ not as good as I think I am'
5. Be Strong	fear of rejection	invulnerability to others, boredom	'I can't get close', 'Nobody appreciates me'

Gradually, from my experience, the miniscripts developed in my mind as far more than just the negative process described by Kahler, rather a total personality typology, comprehensively representing all the ways human beings deeply experience and defend against their basic fears and against full awareness of their own responsibility for the pains associated with those fears. I also discovered that each of the five personality types has associated virtues as well as shortcomings, which are manifest as highly developed permissions, as below.

PERMISSIONS OF THE FIVE PERSONALITY TYPES

Personality Type	Associated permission(s)
Be Perfect	organization
Hurry Up	efficiency
Please	flexibility
Try Hard	persistence
Be Strong	reliability, resilience

Next I realized that Be Perfect and Hurry Up are distinctly 'deeper' than Please, Try Hard and Be Strong insofar as they refer to decisions we made about existence before the age of three, while Please, Try Hard and Be Strong refer to decisions we made about relationships between the ages of three and six. Thus it dawned on me that ALL OF THE FIVE TYPES ARE IN ALL OF US; we differ from each other in the proportional representation of each of them in the totality of our personalities. The table opposite shows the universal decisions that correspond to each of the five types.

Finally, I realized that there is a meaning behind the observable fact that any particular individual usually has two of the five types obviously dominant in his or her overall personality. The two dominant types in an individual represent both an existential dilemma or conflict at the core of his or her being and the means he finds to resolve it. This arises because each type has a deep characteristic in common with each of the other types; and each type has deep characteristics that find their opposites in the other types. Inasmuch as

THE BASIC DECISIONS PEOPLE MAKE

Decision	Personality Type
'Life is worth living.'	Be Perfect
'Life is not worth living.'	Hurry Up
'I am entitled to get everything I want from other people.'	Please
'I am inferior, and so deserve to be humiliated by other people.'	Try Hard
'I am unloveworthy, and so I can only form relationships with people who need me.'	Be Strong

the pairs that make up the compound types (see later in this chapter) are often more observable than the singular, primary types in everyday life, what we are seeing is the bid the person's ego is making to resolve a core conflict in his being through a 'symptom' that expresses both poles of the conflict at the same time. Thus the compound types may be understood as a kind of contamination (see Chapter 2). For example from the table overleaf, a Be Perfect/Be Strong person probably has a deep conflict concerning whether she values most highly emotional intensity or detachment, and in her rationality she manages to express both emotional intensity and detachment at the same time.

The rest of this book is a descriptive elaboration of all that I know about the five personality types, Be Perfect, Hurry Up, Please, Try Hard and Be Strong, in all their complexity within the individual psyche and in interpersonal relationships. They are expressions of the Adapted Child in all of us, which is overwhelmingly dominant in all that we think, feel and do throughout our lives. The examples I have chosen to illustrate how the different personality types can show themselves, both sociologically and in everyday situations, are mostly from British society as this is my experience. Obviously these types are not exclusively British and exist in all cultures and countries.

SAMENESSES AND OPPOSITENESS BETWEEN THE FIVE PERSONALITY TYPES

Pair	Oppositeness	Communality
Be Perfect and Hurry Up	fear of death vs. fear of life	anxiety
Be Perfect and Please	absolute vs. relative standards of righteousness	moral control and righteousness
Be Perfect and Try Hard	superiority vs. inferiority	intellectual rightness
Be Perfect and Be Strong	emotional intensity vs. detachment	rationality
Hurry Up and Please	social maladaptiveness vs. social adaptiveness	nervous insecurity
Hurry Up and Try Hard	futility vs. struggle	anger
Hurry Up and Be Strong	emotion vs. reason	fear and coldness
Please and Try Hard	niceness vs. nastiness	lack of autonomy
Please and Be Strong	compliance vs. autonomy	'do-gooding'
Try Hard and Be Strong	a crippled humiliation vs. resilient strength	resentment

Be Perfect

> It is said that cultures in which the fear of death is not paramount have been the least successful in evolving an indiginous art or a lasting literature. *Peyre*

Be Perfect is the defence against the fear of death. All our fears are derivative from the fear of death, and once this fear is dissipated, anything is possible. But, paradoxically, the most lasting accomplishments of mankind are the outcome of the developed Be Perfect in those who fear death most explicitly. All human accomplishment is the outcome of the bid for a little bit of immortality.

Be Perfect is the religious view of life. 'Religion is the greatest and most important of the efforts by which the human race has manifested its impulse to perfect itself' (Arnold). Religion represents the accumulated wisdom of mankind about how we can live most happily in the face of our knowledge of our mortality. All religions offer us rewards for self-discipline and stoicism accepted in the name of a cosmic Will and knowledge and meaning beyond our capacity to comprehend fully. People who are predominantly Be Perfect live life religiously, whether they are adherents of the orthodoxies of one of the named religions or only of their own idiosyncratic, self-created, self-imposed order and rigid disciplines, by which they hold at bay their fear of death and give 'meaning' to their lives. Be Perfect is in everybody, but how manifestly dominating it is in an individual's everyday life determines whether or not it is an appropriate descriptor of his or her manifest personality. Without a basic minimum of Be Perfect we would each kill ourselves by accident in a very short time.

As a personality type, Be Perfect is a close relative of the psychoanalytic obsessive-compulsive syndrome. It is associated with any too great or too rigid structuring of everyday life in childhood. It is generally a safe hypothesis that anyone with a Roman Catholic or Jewish background, even if lapsed, or anybody brought up strictly in any other faith, has Be Perfect as his or her favourite or second favourite miniscript. Be Perfect is exemplified in the scholastic pastime of arguing how many angels can dance on the point of a needle or the rabbinical one of whether or not it is lawful to eat an egg that was laid by a hen on the Sabbath. In Roman Catholics, and others, Be Perfect is often focused on sex and finds expression in Driver behaviour which abstains from all sex unless it is associated with 'perfect love', or else, in the Blamer position loves some people and has sex with others but never finds love and sex with one and the same person.

Be Perfect is not especially prevalent in any socio-economic class, but it is definitely most prevalent in countries where religion is a powerful part of the culture. It is much less common in Britain and other Protestant countries: Roman Catholicism is much more Be Perfect than most Protestantism.

Be Perfect is usually temporarily dominant in the personalities of all six-to-twelve-year old children, at which stage of development children first become fully aware of the awfulness and horror of death. Children typically become very ritualistic about many things, secretly believing that they will die unless they think or do certain things in rigidly defined ways. Always, or never, stepping on the lines of the pavement is a commonplace manifestation of Be Perfect in childhood. When it is effectively displaced, Be Perfect in childhood finds outlets such as conscientiousness at school, collecting stamps and scout badges and telling parents, with exactitude and in excruciating detail, every single thing that happened at school today or in a horror film they have just seen. Incantations, curses, warding off the evil eye and magic in general are all Be Perfect manifestations.

Overall, Be Perfect is manifestly supersitious, critical, intolerant, righteous, nit-picking, moralistic, meticulous, pedantic, sophistic and joyless. 'Right' or 'wrong' is its usual first response to anybody or anything. Order versus disorder is a core dimension in the script of the individual, and consistency is highly prized. Absolute certainty is sought, often at the very high price of creativity which depends on the willingness to risk being mistaken.

> Give me fruitful error any time, full of seeds, bursting with its own corrections. You can keep your sterile truth for yourself. *Pareto*

Because, as psychoanalysis has pointed out, the obsessive-compulsive personality needs an above-average intelligence quotient to contain it, since its verbal and other ideational gymnastics are so sophisticated, Be Perfect is often the chief syndrome of very intelligent people. That is, Be Perfect can be taken to be a sufficient, although not necessary, indication of an above average level of intelligence. Some of its most adaptive displacements, and its most constricting limitations, are found in the stereotype of the academic.

Typical words used by Be Perfect are: perfect/worthless; clean/dirty; tidy/untidy; should/shouldn't; obviously; as it were; believe; of course; depression; exactly; actually; precisely; It's not my fault; . . . for my sins; to me, personally. Be Perfect's tone of voice is measured, accusatory and didactic; facial expression is stern, severe and flushed; posture is robot-like, rigid, stiff and superior. Verbal and body attitudes include: precision; over-qualification; meticulousness; fastidiousness; refusal to be interrupted; itemizing and numbering of points while talking; pursing of bottom lip between forefinger and thumb; clearing throat; punctuating with finger and hand.

Be Perfect is seeking to reaffirm a decision like, 'I am not good enough' or 'I am a worthless sinner'. Its deadly sin is Wrath, against God. The core defensive aim of the Driver, which by definition is bound to fail, is the reduction of anxiety by behaving in so blameless a way that Providence is not tempted. When introjected, the Driver consists of self-righteous obedience to rules; projected, the Driver gives exact and detailed instructions to others, uses big words, asks many questions, is nit-picking and fault-finding. The Maladaptor position, when introjected, is almost always a racket feeling of guilt and/or apprehensive worry; projected, the Maladaptor refuses others' offers of help on the grounds that it would 'rather do it myself and have it done properly'. Introjected, the Blamer makes a total mess of things, 'So full of artless jealousy is guilt/It spills itself in fearing to be spilt' (Shakespeare); projected, the Blamer interrupts others and gets in the way of their doing what they want to do. 'I am worthless', accompanied by profound disappointment, is the usual Despairer payoff, although it may also be projected as wrathful, judgemental shaming of others and, in extreme cases, murderous aggression.

Be Perfect *saves and makes time and money*. It is hypochondriacal and is more than averagely inclined to die of heart disease. It is an important component of alcoholism and anorexia nervosa. Commonly, Be Perfect is expressed as chronic worry or depression. Most extremely, Be Perfect becomes the insanity of psychotic depression, when the rules the individual imposes on himself leave virtually no scope for any spontaneous behaviour at all, and the whole of the person's life becomes a frenetic struggle to keep pace with 'what has to be done'.

The paradox of Be Perfect is that, when it reaches a critical level, it changes from being the most wholesome, productive and life-affirming attitude to life that there is and becomes an insane living death through its hubristic attempt to be so in control — ultimately of God! — that death is averted forever. Be Perfect's highest values are stability and certainty; and ultimate certainty is death. 'Death is the total defence against anxiety' (Lowen). The truly and fully religious spirit recognizes the need to go on playing the game of life Be Perfectly, as if it has meaning, even though we may just be God's absurd joke. Thus, full-bloodedly joining in God's laughter at the pathos of our attempts to avert death, while still respecting the necessity for the pretence that we may succeed, is Be Perfect at its best. When, in both participation and detachment, we observe the wryly amusing poignancy of our fruitless quests for immortality, we ourselves, others and all humanity become endearing. 'A sense of humour, properly developed, is superior to any religion so far devised' (Robbins). The Be Perfect nature of us all is delineated with genius in Samuel Beckett's *Waiting for Godot*.

Hurry Up

> The man who regards his own life and that of his fellow creatures as meaningless is not merely unhappy but hardly fit for life.
> *Einstein*

Hurry Up is the defence against the fear of life. Its premiss is that the universe is essentially malevolent and that life is to be endured painfully until relieved by death.

Hurry Up is evil. Its central meaning is that there is no meaning, that everything is futile. Nothing is satisfying from the Hurry Up point of view, although it is willing to stay alive while it has the energy to go on looking for the timeless and unconditional love of another human being that it believes would negate the pain of life. The quest for timeless and unconditional love is defeated over and over again, and suspicion and mistrust of other people is accumulated in these defeats. Hurry Up is overwhelmed by fear and consumed with hate. It is the evil in all of us, but how dominating it is in an indivual's everyday life determines whether or not it is an appropriate descriptor of his or her manifest personality.

As a personality type, Hurry Up is a close relative of the paranoid syndrome. It is associated with the experience of abandonment in the first three years of life. The child's response includes the belief that his own intrinsic badness is the cause of his abandonment and that his parents, and the world, would be happier if he had not been born. Sexually, Hurry Up people want exclusively Child to Nurturing Parent relationships with their partners. Sex is the price they are bound to pay for emotional security. Child to Child sex is frightening to them, because to submit is, to them, to be violated. In the sex act itself it is biologically the norm for the man to be the aggressor and for the woman to submit, therefore the sex life of a Hurry Up woman is more obviously disturbed than the sex life of a Hurry Up man.

Moderate degrees of Hurry Up are extremely easy to

induce in children in even the most loving families. A child separated, even briefly, from its mother under an age when the meaning of the separation is clearly explicable to his or her Adult, will experience a sense of abandonment, the consequence of which will be a degree of Hurry Up in the child's personality. I have met many adults whose lives are significantly marred by Hurry Up as a result of no more than a week's necessary hospitalization when very young or a few days' inexplicable absence of their mother (or principal caretaker), who was possibly in hospital when a younger brother or sister was born. Happily, society at large is becoming increasingly aware of the awesome vulnerability of young children to separation from their mothers, and it is now becoming more usual than not for mothers to be domiciled in hospitals with their young children and for young children routinely to be allowed to visit their mothers in maternity wards.

Hurry up, in its moderate as well as its extreme forms, manifests a cornered position. It is usually a response to two separate injunctions, 'Don't think' and/or 'Don't belong'. Typically, the children are called on to obey Mother or Father instantly; either they comply and forgo thinking for themselves or refuse to jump to it and find that when they do arrive nobody has waited for them and they are left out of things and feel they do not belong. There is a curiously relevant relationship between 'Don't belong' and 'Don't be long'! The general atmosphere in such families is tense. Members of the family bicker and screech and shout at each other and rush around frenetically. Things are generally disorganized and chaotic and, from the child's point of view, frighteningly unpredictable. Nobody has time to give the children many strokes at all, and those they do get are usually angry negative ones. The child is treated by the parents as an object that gets tripped over. As often as possible they get the child out of the way, so they don't have to notice him or her at all.

Usually, Hurry Up people have a dim recollection of being loved when they were babies but also of having been suddenly and shatteringly rejected some time between the ages of about eighteen months and three years of age. The recollection of love and trust, together with the memory of that love being shatteringly removed, induce in them an overwhelming mistrust of any love that is subsequently offered. They decide, 'I know how wonderful it is to be loved unconditionally, but it is not trustworthy. Love given is bound to be taken away after a short time and my pain is then so great that I would rather not accept love at all than pay the price of the pain I experience when it is inevitably taken away.' By this means Hurry Up is ensured of going through life loveless. Phenomenally, it is greedy for love, asking for strokes from others all the time and claiming that it is only love that it wants. Although love may be offered, in truth, it never does last long. But it is not the other person who rejects Hurry Up; it is Hurry Up who does the rejecting, although often under the disguise of behaving so badly as to drive the other to leave, on the grounds that the other person does not love it the way it wants to be loved, which is unconditionally and timelessly. That is the dim recollection it has of love, the absolute secure narcissism of the infant at the breast. Hurry Up was never given the opportunity to learn the value of conditional love, which is all that is on offer in the world at large to everybody, once infancy is past.

Sociologically, Hurry Up is more often than not found in Britain in the working-class and upper-class; this perhaps elucidates the nature of the greater understanding it is sometimes claimed the working and upper classes have with each other than either has with the middle class. In working-class families, children in whom Hurry Up is induced are typically latchkey kids who are obliged to come home from school to an empty house and to get their supper from a fast food outlet; upper-class children in whom Hurry Up is induced are usually put in the care of paid nannies from birth and sent to boarding school at the earliest opportunity. The material privileges of the upper-class child in no way mitigate his or her suffering; his or her life becomes equally as painful and futile as the poorest child who lives in a slum, if that child is also fundamentally unloved. The varieties of love and lack of love given to us in childhood are all that essentially determine how happy or miserable are the rest of our lives. Hurry Up has suffered the cruellest blow of all, unconditional lack of love.

Hurry Up is temporarily a dominant theme at puberty, when being 'anti' everything it has previously been taught and accepted as good is a necessary pre-cursor to full adult maturity. Containing the Hurry Up impulse to self-destructiveness is the core component of the stress of puberty experienced by both the child and his or her parents.

Overall, Hurry Up is manifestly chronically fearful and anxious, in a hurry, jittery, demanding, restless, shifty, manic, late and generally unreliable and ungrateful. Core existential dimensions are: madness or murder; life and misery or death and peace; belonging or not belonging, which is often expressed as a childhood fantasy of having been adopted and really belonging, to other, good parents; demand or withdraw; space and aloneness or claustrophobia and people. Hurry Up people are unable to be alone contentedly and yet, when they are with people, they give the impression that they would rather be somewhere else or with somebody else. They are unable to sit still, they tap their fingers and feet impatiently, frown uncomprehendingly at the person talking to them, often giving the impression to the person that he or she has said something offensive. In truth, Hurry Up is on the run, all its life, from one or other parent and is deeply convinced that its own intrinsic badness is responsible for the pain inflicted on it in childhood; and further that if its parents ever actually catch up, they will murder it for its sins.

Typical words used by Hurry Up are: hurry up!; time; panic; anxiety; quickly; energy; tired; crazy; it's pointless; it's futile. Hurry Up says 'I' but never 'we'. Hurry Up's tone of voice is agitated, demanding, staccato; its facial expression is blank or frowningly non-comprehending, with brows knitted into vertical lines between the eyes. Hurry Up speaks rapidly and interrupts itself and others, is breathless and fidgety, impatient, drinks too much alcohol or takes drugs, drives dangerously and generally 'with a crafty madness keeps aloof' (Shakespeare).

Hurry Up is seeking to reaffirm a decision like, 'Life is meaningless and full of pain. The things I want will be given to me very briefly and then taken away forever, so it's best to reject people before they reject me.' Its deadly sin is Greed, and it is tyrannical in its needy demandingness. It asks for everything and ends up with nothing. The core defensive aim of the Driver is to justify continued existence by frenetically seeking to find the one person who will love it unconditionally and forever. Most sexual promiscuity is an expression of this Hurry Up quest. When introjected, the Driver is 'I must keep moving and looking'; projected, it is 'Hurry Up!' The Maladaptor position is racket fear, panic or terror which is projected as, 'Let me be your baby'. The Blamer position is introjected as total immobility which often takes the form of falling asleep in public; projected, it is 'dumb insolence'. 'I am an outsider', 'I am crazy', 'Life is meaningless/futile/painful waiting for death', and 'I suffer therefore I am' are typical Despairer payoffs, projected as, 'My suffering is worse than yours', to which is added, unspoken, 'because if your suffering is worse than mine then my existence becomes questionable.' Colin Wilson's *The Outsider* is a profound and elaborated description of Hurry Up.

Hurry Up *kills time and loses money*. It is prone to all kinds of addiction and to the necessity for surgical operations, and is more than averagely inclined to die of drug abuse or other forms of self-inflicted bodily harm or neglect. It is an important component of alcoholism. Commonly, Hurry Up is manifest as chronic restless anxiety and fear. Most extremely, Hurry Up is manifest as paranoic schizophrenia, in which the person is utterly alienated by his or her incapacity to think any thoughts that are shared by others.

The paradox of Hurry Up is that, as well as being life-denying, it is also the adventurousness in us all, originally seen in the fearlessness of the infant who is totally ignorant of danger. To this extent it is the antidote to the excesses of pure Be Perfect, which, unmitigated in its quest to avoid death, eventually achieves as-good-as-death psychological stultification, or even actual physical death. For example, a Be Perfect housewife I heard of who every week found more and more items she 'had to clean', until eventually she electrocuted herself cleaning the inside of a power point.

> A garden is not a tapestry; if all the weeds are removed, the soil is impoverished. . . This is the general outline for an answer to why pollutions are often used in renewal rites. *Douglas*

When the Hurry Up person comes to terms with the unattainableness of unconditional, timeless love, comes to see itself and others as essentially good and becomes willing to earn and value the conditional love of others, the residual Hurry Up can be the positive, refreshing, adventurous spontaneity that spits in the eye of death and makes life worth living.

> When man no longer regards himself as evil he ceases to be so. *Nietzsche*

Please

> Moral timidity, which refuses to accept responsibility for what deliberately has been suggested.
> *Coveney*, in Encounter, June 1987

> To do nothing is equally to make a decision. *Cloud*

Please is the defense against the fear of responsibility. It is the response of the child to having won the Oedipal battle, that is, of having been more loved by the opposite-sexed parent than that parent loved the same-sexed parent. The consequence is the 'spoiled brat' syndrome of Please, which consists of a presumption of its entitlement to anything it wants from another. Along with this presumption goes a mixture of guilt and resentment towards the same-sexed parent, guilt for the illegitimacy of his or her victory over that parent, and resentment towards that parent for lacking the power legitimately to defeat the child. Please children also over-idealize their opposite-sexed parent and pay the price of being unable appropriately to dissolve their sexual-emotional tie to that parent in order to find another whom they experience as being worthy of whole-hearted love. Please recapitulates this theme in all its relationships by manipulatively getting what it wants and denying responsibility for having 'done' anything. But, in truth, 'the letter that you do not write, the apology you do not offer, the food that you do not put out for the cat — all these can be sufficient and effective messages' (Bates). Please is nervously frightened of being 'found out' and punished. When it is found out and confronted by another's wrath, it smiles abashedly. This smile represents both its triumph of revenge against its parents, who have so stunted its emotional growth, and a seductive bid to be forgiven on account of its child-like charm.

> Adulthood comes at a price; . . . There is no maturity for us unless we suffer and make others suffer, and take our retribution; and . . . when the soul has been purged, it must look not to others but within itself for consolation and courage. *Peters*

Control or be-controlled is the core dimension which Please applies to all emotional transactions. Effectively, it says, 'I will please you (controlled to controller), but when it's my turn, you have to please me (controller to controlled).' The dominant manifest feature of Please is the individual's unwillingness, which he or she perceives as inability, to make any clear-cut or committed statement of his or her autonomous feelings, in case these feelings are morally wrong (which they were deemed to be by its parents). Please's aim is to get all that it wants by covert manipulation and so deludes itself, as well as others, that things just 'happen' to it, for which, of course, it can in no way be held responsible. The appropriate confrontation for this is: 'Oedipus did not know he was sleeping with his own mother, yet when he realized what had happened, he did not feel innocent' (Kundera). Other people generally know they have been manipulated and are often very angry, but so slippery is Please that it is usually very hard to prove the case against it, obvious as it actually is to the manipulated party.

As a personality type, Please is a close relative of the psychoanalytic passive-aggressive syndrome. Please presumes to read other people's minds and considers having its own mind read to be a positive stroke. Because it doesn't know what it wants, Please is glad to have other people tell it what it wants and give it whatever the other person decides is appropriate. When a response is called for, it usually utters a platitude or cliché. Although it is thus denied autonomy or independence, Please finds its compensation in being relieved of responsibility; if things go wrong, it is the other person's fault. Please is so over-adapted that it is virtually cut off from its Natural Child. It has been conditioned to believe that all feelings are made to order; it accepts, above all other considerations, its own obligation only to have *nice* feelings and to behave in accordance with propriety. It demands the same of others and doesn't mind its own business, is a nosey parker and a busybody. It is unable to distinguish between Parent responsibility and Child feelings; for example, in looking after a crotchety old relative, Please demands of itself that it always feel benevolent towards that relative as well as acting in accordance with Parent duty. Please won't say 'no' to any request, but often manages to forget that it ever said 'yes'; it secretly resents any demands made of it, and collects and stores resentment inside itself until, like a balloon, one more puff causes it to burst. The nearest innocent bystander may receive the full force of the explosive accusation that it is being treated like a doormat.

Please can be presumed to be dominant in all only children. It is conditioned in families where respectability is emphasized and expression of Natural Child wishes and feelings, especially bad feelings like jealousy, anger, vengeance or hatred, are considered an embarrassment. Any authentic expression of feeling on the part of the child is likely to be responded to with, 'That's not nice'. Overall, these parents treat their children like accessories that improve their own appearance. But as long as the child responds obediently to such parents by only feeling and doing what it is told to feel and do, it is rewarded by having all its Adapted Child wishes granted before it is even aware of having them. Limitless love is granted so long as it remains a 'good', irresponsible, dependent 'baby'.

Please is overwhelmingly dominant in British society. My estimate is that about eighty percent of the population exhibit it as their most often used miniscript. It typifies the English middle-class personality and is especially a feature of lower middle-class respectability. 'What will the neighbours think?' rules such families' lives.

> ... That interest in the universal which the average Teuton possesses and the average Englishman does not ... The good, the beautiful, the true, as opposed to the respectable, the petty, the adequate. *Forster*

Developmentally, Please is most evident between the ages of about one and six years of age, during which stage the child is predominantly compliant and uses coy manipulation to get what it wants.

Overall, Please is manifestly manipulative, 'nice' and 'nasty', affected, pretentious, snobbish, inauthentic, histrionic, nosey, 'proper', socially devious and querulous about the acceptability of his or her behaviour. 'Am I good or naughty?' is a core issue. Safe pleasantness is sought rather than risky passion; blame and innocence, nurture or be nurtured, control or be controlled are its chief existential dimensions. Wriggling out of responsibility is its greatest triumph. The free expression of these individuals is suffocatingly stifled for the sake of emotional security, and yet Please never feels fully assured that he or she is being 'good enough' not to be abandoned.

Typical words used by Please are: dear; really? nice; pleasant; y'know; kinda; sorta; I mean. . .; please youself!; embarrassed; super; you misunderstand me. Please says 'we' rather than 'I' to avoid autonomy and responsibility. Paradoxically, beginning a request with 'please' is a sign of not being in Please, since it forces the user actually to state his or her wishes, and implies the freedom of the other person to respond positively or negatively. Please's tone of voice is pleading, whining, dictating, questioning and patronizing; its face is usually averted from directly looking at another person, its eyebrows are often permanently raised, resulting in deep horizontal lines on the forehead; posture is humble and round-shouldered. Verbal and body attitudes include: nodding the head repeatedly while another person is speaking, running fingers through or patting hair, checking appearance in a mirror.

Please is seeking to reaffirm a decision like, 'No matter what I do, others are never satisfied' or 'Nobody gives me what I want'. Its deadly sin is Falsehood. The core defensive aim of the Driver is to avoid being devoured or abandoned, by being good. If a defining characteristic of all the miniscripts is inauthenticity, Please is inauthenticity squared. When introjected, the Driver is compliant to the overall position of 'I have to please you'; projected, it demands, 'You have to please me'. The Maladaptor position, introjected, is usually a racket feeling of embarrassment; projected, it says resentfully, 'That's not nice'. Introjected, the Blamer withdraws sulkily and may say, 'Please yourself!' Projected, the Blamer is an angry outburst that usually takes the other person completely by surprise. More than for any other of the miniscripts the strain of staying in the Please Driver is more than the individual can bear for very long, so he or she almost inevitably has vehement outbursts of the Blamer position, usually taking the form of rudeness and lack of consideration for others, justified as being sick of being put upon. 'I am misunderstood', 'Nobody ever gives me what I want', and 'People treat me as if I am bad, but really I am good' are typical Despairer payoffs, which may be projected as 'Forget it!', meaning 'Go to hell! You're the bad one, not me.'

Please *fritters time and money*. It is prone to indigestion — difficulty in stomaching the bad feelings it swallows — and psychosomatic ailments; and is more than averagely inclined to die of cancer. Commonly, Please is expressed as an overwhelmingly conventional and banal personality. Most extremely, when its feelings are thoroughly repressed, it becomes classical hysteria with conversion symptoms.

The paradox of Please is that through its bid to please all of the people all of the time it rarely really pleases anybody, because it totally discounts people's individuality. 'The desire to be loved by everyone often leads to being loved by no one at all' (Rossel). Conformity is Please's most speciously valued virtue and, at best, it lives its life in the confines of a tiny gilded cage. Maintaining its sense of its own blamelessness is a desperate need for Please, to which all other social aims are subsumed, and every transaction it has with another needs to culminate in it giving itself a merit stamp for good behaviour. It would be and do far more good if it were willing openly to acknowledge its guilt and resentment, which are hugely exaggerated by virtue of its compulsion to keep them hidden from itself and others.

> Man is neither angel nor brute, and the unfortunate thing is that he who would act the angel acts the brute.
> *Pascal*

Try Hard

> Self-love, my liege, is not so vile a sin
> As self-neglecting. *Shakespeare*(King Henry V)

Try Hard is the defence against the fear of failure. It defines the world's losers, and the words 'try' or 'try hard' may very reliably be used to infer that whatever the person using it is setting out to do, he or she will fail. In a recent television documentary about World War II some film was shown of Neville Chamberlain returning from his second visit to Hitler, with his second bit of paper, and greeting the waiting crowds by saying, 'When I was a little boy, I always used to say, "If at first you don't succeed, try, try, again".'! Try Hard is the response of the child to having lost the Oedipal battle in a wrong way, namely by the excessive aggression of the same-sexed parent. The consequence in the child is fearful timidity towards the same-sexed parent and an absence of self-esteem. The love of the opposite-sexed parent may be assured, but the child experiences the same-sexed parent as a powerful barrier preventing him or her gaining intimate access to the opposite-sexed parent. The child is humiliated and full of rage towards the same-sexed parent, and is ambivalent about whether or not to dare to fight the same-sexed parent for the right to intimacy with the opposite-sexed parent. Try Hard believes that if it fought it could be defeated and even more humiliated than it is already in its passive acceptance of inferiority; if victorious, it would feel itself to be the murderer of the same-sexed parent. So Try Hard hovers between the contrary impulses of impotent passivity and rageful pugnacity, which it resolves by trying to gain its share of success. This 'trying' is carefully calculated, by the Adapted Child, to achieve neither of the fearful outcomes of murdering the same-sexed parent or of resignedly accepting essential inferiority. Try Hard uses an enormous amount of energy as if treading water and so not drowning, but also getting nowhere; procrastination is a favourite device. Try Hard recapitulates this theme in all that involves self-esteem, particularly in relationship to worldly success but also in its intimate relationships. Try Hard's pose may be humble or arrogant, or alternating, but whichever side of the coin is its chosen mask, the other side will be very evident to any sensitive observer. Its own and others' aggression cause it a lot of trouble.

As a personality type, impotent envy or admiration, or arrogant pugnacity or self-deprecating humility, is the core dimension of Try Hard.

> We are not here to be admired... 'Admirer', this is a feeling which is based on the sense of being inferior to the admired one.
> *Sartre*

It is important to distinguish between envy and jealousy. Envy is purely destructive and is based on two false premises: that if I had what another has I would surely be happy; and that the other person, having what I believe would make me happy, must be happier than I am. Jealousy, when exaggerated, is also an expression of destructive, low self-esteem, but when it is unexaggerated, it is a natural and healthy expression of the wish to be loved by a loved other mixed with hatred of a rival for that other's love. Jealousy is a mixture of love and hate; envy is pure hate.

Try Hard is always putting all its eggs in one grandiose basket, forever being about to make the big time in whatever realm its essential need to fail is focused. In its head Try Hard is forever competitive and forever comparing itself to others as either superior or inferior to them in some way or other. The typical Despairer payoff of, 'I'm not as good as I think I am', is a close relative of Adler's inferiority complex, whose compensation is found in both the Driver position of being 'about to make it' and the Blamer position of copping out of all competition with a rationalization such as, 'I could be the greatest if I could be bothered.' In reality, the Try Hard person is neither as great as he or she believes in the

Driver and Blamer, nor as incapable of achievement as it experiences itself in the Despairer. Try Hard buys a ticket in a lottery and excitedly thinks of nothing else but winning until the lottery is drawn; or is out of work and expects that something will turn up; or blames its tools when it does a botched job, or doesn't attempt the job at all on the grounds that it is 'impossible'. Try Hard is a great believer in luck; others get the good sort, while it gets the bad. In fact, as mentioned in Chapter 1, luck, good or bad, hardly exists. It only exists in such matters as just catching or just missing a bus, but these can be seen to cancel out to zero after a very few occurrences.

Try Hard is made in families where one or both parents are resentful or bitter about their lot and blame other people or society for the fact that they have not got what they wanted in life. Their children are not allowed to be pleased with themselves; if they dare to achieve things and be proud of the fact, they are quickly put down with, 'Who do you think you are?' Try Hard is the response to a very powerful injunction against competing with Mother or Father. It is sex-linked, that is, a Try Hard woman is unwilling to compete with her mother, and a Try Hard man is unwilling to compete with his father. The Child of the child is terrified of losing Mother's or Father's love by making them envious, if they dare to achieve something their parents wanted to but never did. Often, the Parent messages given are vociferously, 'We want you to do/have all the things we never had the opportunity to do/have'. The Depression, the Second World War and early motherhood are often invoked by recent generations of parents as the external circumstances that account for their failures in life; the children believe them and are thus made loath to take what they see as the unfair advantages that the world is offering them compared with what it offered their parents. True, there are external social circumstances that stand in the way of people getting all that they want when they want it, but external circumstances are never the whole truth. A spirit of aliveness and joy can be found in the direst external circumstances, as can misery and bitterness be found in abundance amongst the materially most privileged. Even in concentration camps where luck was truly in evidence and giving up could be justified, there were winners and losers. Obstacles empower winners and defeat losers; winners see the doughnut, losers see the hole.

Sociologically, in Britain Try Hard is eminently working-class Conservative to the point of 'fascism' in the Driver position and militant trade unionist in the Blamer position. 'Knowing one's place' rules such families' lives.

Developmentally, Try Hard is very much in evidence in adolescence, when aggressive hostility towards the same-sexed parent is expressed by the child as he or she struggles to achieve his or her confidence as a competent adult. The demands on the child to work hard to pass examinations exploit, in a positive way, the natural aggressive-competitive impulses of this stage of development.

Overall, Try Hard is competitive, angry, aggressive, pathetic, humble, helpless, grandiose, conceited, bitter, militant and sarcastically discounting of others. Above all it is envious of others. The Try Hard person starts a dozen projects and finishes none of them. Try Hard seeks out the company of people who are even more Try Hard than itself so that it can look down on them; although it is also eager to be a hanger-on of some other people whom it looks up to. What Try Hard cannot cope with is the essential reality that we are all better than most people at a few things, not as good as most other people at a few things and equal with every other human being in nearly every respect. For Try Hard it is competing on the centre court at Wimbledon or not playing tennis at all; winning the Nobel Prize or discounting all its achievements; being the most beautiful woman in the room or not going into the room; being able to afford a mink coat or having no coat at all. Try Hard wants all or nothing and so gets nothing.

Typical words used by Try Hard are: Can you. . .?, could/couldn't; impossible; superior/inferior; fail/succeed; I don't know; it's hard; lucky/unlucky; I'm better than/not as good as you/him/her. Try Hard's tone of voice is angry and sarcastic; its facial expression is puzzled, irritated and worried. Verbal and body attitudes include sitting forward, elbows on knees, chin in hand; asking more than one question at a time; not answering the question asked; a stuttering, impatient manner and clenched fist.

Try Hard is seeking to reaffirm a decision like, 'I'm a failure' or 'I'm not as good as I think I am'. Its deadly sins are Envy and Sloth. The core defensive aim of the Driver is never to finish anything, so as to leave open to doubt whether it is a success or failure. Success would mean symbolically murdering the envious parent; failure would be wholeheartedly to admit that the parent was right. More than any of the other personality types, Try Hard bears witness to the Biblical 'sins of the fathers being visited upon the children even unto the third and fourth generation'. When introjected the Driver 'tries'; projected, it tells others to 'try'. The Maladaptor position, when introjected, is withdrawal in response to the racket fear of failure; projected, it is, 'Who do you think you are?' The Blamer position, introjected, is 'I could do that if I wanted to', or 'It's not worth it'; projected, it is 'That's good enough', or 'Well, it's better than nothing'. The typical Despairer payoff of 'I'm a failure', or 'No amount of effort pays off for me' is projected as, 'Well, you were overstepping yourself, weren't you?'

Try Hard *wastes time and money*. It is prone to headaches and all stress-related illnesses such as ulcers. It is more than averagely inclined to die as a consequence of accidents. Commonly, Try Hard is manifest as conceit or envy and bitterness. Most extremely, it becomes pathological narcissism and/or schizoid grandiosity.

The paradox of Try Hard is that its defence against its fear of failure makes the success it longs for impossible, because all success involves failure along the way. It avoids Hell and Heaven; it lives in Purgatory. Only when it stops making excuses for its parents' failures and bitterness will it stop, likewise, making excuses for itself and instead, by appropriate persistent effort, achieve its own healthy self-esteem and be able to take pleasure in others' self-esteem, without envy or admiration, but as equal to equal.

> Lack of reverence for oneself revenges itself through every kind of deprivation, health, friendship, well-being, pride, cheerfulness, freedom, firmness, courage. One never afterwards forgives oneself for this lack of genuine egoism. . . I wish men would begin by respecting themselves: everything else follows from that.
>
> *Nietzsche*

Be Strong

> A person who does not lose his reason over certain things can have no reason to lose. *Freud*

Be Strong is the defence against the fear of rejection. It is the Oedipal response of the child to feeling redundant to the self-sufficient, closed, symbiotic relationship between his or her parents, irrespective of whether the relationship between the parents was essentially happy or essentially unhappy. The consequence is that the child neither identifies with his or her same-sexed parent, nor feels appreciated by his other opposite-sexed parent. Consequently, Be Strong children believe they lack the characteristics that are needed to be loveworthy, and they respond with lonely self-sufficiency. Be Strong recapitulates this theme in all relationships by a mask of aloofness and invulnerability to others, which prevents others making intimate contact and so avoids being rejected at the price of avoiding intimacy. 'I don't need or want anybody' is the lie it tells itself and others.

As a personality type, self-sufficiency or rejection is the core dimension which Be Strong applies to all relationships between people. It longs for closeness, but believes it is intrinsically unloveworthy and, therefore, has to do without intimacy altogether or be satisfied with a relationship with a very needy other, whose neediness alone will bind that other to him or her.

> I hope I never lose control of myself in anything. I never have, not even with a girl I wish I wanted to. I'm glad I don't. . . I wonder what kind of person would come out if I ever did erase all my inhibitions at once, what kind of a being is bottled up inside me now. Would I like him? I think not. *Heller*

Be Strong makes a virtue out of what it sees as a necessity to be solely dependent on itself for strokes to its Child. Convinced that its Child is essentially unloveworthy, Be Strong never asks for any strokes from others for its Child and puts it last when choosing, on any occasion, which ego state is the most appropriate one to be in. Because, biologically, it is natural for the man to 'ask' the woman for intimacy and for the woman to respond to this asking, the sex life of a Be Strong man is more obviously curtailed than is the sex life of a Be Strong woman. Even when Be Strong cannot avoid noticing that people are stroking its Child, it disbelieves in the authenticity of the strokes being offered, and either huffily dismisses the other person on the presumption that he or she is a crawler or else politely accepts the stroke without allowing it to give nourishment. He or she is only able to accept a few strokes for its responsible Parent and its sensible Adult.

Be Strong is induced in families where children are expected to be seen and not heard. Expressing emotion, particularly painful emotion, is frowned on as bad form, and kissing and cuddling are positively discouraged. Be Strong is also induced in families where there is no Parent currency to support it, but it is simply a response to circumstantial unlovingness towards and general emotional neglect of the child.

Typically, one or other of the parents is so narcissistically embroiled in his or her own Child's needs and the other parent so busy coping with the narcissistic parent's demands, that neither parent has energy left over for giving to the Child of the child. The child assumes the Rescuer role towards the needy parent's Victim, by which means he or she makes continual but doomed-to-fail attempts to 'make Mummy or Daddy better'. The Victim parent often explicitly invites the child to 'Parent' him or her but inevitably turns Persecutor so that the child ends up the true victim of the parent's exploitation. Be Strong children are never allowed to be real children — carefree, playful, demanding and indulged — only little adults, worldly-wise, sad and constantly burdened by their awareness of others' suffering.

Like all the other types, Be Strong may predominate in any individual in any culture, but sociologically, Be Strong is a very English middle-class and upper-class syndrome, and the British public school ethos systematically indoctrinates it. Children at public and other boarding schools typically have Be Strong imposed on them by teachers and caretakers as a moral imperative, with the aim of producing stiff-upper-lipped ladies and gentlemen, ready to serve the community with impermeable emotional invulnerability. Stoicism is the chief Parent currency supporting Be Strong.

Developmentally, Be Strong is most evident during latency, six-to-twelve-years of age, when the Adult ego state predominates in the personality, and children are less emotionally involved with others than they were in their earlier years or will again be from the onset of puberty.

Overall, Be Strong is manifestly cold, aloof, self-contained, uninvolved, invulnerable, unemotional, independent and a loner. Be Strong talks about feelings, but never shows them. 'Strength' versus 'weakness' is a core dimension; self-discipline is displayed and respected in oneself and others, while mawkishness or any form of wearing one's heart on one's sleeve is deplored. Duty is pleasure. People who express their emotions are judged boring. Be Strong longs most of all to be given the love that it, in fact, rejects if gratuitously offered it, because it cannot believe in love. Be

Strong asks for nothing and so gets nothing.

> Against the suffering which may come upon one from human relationships, the readiest safeguard is voluntary isolation, keeping oneself aloof from other people.
> *Freud*

It was Be Strong in Captain Oates that 'went out for a while' to die on Scott's last voyage. It is Be Strong who is the last to leave a sinking ship, is marvellous in a crisis, gets on with things, goes for brisk walks and gets up at 6.00 a.m. every day of the year to go for a swim. It never cries or whines or complains, and a Be Strong man often wears a moustache, 1982 to keep his upper lip hidden just in case, despite his best efforts, it should slacken. Be Strong is deeply lonely and stroke-deprived but is usually only seen by others to be aloof and stand-offish.

Typical words and phrases used by Be Strong are: strong/weak; boring; pull yourself together; I don't care; no comment; vulnerable; duty; childish; it's no good getting upset/crying over spilt milk; you don't appreciate what I'm saying; I feel that. . .; that makes me feel. . . Be Strong says 'you' or, even more Be Strong, 'one' instead of 'I'. Be Strong's tone of voice is monotonic and dispassionate; its face is moulded, cold, hard, expressionless; posture is erect, rigid and frozen. Verbal and body attitudes include an over-straight back; legs crossed, apparently being totally in Adult but actually in Adapted Child; having, if male, a moustache and pulling up socks; excessive expression of appreciation for anything received.

Be Strong is seeking to reaffirm a decision like 'I am unappreciated' or 'I am unloveworthy'. Its deadly sin is Pride. The core defensive aim of the Driver is to avoid rejection by not asking for anything. When introjected, the Driver may be observed as not complaining whatever the circumstances; projected, it is Rescuer behaviour that offers unwanted help to others.

> Sparsit . . . was so excessively regardless of herself and regardful of others, as to be a nuisance.   *Dickens*

Be Strong loves playing the 'Why don't you. . .?' hand in the game 'Why don't you. . .? Yes, but. . .'. The Maladaptor position, when introjected, is usually a feeling of fear of rejection; projected, others are accused of being too demanding. Introjected, the Blamer waits passively and inflexibly for others to make the first approach; projected, the Blamer finds others boring and expresses invulnerability to them. 'I am unappreciated/unlovable' is the usual Despairer payoff, which may be projected as accusing others of being unappreciative and insatiably demanding.

Be Strong *uses time and money*. It keeps itself very healthy to avoid the 'weakness' and vulnerability of being ill, but Be Strong is commonly the predominant miniscript amongst people who commit suicide without warning, taking others completely by surprise. Be Strong is more than averagely inclined to die of a stroke. Note the canny connection to its 'stroke' deprivation, which suggests that Eric Berne may have drawn on a deep psychological truth embedded in language when he coined the term 'stroke' for TA. Commonly, Be Strong is expressed as resigned loneliness. Most extremely Be Strong becomes autism, in which there is total non-reactivity to other people, that is, no strokes whatsoever from other people are acknowledged.

The paradox of Be Strong is that its defence against its fear of rejection makes the intimacy it longs for impossible, because the achievement of intimacy involves being open to others, which involves the risk of rejection. Its adherence to the myth that the avoidance of the pleasures of intimacy is a fair enough price to pay for the avoidance of pain is tantamount to emotional death. Only when it drops its pride and its selfishness in only giving and never allowing others the pleasure of giving to it, can it receive the love it longs for and intrinsically deserves as much as anybody else.

SOME TYPICAL AND VERY RELIABLE INDICATORS OF THE FIVE PERSONALITY TYPES

Personality Type	Words	Non-verbal signs	Facts of life
Be Perfect	'perfect', 'guilty', 'for my sins', 'thank God'	pursing of bottom lip between forefinger and thumb, itemizing points while speaking	having (even one) Roman Catholic or Jewish parent
Hurry Up	'Hurry up!' 'futile' 'pointless'	being regularly late, noticeable vertical frown marks between eyes	having been to boarding school, having been separated from mother before the age of three for even a few days
Please	'Y'know', 'embarrassed', 'I know you think that...' 'Really?'	hero-worshipping opposite-sexed parent, questioning expression with noticeable horizontal lines on forehead, running fingers through hair	being an only child or more than six years apart from nearest sibling
Try Hard	'try', 'superior/inferior', 'lucky/unlucky' 'I envy/admire...'	hero-worshipping same-sexed parent, sitting forward, chin in hands, with concentrated and puzzled look	the premature death of the same-sexed parent
Be Strong	'one' instead of 'I', 'bored', 'weak/strong'	(man) having a moustache, pulling socks up	having been to boarding school

The Compounds of Personality

By and large, every personality contains characteristics of each of the miniscripts. Together, the five elements of Be

Perfect, Hurry Up, Please, Try Hard and Be Strong make up the substance of everybody's Adapted Child; and the Adapted Child is involved in nearly everything we feel, think and do in the course of our waking lives. But these elements are mixed and matched in a large variety of ways in individual human beings. Some people have one element dominatingly and overwhelmingly present in most of their everyday transactions, while others seem to make use in quick succession of all five elements. However, generally speaking, most people seem to concentrate on two miniscripts to confirm their core painful existential position, whose continual reaffirmation is the chief motivator of all that we think, feel and do throughout our lives.

Thus the ten possible pairings of the five miniscripts describe ten common personality sub-types. Usually the elements seem to combine in an additive way. That is, they combine in such a way as to underline some feature to be found in both of the constituents. One of the elements usually describes the kernel of the individual's being, while the second provides the flesh to protect and reinforce the central existential position with additional rationalizations and justifications. Sometimes one of the pair, notably the other element in most combinations with Hurry Up, is an attempt to nullify the meaning of the principal element at the core of the personality. However, at the deepest level, each pair represents both a conflict and the resolution of that conflict in an individual. See the table, *Samenesses and Oppositeness between the Five Personality Types* (p.130).

Sometimes people experience themselves as being less profoundly committed to one of the miniscripts they habitually use than to others. When this is the case, the miniscript that is more superficial is usually a third miniscript that has been acquired imitatively, at a behavioural level only, from one or other of the parents, without serving a deep existential commitment of its own. Its expression in the personality represents obedience to an injunction rather than the reaffirmation of a decision.

While the isotopic manifestations in thought, feeling and

behaviour of the singular miniscripts are multifarious, their essentially elementary nature makes a fairly comprehensive account of each of them possible. The compounds, on the other hand, are manifestations of the enormous overall complexity of any particular personality, so any compound description is bound to be a caricature of any particular human being it is describing. Nevertheless, the stereotypes described by the compounds of pairs made out of the five elements are enormously useful means of inferring, from even the briefest transactions that we may have with a stranger on a bus, the core existential positions of people we encounter. The vignettes that follow are outlines of the usual attributes contained in each of the simplest compounds of personality including the usual childhood background associated with it, the core existential dichotomy of the compound, the defensive armour associated with it and the typical compound decision being served.

Be Perfect/Hurry Up This is the *uncommitted doubter*. Potentially, because it holds in balance the most atavistic and archetypal impulses in us all, the fear of death and the quest for excitement, it represents the ideal of psychological health, but it also contains within it the seeds of some of the best-known and intractable dis-eases that are familiar to psychotherapists including alcoholism, manic-depression and anorexia nervosa. Whether the net result of the internal balancing act of the personality is equanimity and healthily sceptical open-mindedness, or an excruciating and overwhelming combined terror of and wish for insanity or death or something in between, depends on how intensely the two elements are experienced in the individual. From my experience, the difference between essential health and essential pathology in this compound is reflected in whether or not the individual has found a meaning of life, which transcends the mundane goals of everyday living, and can be expressed through purposeful endeavour. For many people, parenthood is the prototype of all such endeavours, but anything that the individual decides is in the long run profoundly worth doing serves the same need. If such a purpose is not found, the individual forces himself to consume all the energy of his dilemma in the dilemma itself, in an escalating spiral of Be Perfect catching up with Hurry Up and overstepping the mark, which necessitates an extra spurt of Hurry Up to catch up with Be Perfect, which oversteps the mark . . . to the limiting equilibrium, in its most pathological form, of manic-depressive psychosis or death by suicide or accident. Like right-wing and left-wing political parties, Be Perfect and Hurry Up are manifestly opposites and capable of holding each other in check, yet they meet in an implosive fusion of fascism/communism when each becomes extreme. Uncommitted doubters need their work to provide them with personal meaning as well as money. They make very good salespeople if they 'believe in' what they are selling. I am grateful to a colleague and friend of mine, Dianne Salters, who has told me of a man in one of her therapy groups who manifests his Be Perfect/Hurry Up nature adaptively and with remarkable literalness in his job; he is a safety officer in a nuclear power station!

It often seems to be the case that the personality compounded into an unhealthy combination of Be Perfect and Hurry Up is playing out a protracted vengeance on one of its parents. A Hurry Up response by a child to its perception of some form of abandonment by the parents is often the beginning of the syndrome, at which time the child says to itself, 'I must have done something bad to have been so punished'. But the child also notices Be Perfect in its parents, and learns from them how to use it both introjectively to confirm its perception of itself as a sinner, and projectively to blame its parents, who are eminently vulnerable to blame by virtue of their own Be Perfect, for being bad parents. 'I am bad, but so are you' is the conclusion. This conclusion is displayed by some form of chronic illness in the child, physical or psychological, which serves as a punishment of affliction for all parties to the sin. The parents feel overwhelmed by distress and guilt for the sickness of the child, who chronically Tries Hard to get better while gleefully avenging itself on itself and its parents. The breaking down of the impasse rests with the child; once it is willing openly to confront its parents with what it blames them for and to hear their self-flagellating apologies and to forgive them in a once-and-for-all way, both parents and child can each be freed to deploy their energies outside their previously all-consuming mutual symbiosis.

In its moderate degrees, the Be Perfect/Hurry Up compound is often expressed as a very equable personality. If it sabotages the individual's overall happiness, this can often only be inferred by statements the individual makes about himself like, 'I don't know why, but I always feel I'm not fulfilling my potential'. This remark reflects the individual's awareness that too much of his energy is consumed in his internal balancing act.

Some behavioural and verbal clues may be observed in individuals who seem to alternate between thinking too long and too hard, and rashly rushing into things; or who are reliably unreliable to a precise degree, such as always being seven minutes late for appointments; or who express intense needs to belong and not belong at the same time, which is well-exemplified in people who are members of an unusual or unorthodox religious or other community.

The core existential dichotomy of this compound is security or danger, which justifies the expression of excessive caution and bravado. The compound decision being served is something like, 'I and the whole world are either mad or bad, but I'm not sure which'. When the uncommitted doubter transforms guilt into organization and panic into efficiency, he or she may become the truly *passionate philosopher*.

Be Perfect/Please This is the *righteous blamer*. Be Perfect morality is powerfully brought to bear as a justification for the conventional goodness that defends Please's emotional insecurity. This personality is a proclamation of unresolved symbiotic attachment to the opposite-sexed parent; Child feelings and Parent beliefs are heavily contaminated, and the individual expresses intense emotionality in response to everybody and everything. Portnoy is the prototype, and the caricature of Jewish parenthood as morally upright, argumentatively controlling, indulgent and smotheringly loving is the archetypal cause. Righteous blamers are typically very successful 'organization' people, eminently capable as they are both of controlling and being controlled, and they are often workaholics.

This compound can be seen also as a consequence of the premature death of the opposite-sexed parent, resulting in a forced incompletion of the healthy emotional-sexual 'letting go' of that parent. The parent's death is rationalized by the child as punishment for her sins, and she adds Please to Be Perfect in a desperate bid to be so very, very good in future that no such punishment will ever again be justified. The core dichotomy of this compound is control or be controlled, which justifies the expression of pious self-righteousness. As Polonius put it:

> Tis too much prov'd, that with devotions visage
> And pious action we do sugar o'er
> The devil himself.   *Shakespeare*

The compound decision being served is something like, 'If I make the wrong decision I will be culpable and feel guilty, but so long as I make no choice I am being good, so nobody can blame me for what goes wrong.' When the righteous blamer transforms guilt into organization and feeling misunderstood into flexibility, he or she may become the truly *responsible leader*.

Be Perfect/Try Hard This compound is the *fighter of lost causes*. The Be Perfect component is an obsessive *idée fixe* about what should be done to set the world to rights, but Try

Hard makes sure that the goal is unrealistic. This personality is aggressively single-minded and dismissive of all topics of conversation but its own hobby-horse. In non-communist countries, communism is a favourite belief system espoused, containing as it does, within its own self-definition, a core existential component of this personality: that Adult, reason and Parent belief are one and the same thing. 'Moral and stupid' is opposed to 'rebellious and clever'; super-reasonableness flatly rejects as irrelevant any Child feelings which may question the absolute righness of the cause. Often this personality is an expression of antiscript against a dogmatic and bullying parent, whose ethical or political views were the direct opposite of what the child now stands for. It may also be a consequence of the premature death of the same-sexed parent. There is unresolved competitive attachment to the same-sexed parent, resulting in Try Hard, to which the individual, as an adult, adds Be Perfect as a compensatory bid for power that it does not feel and which convinces nobody but his own frightened children.

Power and pride or submission and humiliation is the core dichotomy in this compound, which justifies the expression of blame and envy. The compound decision being served is something like, 'Nobody lives up to my ideals and I'm not as good as I should be either. If I do bad things other people may let me off, and then I am relieved, but I would feel more loved if they punished me and told me what I've done wrong'. These people usually struggle long and hard to feel successful in their work because of their chronic equivocation between wanting to stay non-conformist rebels and wanting the privileges, but not the responsibilities to others, of becoming members of the Establishment. When the fighter of lost causes transforms guilt into organization and fear of failure into persistence, he or she may become the truly *committed champion*.

Be Perfect/Be Strong This is the *cold intellectual*. The two elements in this compound are the only two elements which do not, in some way, imply inhibition of thought. This compound throws interesting light on British, as contrasted with European and particularly French, thought. Since the rationality of Be Perfect is an essential ingredient of all intellectuality, and Be Perfect is much more predominant a cultural element of continental Europe than Britain, Britain is a comparatively non-intellectual country. But when, in Britain, an individual Be Perfect thinker produces an idea, it is likely to have the special British advantage of Be Strong empiricism as well as Be Perfect rationality. Historically, it is probably a fair claim that as a nation we don't think much, but when we do, Be Strong pragmatism gives our ideas an ultimate advantage over the purely rational ideas of our singularly Be Perfect French rivals.

The childhood background invoking Be Perfect/Be Strong is usually puritanically achievement-oriented. Hard work is the purpose of life and achievement is its meaning. The personality is fiercely independent and self-sufficient. Cold intellectuals dislike 'bossing' or 'being bossed' and are happiest self-employed.

Being rejected or self-denial is the core existential dichotomy of this compound which justifies the expression of superior aloofness. The compound decision being served is something like, 'Other people cannot cope with my needs as well as their own. Since their needs are greater than mine, I have no right to ask for anything from them. So long as I need nothing from others I will not be tempted to ask for anything, and so I can remain blameless.' When the cold intellectual transforms guilt into organization and feeling unappreciated into being resilient, he or she may become the truly *independent thinker*.

Hurry Up/Please This is the *sorry sinner*. Hurry Up is usually at the core of this compound, with Please taken on board in a desperate bid to find the rules of interpersonal behaviour that will release the individual from his or her pain and isolation. Existentially this compound has much in common with Be Perfect/Hurry Up, but Hurry Up/Please is usually less well adapted to the world at large, because Please is less powerful than Be Perfect as a counterforce to Hurry Up. Please's values are relative; Be Perfect's are absolute. Whereas a powerful enough Be Perfect purpose of life can often control and contain Hurry Up in an individual, any Please rules only work with some of the people some of the time; so Hurry Up, seeking reassurance of goodness from Please, is called on constantly to amend its rules with changing people and circumstances. Overall, the individual tends doubly to defeat her goal, since the uncertainties of Please merely add nervousness to her consciousness of herself, and so further exacerbate her Hurry Up. Sorry sinners are usually popular for being lively amongst the people they work with, but they are inclined to have episodic outbursts of rudeness and bad temper that may threaten their job security.

Hurry Up and Please separately each presume to read other people's minds, and compounded they are obsessed with knowing what other people are thinking. By this knowing they seek positively to obey Please rules, but they switch rapidly and unpredictably into screaming, paranoic 'knowing' that the other person is out to get them, which they will not put up with one moment longer!

The family background that produces this compound is one where the child is fundamentally rejected, but the rejection is cloaked with middle-class niceness that protects the parents from accepting responsibility for the harm they are inflicting on their child. I once spoke, every so nicely, to one such mother, suggesting that perhaps some of her attitudes had a bearing on her now grown-up daughter's problems. Her response was, 'But I don't think parents can influence their children, do you?'

The core existential dichotomy of this compound is terrifying aloneness or suffocating reassurance which justifies the expression of clinging dependency and paranoid rejection. The compound decision being served is something like, 'I could love life if only I could find somebody to love me in the way I want to be loved, that is with unconditional love from the other's Parent to my Child. I try so hard to be good, and sometimes I think I am loved, but then the other person always soon stops loving me and tells me to go to hell'. When the sorry sinner transforms panic into efficiency and feeling misunderstood into flexibility, he or she may become the truly *lively conformist*.

Hurry Up/Try Hard   This is the *angry outsider*. It is formed out of rejection in childhood combined with aggressive negative strokes usually including physical violence. It is Hell's Angels, bully boys, and criminals. Less extremely, it is con men, militant trade unionists or militant women's libbers . . . or militant anything. The passive version is the derelict or the laid-back drop out. In general, this personality is snarling, derisive and cynical. Often it is utterly joyless, but sometimes the underlying Natural Child quest for joy finds expression in a hare-versus-tortoise-like attitude to life, in which the individual is always moving on from one short-lived enthusiasm to the next. Each enthusiasm is a doomed-to-fail bid for success that Try Hard denies it, and/or the salvation that Hurry Up prompts it to seek and never to find. Angry outsiders hate 'the system' and only work at all for the money they need for their personal, usually profligate, pleasures.

The core existential dichotomy of this compound is rage or futility which justifies the expression of pugnacious sarcasm. The compound decision being served is something like, 'There's nothing you can do for me or give me and I'll sock you one if you try. I'm no good but neither are you. The world is one big shit heap'. When the angry outsider transforms panic into efficiency and fear of failure into persistence, he or she may become the truly *roving adventurer*.

Hurry Up/Be Strong   This is the *frightened loner*. Any individual in whom this compound is a central feature has unequivocally been stroke-deprived in childhood to a criminal extent. These are the battered babies, the children in care and, horrifically — in my direct experience — many of the most materially privileged children in Britain, the sons and daughters of the upper class. So lonely are these people and so painful and futile does life seem inescapably to be to them, that they are compelled continuously to do battle with self-destructive impulses that goad them to find, in death, the only possible release from their torment. They recognize Hurry Up and Be Strong in themselves as two independent components in their being. Hurry Up is the bad part, and Be Strong the good. True, at least Be Strong in them is allowed to think, but it never occurs to them that life has anything better to offer than stiff-upper-lipped loneliness. Their profound social alienation often disenables them to remain in any job, except briefly.

The typical British upper-class childhood of frightened loners is one of very early rejection by busy mothers and militaristic fathers, who pay for their infants and young children to be cared for by, often, a succession of nannies. Hurry Up is well established by the time these children are sent off to boarding school at seven or eight years of age, at which time their sense of desolate aloneness probably reaches its peak. Thereafter, if not before, Be Strong is imposed imperiously to produce the deeply lonely, joyless, duty-bound member of the Establishment that is intended. By and large, such an education is 'successful': Be Strong wins and Hurry Up is submerged more or less out of consciousness, leaking out perhaps in 'drinking a bit much' or 'losing a bit much' gambling. I see the failures of the system, the souls too sensitive to create an armour thick enough to defend themselves against awareness; individuals tragically bound in a Dr Jekyll and Mr Hyde existence, oscillating wildly between morally upright Be Strong and crazy, rejecting, often drug-addicted Hurry Up. The boys are often heroin addicts; the girls are often promiscuously loveless. One man, who was a member of the aristocracy, twenty-four years old, an old-boy of England's most prestigious public school and a heroin addict, told me he personally knew of the deaths, by drug overdose or car accidents, of five of his schoolmates during the past few years.

Brave adventurers and heroes, such as solo yachtsmen, are probably the people best adapted to this compound in themselves. Women with this compound at the core of their being sometimes enjoy a brief period of contentment during the first year of their children's lives, when they psychologically invert the utter dependency of their infants into an experience of unconditional love given by their infants to them.

The core existential dichotomy of this compound is reject or be rejected, which justifies the expression of futility and boredom. The compound decision being served is something like, 'I can make no sense of people or the world. The world is strange and cold and I am lost in it. Anyone who loves me is a shit'. When the frightened loner transforms panic into efficiency and feeling unappreciated into resilience, he or she may become the truly *brave individualist*.

Please/Try Hard This is the *humble servant*. It is stereotypically working class and lower-middle class respectability. This personality is timid, proper, utterly conventional, knows its place and does not question life as it finds it. But it is not without pride. Knowing its own place implies the obligation for others to know their place too, exemplified in the lady's maid who defines herself as above her background by virtue of the status of her employer but, equally important, below her employer. This compound is both patronizing and servile, reflecting as it usually does a childhood background that made the sons be good to be worthy of Mother's love and obedient to avoid Father's aggression, and made the daughters be good to be worthy of Father's love and obedient to avoid Mother's aggression. Humble servants are usually content to stay in dead-end jobs, so long as these jobs are secure.

The core existential dichotomy of this compound is niceness or success which justifies the expression of resentful sarcasm. The compound decision being served is something like, 'As long as people do as they are told, no harm will come to them'. When the humble servant transforms feeling misunderstood into flexibility and fear of failure into persistence, he or she may become the truly *contented worker*.

Please/Be Strong This is the *do-gooder*. While it may predominate in an individual of any nationality, it is the stereotypical picture of the English: courteous, considerate, nice but sometimes nasty; practical and helpful but also aloof, uptight, and secretly resentful of the impositions of others on their goodwill. The commonplace admiration of other nationalities for British tolerance and agreeable acceptance of eccentricity in others, seems to me to describe the comparatively rare combination, amongst nations, of Please plus a lack of Be Perfect.

At an individual level Be Strong is usually the core element, with Please added as a means of ritualistically accepting positive strokes within the strictly circumscribed bounds of convention. Reciprocally, Be Strong subdues the nervousness of Please by lending it some invulnerability to counteract Please's feelings of being misunderstood. The childhood background is an ethos of 'Think of those less fortunate than yourself, and always remember to be polite'. The thinking permission of Be Strong is fundamentally subsumed to the propriety of Please but finds expression as practicality and commonsense. This compound concentrates on putting others at their ease, so reassuring itself that it is relating effectively to others.

The core dichotomy of this compound is control or vulnerability which justifies the expression of resentful withdrawal. The compound decision being served is something like, 'I look after others when, by rights, they should be looking after me'. When the do-gooder transforms feeling misunderstood into flexibility and feeling unappreciated into resilience, he or she may become the truly *generous carer*.

Try Hard/Be Strong This is the *proud loser*. The childhood that invokes it usually has the quality of military-type subordination of the child by his or her same-sexed parent. The child is stroke-deprived and humiliated. As adults, these children continue deeply to fear and hero-worship their same-sexed parent, and unconsciously decide never to threaten that parent's supremacy by never matching the parent's accomplishments. In contrast with the Be Perfect/Try Hard compound, which is existentially similar in some ways, proud losers do not make a fuss about their loneliness or despair; rather they timidly Try Hard to make their feelings and wishes known and to fulfil their ambitions, but they so under-express themselves as to ensure that their cries and ideas remain unheard and unvalued. Proud losers typically dislike but endure their work, whatever it is. But they are not much noticed in their jobs, and they tend to withdraw into their private dreams.

The core existential dichotomy of this compound is frustration or resignation which justifies the expression of envious aloofness. The compound decision being served is something like, 'The struggle to get what I want is not worthwhile because successful people never appreciate my worth, so I'd rather be with losers who I know are inferior to me'. When the proud loser transforms fear of failure into persistence and feeling unappreciated into resilience, he or she may become the truly *quiet achiever*.

At a sociological level, my experience of the compound types being associated with particular classes in society is limited to England. However, through my travels and my vicarious experience I feel confident enough to make some broad generalizations about some other societies as wholes, although not to sub-sections within them. Non-English readers may judge for themselves whether my broad assessments of their own societies are accurate. Readers may also like to make their own assessments of the meanings of friendships and enmities between nations based on the interactions of the stereotypes (See Chapter 9).

The English are Please/Be Strong.

The Irish are Be Perfect/Hurry Up — Hurry Up tending to dominate.

The Welsh are Try Hard/Be Strong.

The Scots are Be Perfect/Be Strong.

The French are overwhelmingly Be Perfect — focused mostly on sex and food and the pronunciation of their language.

The Germans are Be Perfect/Please — to be successful and respectable.

The Italians are Be Perfect/Hurry Up — Be Perfect dominating in the aesthetic aspects of life, Hurry Up in government.

The Americans are Hurry Up/Try Hard — to be loved and make a billion dollars.

The Israelis are Be Perfect/Please — to be righteous in their own and others' estimation.

The Arab nations are Be Perfect/Try Hard — to get revenge.

Northern European countries tend, like the English, to be Please/Be Strong.

The Australians are Hurry Up/Try Hard — to have a good time and be culturally respected.

The Japanese are Please/Try Hard — to be nice and rigidly to persist.

Chapter 5

Life Tasks

The best man is he who most tries to perfect himself, and the happiest man is he who most feels he *is* perfecting himself.
Socrates

A man should not strive to eliminate his complexes but to get in accord with them. They are legitimately what directs his conduct in the world.
Freud

Transmuting Pain into Joy

Our hang-ups and our talents are one and the same. It is the human drive to find positive meaning for our pains that, individually and collectively, has produced all the ideas and artefacts of civilization. I believe it is far from fortuitous that Beethoven was deaf, Monet blind, and Freud had cancer of the mouth. Without our uniquely human consciousness of 'self' we would live instinctively, as animals do, and the only 'aim' of our lives would be unself-conscious play. There would be no despair and no exultation.

Paradoxically, the ultimate achievement of the mystic in

'transcending the ego' comes very close to the mindlessness of animals who seek no meanings in life and merely live it. So, too, an infant before he demonstrates the emergence of his ego by his use of the word 'I' is at one with the universe. In between these two extremes of innocent infancy and the serene wisdom of old age — attained by very few! — lies the vast territory of the ego which, mundanely speaking, is what our individual destinies and our relationships are all about.

It is the difficulties we encounter in establishing our egos, that is, in establishing our full self-esteem, that constitute our fears and their associated pains. The most primitive response to the fears in our egos is denial of their existence, and people who choose this option reduce themselves to the status of animals in inescapable captivity, apathetically staring at the iron bars of their cage with never even a dream of the jungle. There are others who are aware of their fears and pretentiously seek to evade the challenge of developing their egos with pre-emptive pseudo-wisdom, mouthing 'Vanity of vanities, all is vanity. . .', being 'transcendental' on drugs and generally 'copping out'. They remain miserable and self-destructive despite their protestations.

But the majority of us acknowledge our humanity and struggle valiantly to grow our egos within our acknowledged personal limitations. These limitations are our fears which, irrational as we know them to be, seem like insuperable barriers to the attainment of our deepest longings. Our fears are manifestations of our knowledge, which we desperately seek to be unconscious of, that we compulsively reiterate our obedience to our painful as well as our joyful messages and decisions. For as long as we deny the existence in our psyches of our compulsions to pain, they remain our hang-ups; brought into consciousness, they can be harnessed to provide us with passion to transmute them into the heroic, rather than the tragic, fulfillment of our personal destinies. We are all alike in having some painful messages and decisions that we live by; we are all different in the specificity of our pains. Knowledge of the five personality types is a powerful shortcut to knowing our personal pains, because all our specific pains are variations on these five themes.

Our fears derive from our defeat in our very early socializing experiences, when our compliance to our parents was a survival issue; now, we continue to behave as if our obedience to our parents is still the choice we must make for our survival, even though it no longer is. And yet we cannot simply throw away our inculcated messages and decisions, for obedience to our messages gets us strokes, our psychological food; and continued belief in our decisions enables us to make sense of experience, and without this facility we would be helplessly insane. Biologically, it is too late for us to be re-programmed with different messages and decisions; but what we can do is make the most and the best rather than the worst and the least of our total natures. Thus healing occurs for each of us through re-connecting the feared and suppressed 'bad' parts of our psyches with our conscious quests for joy. The connections are made by means of our imaginative Little Professors creatively transmuting the meanings of our involuntarily received pains into present and future chosen purposes. 'To redeem the past, and to transform every "it was" into "I wanted it thus" — that alone I would call redemption' (Nietzsche).

The extent and intensity of pain in people's scripts varies, and those people whose pains are great may need the help of formal psychotherapy to gain the power to obey the letter of the law of the Adapted Child and yet serve the spirit of the Natural Child and so find positive fulfillment of their decisions. This is particularly the case for all people in whom Hurry Up is a prominent part of their personalities. While no book can create the dynamic tensions which a therapist's skills produce to precipitate the radical release people seek from the most constricting messages and decisions in their Adapted Child, there is, nevertheless, some general good counsel that can be given to people concerning how to act towards themselves and others in ways that can significantly improve their overall sense of well-being. And even without the lengthy process of creatively transmuting our compulsions to pain into zealous positive purposes in our lives, a great increase in our well-being can be attained simply by becoming fully and honestly conscious of the pains we set ourselves up repeatedly to experience.

There is one immutable truth about all our fears, whatever personality types we happen to be, and that is that to triumph over them we have to have the courage to work through them. It is simply not possible to overcome a fear by rational assault on its irrationality and then to do the thing we most long to do without fear. The Adapted Child is far, far too powerful to capitulate to Adult reason. There is certainly no harm done in mocking our fears with our reason and thus having a sense of humour about our hang-ups; but the only way we can actually diminish our fears is to do what we most fear even while we are frightened.

Doing what we most fear is courageous, creative living. It stretches our boundaries and rewards us with immense relief, and the frightening experiences we previously sought so hard to avoid but couldn't, as if by magic, begin to dissolve into nothingness. Our fears never entirely disappear, but the threshold of our reactivity gets higher and higher, until only the rarest occurrences have the power to prompt us back into fear. Shakespeare knew, of course.

> Assume a virtue, if you have it not.
> . . . Refrain to-night;
> And that shall lend a kind of easiness
> To the next abstinence: the next more easy;
> For use almost can change the stamp of nature,
> And master ev'n the devil or throw him out
> With wondrous potency. *Shakespeare*

The issues for each of us are idiosyncratic to our scripts, but the process is the same for all of us. Nietzsche put it very eloquently.

> One thing is needful — To 'give style' to one's character — a great and rare art! It is practised by those who

survey all the strengths and weaknesses of their nature and then fit them into an artistic plan until every one of them appears as art and reason and even weaknesses delight the eye.... Whoever is dissatisfied with himself is continually ready for revenge, and we others will be his victims, if only by having to endure his ugly sight. For the sight of what is ugly makes one bad and gloomy.

Thus, by virtue of being human, we are driven by the fears in our Adapted Child, and the only choices we have are to evade our fears by one device or another and get nowhere; or to struggle through our fears consciously and courageously preferring both joy and pain to nullity.

The outcome of struggling to overcome our fears is bound to be manifest as tangible accomplishments of one form or another. It is the obsessive desire to transcend our hang-ups which is, I believe, the hidden energy in anything and everything that has ever been created by individuals or by mankind collectively. I believe that all accomplishments are the outcome of the struggle to reconcile desire with reality. That is, all accomplishment is energized by discontent. In our individual psyches 'reality' is our Adapted Child constrictions, and 'desire' is the impulse in our Natural Child towards joy. The more powerfully opposed are the forces of our Natural and Adapted Childs the greater is our neurosis and our creative potential. We have no choice in the matter of what hand we have been dealt. Happy genes and a contented childhood are the lot of some and, consequently, a simple and contented life. Innate psychological or physical handicaps and a sorry childhood are the lot of others and, consequently, a neurotic life or a life of creative peaks and troughs beyond the capacity of the simply contented. No hand is better or worse than another; we can only choose to play our own, well or badly. It is the courage and the struggle, not the outer achievement, that is the measure of an individual's worth.

In what follows I have collected out of my accumulated experience some tips for each of the five basic personality types that may facilitate people, without recourse to formal psychotherapy, to enhance the quality of their relationships to themselves and to other people. For any individual reader some of the suggestions I make to his or her central personality type may seem less pertinent than others; I have done my best, for each type, to include all the advice that seems comparatively simple to follow and that people have most frequently informed me is useful, although I make no claim to comprehensivity.

For some people, eliminating the most negative aspects of one or other of the types from their personality is much easier than for other types in their personality. This is often the case because the easy-to-eliminate part of their total personality represents obedience to a message rather than a decision in their Adapted Child. Decisions are more profound and more immutable than messages; we can afford to disobey some of our messages and forgo some strokes to our Adapted Child, but our decisions are our profound reality and as precious to us as our sanity. So, for example, the daughter of a Please mother might, in principle, have formed no profound Please-type decisions but nonetheless exhibit Please behaviour which she acquired imitatively from her mother as a way of coping in social situations. Thus her Please symptoms will be comparatively simple to eradicate by merely informing her Adult that they are unnecessary. If you suspect that your personality contains one of the types in this superficial form it will probably be one of three types you recognize in your manifest personality, the other two types being manifestations of the profound decisions you have made.

Be Perfect

If you are mostly Be Perfect there is no doubt about it you have a better idea of how to live well than most other people. You realize that, irrespective of whether or not there is an ultimate meaning to life, the only appropriate way to live life is purposefully and morally. You set your own very high standards for everything you do, and it makes no difference to you what other people's standards are.

Your major distresses are associated with the impingement of other people's less perfect standards on the order you create in your life. Other people's casual unconcern for the things that matter most to you induces anxiety in you and prompts you to demand of them that they abide by your standards. They may be cowed into resentful submission by you but will hate you in the process. If, on the other hand, they rebelliously resist your autocracy, your anxiety and rage may escalate to murderous proportions with a backlash, in due course, of profound even suicidal depression.

Your life task is to appreciate the ultimate relativity of all values and to calibrate into degrees of importance your standards in the various areas of your life to which you apply your perfectionism. Can a muddy footprint on your newly polished floor or somebody arriving ten minutes late for an appointment truly be assessed as deserving the same degree of punitive rage from you as if you had been robbed at gunpoint? And yet this is how you tend to behave. You benefit from the standards you set yourself; other people have the right to choose lesser benefits for themselves for laxer standards. When you appreciate this you will be enabled actually to get other people more readily to meet your criteria. Recognizing and tolerating that other people have the right to care less than you do about things, you can begin to ask them, from your honest Child rather than demand from your righteous pseudo-Parent, that they maintain your standards when they are around you. Tell them, with a bit of self-mockery, that you know you're a bit of a nutter about these things but you'd really appreciate it if they would maintain certain standards, for your sake. You'll be amazed how positively responsive people will be to your requests once you de-contaminate them from self-righteousness, and other people may even come to adopt your standards for themselves.

Stop thinking! Stop making lists and lists of lists... Just get up and get on with things, in any order. Don't stop doing and don't start thinking until everything that has to be done is done. And see if you can sometimes dare to disobey the injunctions: 'Don't give in to temptation'; 'Don't be carefree'; 'Don't take chances'; and 'Don't be tolerant'.

Be aware, too, that irrespective of your relationships to other people and satisfying as you find your life, you could enormously enhance your exuberance in life by introducing a bit of chaos into it. Once in a while respond to a Natural Child impulse in yourself to do something spontaneously enjoyable now, before you have performed all the tasks that 'must' be done today. The universe will not disintegrate, and even you will survive. Above all, cultivate laughter at the essential absurdity of the human condition including your own obsessions. You are potentially very wise, and nobody has a greater capacity for achievement than you do. The difference between fulfilling your creative potential and wasting your life in pointless rigidity and superstitious obsessiveness resides in your choosing to focus your perfectionism on things that have a productive outcome rather than on meaningless rituals that simply keep your anxiety at bay. A little bit of calculated chaos and uncertainty and a developed sense of the absurd makes all the difference.

Hurry Up

If you are mostly Hurry Up you are lively, adventurous, spontaneous and active. You have a devil-may-care attitude to most things and you are ready and willing to do anything that promises immediate excitement. You are often the life and soul of the party. You are eager to form friendships and are extremely enthusiastic about any new person you meet who takes your fancy.

But anybody who is with you for more than a few hours discovers the reality that lies just beneath the surface of the very thin veneer of your social personality. Life actually terrifies you, and all your frenetic activity is a desperate bid you make to never have time to think of the aeons that stretch ahead, somehow to be filled, before you will be allowed the painlessness that only death can provide. Some of your activities may be quite clear manifestations of your death wish: alcohol; drugs; fast cars; dangerous sports. You do your best not to have enough sleep so as to incapacitate yourself for the ordinary demands of everyday life, and to blunt your awareness, thereby producing immunity to the blackness of the thoughts you believe you would have to endure if your mind was fully alert. Nevertheless, you have one continuous hope that works in favour of your staying alive, that you will find someone who will love you unconditionally and totally, forever.

Your life task is to learn to love life for its own sake and to be willing to earn the love you want from others. The only way you, or anybody, comes fully to love life is by endowing it with meaning, however obscure that meaning may be. Such meaning is what religion has always provided for mankind, but there are individuals who eschew any established religion and still find meaning through some individualistic but profound beliefs that they hold dear. You believe in nothing but the futility of all endeavour. In this you are both very far from and very close to the attitude to life that brings the greatest satisfaction and joy, namely that life is absurd. Yours is the cold, hard, pointlessness of the quest for love, espoused in Pinter's plays; warm, soft loving, that transcends sexuality, is espoused by Beckett's characters, who continue to make the most of every moment, notwithstanding their intelligent understanding that it all may be meaningless. Joy in the moment is the consequence of an absurd view of life; pain and panic are the consequences of a futile view of life.

Such preaching, though, is far from sufficient for you to make the tiny existential shift that would relieve you of your agony and bring you peace and contentment. For you, the distance is a yawning chasm that can only be bridged by the feeling that you are loved. And that is not an unrealistic demand. What is unrealistic is your demand that you do nothing to earn that love. Our only entitlement to unconditional love is from our mothers when we are babies. Maybe you didn't get it then, but you will never be happy until you give up all hope that you will get it now or in the future, from your mother or anybody else. Only then will you allow yourself to do what is necessary, slowly to build up your contentment and emotional security.

You will be considerably helped to feel in harmony with life by legitimizing your core existential position of being an outsider. For example, you could choose to live 'outside London' and have to travel in to work; or marry a foreigner and/or live in a foreign country. You will be happiest in jobs that involve movement in some way, for example: being a travelling salesman, an explorer, a fireman, an ambulance driver or an air traffic controller. Above all, in everyday life you need to Stop! Sit down and think, and don't do anything until you have made a careful plan of everything you are going to do. Then, and only then, may you get on with things in a systematic and ordered way, crossing items off your list as you complete them. (Note the paradoxical oppositeness of Be Perfect and Hurry Up. In order for Be Perfect healthily, rather than excessively, to express its chief virtue of organization it has to modify itself with efficiency which is the chief virtue of Hurry Up. Conversely, Hurry Up needs to invoke organization first in order for its chief virtue of efficiency to be expressed adaptively rather than as self-destructive impulsiveness.) And see if you can sometimes dare to disobey the injunctions: 'Don't think'; 'Don't exist'; 'Don't take your time'; 'Don't be sane'; and 'Don't be satisfied.'

You act towards people with hatefulness if they fail to give you what you want now. Why should they put your needs and wants above their own? What's in it for them? Start giving ahead of getting and give people who love you space and time to do the things they want to do that are unconnected with you. Even let them enjoy other people's company in preference to yours sometimes! Be on time for appointments. Express heartfelt gratitude for what others give you even though it isn't all you want. Decide to interact with others on the assumption that goodwill is the norm and badwill the exception, rather than with the paranoid suspiciousness of others' motives that is your usual orientation. Make lists of things you decide to accomplish each day, then do them, feeling good when they are done and crossed off the list. In general, create structures and order in your daily life and abide by them, irrespective of how you feel.

None of what I have suggested works like magic, but it will work slowly but surely to bring you the peace and contentment in life that you find so hard to believe is possible.

Please

If you are mostly Please you are as pleasant as possible to everybody. You are law-abiding, always help blind men and cripples across the road, contribute your bit to charity, send all the people you know birthday and Christmas cards and are generally committed to 'doing the right thing'. You enjoy socializing and entertain hospitably and in as lavish a way as you can afford. You are happy to be one of the silent majority of 'nice people'. It is probably unusual for you to read a book like this because you are inclined to the attitude that 'psychologizing' is unnecessary in life because, by and large, if everybody had good manners towards each other nobody would have any psychological problems.

The chink in your armour is your awareness of the trouble your own episodic outbursts of rudeness and bad temper cause you. Even so, on these occasions you usually judge the retaliatory anger you invoke in others as 'worse' than your own, so you end up feeling misunderstood but righteous.

Your life task is to accept responsibility for what happens to you and for the pain you inflict on others. It is true that your general *modus vivendi* of conventional pleasantness is a very great asset to you in the vast areas of life where people appropriately interact with each other in superficial, transient ways; but, for you, there is no real difference between these kinds of encounters and the interactions you have with the people with whom you are intimately involved. You hurt these people very deeply indeed by the thoughtless, stereotyped clichés and platitudes with which you respond to them. At the deepest levels of their being people are not all the same. Loving somebody involves responding to their unique individuality from your own feelings, from your heart, not from a rulebook of good manners. A bunch of roses may be a safe bet as a present for somebody you don't know; but for a friend, it behoves you to know, if it is the case, that he or she actually prefers daffodils! This is using your flexibility as a real virtue, rather than as thoughtless conformity. Loving somebody involves fully listening to them, right to the end of what they are saying, irrespective of your mental anticipation of what they are going to say. In fact, in your nervous haste you accurately anticipate what others are going to say far less often than you believe, and when they are angry in response to you it is often because you have heard what you decided in advance they were going to say even when they actually said something quite different.

All of this derives from the simple truth, deeply hidden from yourself, that you refuse to act or respond as a fully autonomous individual because you are terrified that if you turn out to be 'wrong' in some way you will disintegrate into a non-person and/or be punished with abandonment.

Next time someone close to you asks you if you would like to go to the pictures, have a meal out, watch a programme on television . . . or whatever, make the effort to find out in your own mind what your impulses in the matter are and then answer 'yes' or 'no' unequivocally. You are not being kind or considerate to the other person by saying, 'I don't mind' or 'If you like'. What you are really doing is making sure that you won't be responsible if you don't enjoy whatever it is; it will be the other person's fault. Is it such a terrible thing to make a mistake and not enjoy what you hoped you would? Would it be absolutely unbearable for you sometimes to persuade somebody to do something for your sake and take the responsibility for their pleasure as well as your own? And if they didn't like it to say, 'I'm sorry. I made a mistake?'

You are happiest in jobs in which you wear some actual or symbolic uniform, for example, being a policeman, fireman, judge, actor, soldier, teacher or fashion model; and in jobs serving the public or in a hierarchical organization where you can be both the boss of some people and the subordinate of others.

See if you can sometimes dare to disobey the injunctions: 'Don't feel what you feel, but what I tell you to feel'; 'Don't leave me'; 'Don't grow up'; 'Don't express bad feelings'; and 'Don't know what you want'. Your compliance to conventional and acceptable norms of behaviour takes you a long way, and many people could advantageously learn from you the needed skills for getting on with people in general. Dare to add to your repertoire of skills the challenge of being a deeply feeling, autonomous individual as well, and you will discover the joys of real intimacy that you would never previously have dreamt possible.

Try Hard

If you are mostly Try Hard you are intense and passsionately committed to righting wrongs in society and/or the world. You are deeply sympathetic to the cause of the underdog and you bravely stick your neck out to defend him or her against the aggression and oppression of the powers that be. You are an ardent and tireless worker for the political party, usually left-wing, or any other cause that you believe in, and you use your acerbic wit to deflate the pompous and smug. You stay on to fight for your cause, however difficult the going may be, long after nearly everyone else has quit. No matter how much other people may disagree with your opinions they respect your passionate aliveness. (Note the overlaps and differences between Be Perfect, Please and Try Hard in matters of 'rightness'. Be Perfect is concerned with factual and moral rightness; Please is concerned with moral rightness only; and Try Hard is concerned with factual rightness only.)

What bothers you most is that, notwithstanding all your passionate endeavours, you so rarely achieve your goals compared with so many others who seem to get what they want effortlessly. You know, but rarely admit, that you have a terrible inferiority complex which you mask with your stand-up-and-fight aggression. You can't see or hear or feel the difference between confident self-assertiveness and the aggression that seeks to compensate for the timidity you actually feel towards other people, especially those in any kind of authority over you, so you don't understand why it is always you who is 'put in your place'. You know you rarely fulfil your potential, despite the huge amount of energy you invest in working for your goals, and you are consequently deeply frustrated and bitter.

Your life task is wholeheartedly to accept the responsibilities and authority of full adulthood and so fulfil your ambitions. Your first step is to realize that the causes you so passionately espouse are displacements and evasions of the rebellious passion you feel towards your same-sexed parent, which you are too frightened to express directly. One way or another your same-sexed parent has over-powered you because of his or her own inferiority complex and consequent unwillingness to allow you the expression of your natural, adolescent, developmental need to challenge his or her authority. You have covertly been told never to dare to compete with that parent and threaten his or her tenuous, bullying self-esteem. So you are stuck in adolescent antis-cript, not knowing whether you prefer to be a difficult, defiant child or a member of the grown-up establishment. You are treading water and getting nowhere. Your relevant parent depends on the excuses he/she gives him/herself for the lack of fulfillment in his/her life, and so you dare not fulfil your potential for fear that you would thereby 'murder' that parent.

You must turn your pity or admiration for your parent into a deep gut-level, as well as rational, realization that, irrespective of the facts of people's lives over which we may have very little if any control, all human beings have the freedom to choose whether to be affirmative or negative in the living of their given circumstances. Then you will realize the unforgivable cruelty of your parent's desire to prevent you from being fulfilled so that you, their nearest and dearest, will not show up the shame of their own excuses for not fully having got what they wanted from life. Don't let them do this to you!

Stop using the word 'try' — it means you have decided in advance that you are going to fail. If you asked me to come to dinner tomorrow night and I said, 'I'll try', would you expect me? If you had appendicitis and the surgeon you consulted said, 'I'll try to take your appendix out', would you go through with the operation? 'Attempt' or 'endeavour' won't do either; they mean the same thing. Instead, you need to 'have a go', implying that you are willing to succeed, and revenge yourself on your relevant parent, or fail. But in failing you will not be letting your parent have the outright victory he or she would like to have over you, because your failure will be a stumbling block on your way to success. Don't tell your parents, or anyone else, about your ambitions until they are fulfilled, so you need not suffer the chagrin and humiliation of their triumph at your temporary defeats.

Stop comparing yourself to other people, either in envy or admiration, which are two sides of the same Try Hard coin, or with patronizing pity. Make your standards absolute not relative to other people. And don't pretend you don't want esteem and power in the world as much as anyone else. Nobody has yet 'transcended their ego' without an ego to transcend! Start now, not tomorrow, on the path to the fulfillment of your goals, which should be given momentum by a passionate desire to prove your superiority, not to the world, but only to your relevant parent in the area of life where he or she wants to keep you down. Be honest enough and brave enough to admit it is your parent you want to defeat, rather than continuing to shout angrily and impotently at the Universe for the way it is. This does not mean you need to drop the causes you espouse, but only to change the quality of the energy you expend on them, from hostile pugnacity which arouses the resistance of others and makes you fail, to enthusiastic commitment which persuades others to co-operate with you and enables you to succeed.

You will most enjoy jobs or ventures where talent or luck are clearly irrelevant, but where simple, patient, application ensures eventual success. Irrespective of the way you earn your living, physical activities such as gardening, mountain climbing, collecting or cataloguing objects, or spending years making an exquisite model railway are the kinds of activities you need to apply your persistence to as a virtue rather than as a self-defeating insistence on banging your head against a brick wall. As often as possible make play of all that you do because, irrespective of what happens, the outcome of play can never be experienced as failure. Above all, shut up with your excuses, and bloody well get on with it. And see if you can sometimes dare to disobey the injunctions: 'Don't succeed'; 'Don't be pleased with yourself'; 'Don't do better than

I did'; 'Don't get what you want'; 'Don't be confident'; and 'Don't be ambitious'.

You will have to work harder than most other people to fulfil these special goals of yours, because at every step along the way you will have to continue to do battle with your fear of your mother's or father's envy and wrath, as well as expending the amount of energy naturally needed for the achievements you seek. But when, eventually, out of your persistent grit and determination you do defeat your parent and achieve your goals, your satisfaction will be as profound and lasting as any human being ever experiences.

Be Strong

If you are mostly Be Strong you are wonderfully self-sufficient. You have got all that you have by dint of hard work and getting on with life without any appreciable help from anybody. You always do your best to fulfil the needs of those around you, go out of your way to help people in trouble, are utterly reliable and meet any set-backs you encounter with stoicism and cheerful resilience.

What you most long for, though you barely admit it to yourself, let alone others, is to have your own Child loved and indulged. Whatever you believe about love intellectually, emotionally you believe there is a limited amount to go round and the most needy must have first priority. You know yourself to be so competent and capable that you accept that your position must be very close to the bottom of the waiting list. You are so convinced of your essential unloveworthiness that you would rather nobody ever knew your loneliness and longing rather than suffer the shame and pain of being rejected, which you believe would be the inevitable response to your daring to ask for love. (Note the oppositeness of Hurry Up and Be Strong in this respect. Hurry Up needs to learn to accept that the love he or she seeks must be earned; Be Strong needs to learn to believe that he or she is intrinsically worthy of love and does not have to earn it: such is the relativity of 'truth' and 'falsehood' in human nature.) You feel very sad but will never let anyone else know it and you do your best to deny it to yourself as well. You have effectively withdrawn from the possibility of a truly intimate relationship.

Your life task is to learn to take as well as give love. You know how much pleasure it gives you to look after others and make them happy. Has it occurred to you that you are selfish in denying other people the pleasure of giving to you and making you happy? Perhaps Jesus got it wrong: perhaps it is more blessed to receive than to give, because receiving means giving other people the pleasure of giving. Consider the reality of the worst that could happen if you dared to declare your love for somebody without any confident assurance that your love would be reciprocated. They could only say, 'No thanks, I don't love you', but even then, being human, they could not help but be flattered and nourished by your love for them. At first you need to keep your loves secret from other people until your love relationships are properly established so as not to underline your pain in being rejected by other people's knowledge of it. (Note the similarity of Be Strong to Try Hard in this respect. Be Strong is actually Try Hard of the emotions.) But, in truth, nobody will look down on you for expressing your sadness or loneliness and your vulnerability, and you will have become fully human by letting go of your stance of aloof superiority which so frightens other people. ''Tis better to have loved and lost than never to have loved at all' (Tennyson).

You will be happiest in jobs where you can serve others' needs, but you will never be fully human until you admit that you have needs, too. Set limits to your stoicism and be vulnerable enough to show your pain and allow others to comfort you, so that your resilience and reliability can be your virtues rather than the cold defence against allowing others to make any real emotional contact with you. And see if you can sometimes dare to disobey the injunctions: 'Don't be a child'; 'Don't ask for things for yourself'; 'Don't be close'; 'Don't show your feelings'; and 'Don't lose your dignity'.

If you have children you are probably a wonderful parent because parenthood legitimizes your need to give and give and give and expect and want nothing in return. And you know that your children need your love in abundance and will take it limitlessly. Find someone who knows how to take and needs to learn to give, and make each other whole. You know so well the difference between 'need' and 'love'. Be willing to need someone because you love him or her which is not the same as loving someone because you need them. Then your cup will be full.

Summary of Assets and Liabilities of the Five Personality Types

Be Perfect, Hurry Up, Please, Try Hard and Be Strong are all syndromes in the Adapted Child of each of us. While we also have our Natural Child, Little Professor, Adult and Parent ego states to use as well, our Adapted Childs are overwhelmingly involved in nearly all that we think, feel and do in our lives. None of us can completely avoid the pains of our Adapted Child, let alone the truly unbidden pains that afflict all mortal beings, but the individual who chooses courageously to struggle through the fears peculiar to his or her own personality is rewarded with a sense of triumph and joy unknown to those who lack such will.

Below is a summary table of the assets, liabilities and needed new permissions for the fulfilment of the life tasks of each of the personality types.

ASSETS AND LIABILITIES OF THE FIVE PERSONALITY TYPES

Personality Type	Assets	Liabilities	Needed new permissions
Be Perfect	wisdom, purposefulness, high moral and other standards	depression, rage, criticality, autocracy, dogmatism, bigotry	tolerance, self-mockery, spontaneity, general risk-taking
Hurry Up	adventurousness, responsiveness and sensitivity to others' feelings	anxiety, hostility, emotional resistance, self-destruction	willingness to earn others' love, willingness to love life for its own sake
Please	pleasantness, compliancy to others' wishes, generosity	passive aggression, lack of consideration for the individuality of others, self-righteousness, social deviousness	acceptance of responsibility for pain caused to others, autonomous expression of own feelings and desires
Try Hard	passionate commitment, sympathy for the underdog, persistence	pugnacity, aggression, arrogance, blaming external circumstances for own failures	willingness to succeed and fail, willingness to 'do better' than same-sexed parent
Be Strong	self-sufficiency, consideration of others' needs, reliability, resilience	loneliness, coldness, aloofness, invulnerability to others	acceptance of love from others, risking rejection by others

Being a Couple

Chapter 6
Making Love

Love looks not with the eyes but with the mind.
Shakespeare

Sex would be nothing but dull reflexes without fantasies' secret yearning.
Kovel

Being Loving

Being loving means willingly making other people feel good about themselves. It is consciously choosing to communicate to others that which will please them. It is giving thoughtful positive strokes.

The more idiosyncratically pleasing a stroke is to the person we give it to, the more nourishing it is to that person. So the better we know a person's individuality the more loving we can be to him or her. In our most loving relationships we seek to know more and more about the other, so as to increase and refine the ways in which we can please him or her. '. . . love is a constant interrogation. In fact, I don't know a better definition of love' (Kundera).

There are universally appreciated positive strokes; and ritual 'good manners' are the devices we are taught for being automatically minimally loving to everybody. There are stimuli that are usually understood to make the giving of a small positive stroke to another mandatory, such as saying 'please' and 'thank you' and 'excuse me' a multitude of times every day in our mundane transactions. A loving person gives small positive strokes, gratuitously, to many people, even when to give a stroke is not required by convention.

Being loving always takes at least a little bit of effort; it involves giving the thought and time required to communicate a positive stroke to another; thought and time that might otherwise be given to our self-centred concerns. Sometimes only a little thought and time given to another will be experienced as a large stroke by that other; sometimes a large amount of thought and time given to another will be experienced as a small stroke by that other. 'The value of a communication cannot be set by the communicant, but only by the receiver' (Berne). But by and large the amount of thought and time given to stroking another is proportional to the amount of nourishment received by that other. However, loving people do not keep accounts of strokes given and received; neither in terms of the valuation put on a stroke given to another person by that other person, nor in terms of how many strokes are returned for strokes given. Lovingness is its own reward inasmuch as it increases the sum total of happiness in the world.

The better we understand and know a person's individuality the more nourishing are the strokes we are able to give him or her, because knowing a person well means interacting with him or her in contexts that give us the opportunity to reinforce those qualities the other person most likes about him- or herself. 'One always loves the person who understands you' (Nin). The strokes that nourish people most are their idiosyncratic positive target strokes, which usually refer to what they are rather than to what they do, and we need to be with them to gain authentic opportunities to give them these strokes. The evident pleasure of a person receiving his or her positive target stroke is a positive stroke returned to the original giver. Thus love is made. 'Intimacy is built on eliciting responses' (Bandler & Grinder).

While we need to know a person well to give him or her deeply nourishing strokes, it is easy to be loving in small ways to anybody, even in the most non-specific contexts, such as when we gratuitously smile and say, 'Lovely day' to a stranger we pass in the street. We can give a stroke of considerable value to another, with only very little contextual definition and only a small amount of effort and time, such as appreciatively remarking on how efficiently a taxi driver has got us to our destination despite the traffic and, in general, showing how pleased we are with some service another has performed for us, even though we are paying for it!

We can choose to transact, that is, give strokes to another person, from any of our three ego states — Parent, Adult, or Child; and our transactions can be directed to the Parent, Adult or Child ego state of another. So, in any communication we have with another person, there are nine different qualities of communication from amongst which we may choose in each and every transaction we initiate. While, in practice, some of the nine possible qualities of transaction are much more commonplace than others, in principle, any statement can be given any of the nine qualities. For example, 'What's for supper?' may be asked completely matter-of-factly, Adult to Adult; or critically, in anticipation of the other having failed in her responsibility, Parent to Child; or appealingly, Child to Parent; or in a spirit of mutual concern, such as when an unexpected guest who is vegetarian has just been invited to stay, Parent to Parent; or . . . you do the rest!

While we may receive strokes to our Parent for our caringness, morality, responsibility, etc. and to our Adult for our competence, knowledge, skillfulness, etc., in as much as all positive strokes make us *feel* good about ourselves, in essence all the strokes we receive are chewed up and digested, as it were, by our Child ego states.

However, in giving strokes, the ego state in ourselves from which we choose to communicate to another makes an enormous difference to the quality of our communication and the value it has to the receiver. Broadly speaking, a stroke given by our Parent implies a presumption of our superiority to the other person and a belittling of the significance of the other, no matter how warmly such a stroke is given. Broadly speaking, a stroke given by our Adult implies acknowledgement given to the other out of fairness, but with a cold detachment that makes the receiver shudder. Thus strokes given by our Parent and Adult to another are not usually loving with the notable exception of strokes given by actual parents to their children, but are dutifully given, and serve the giver's sense of self-righteousness.

The only fully loving strokes we give another are from our Child, which strokes effectively say, 'You make me feel good'.

> *Love* is nothing else but pleasure accompanied by the idea of an external cause: *Hate* is nothing else but pain accompanied by the idea of an external cause.
>
> *Spinoza*

'You make me feel good' is paradoxically what makes the other person feel good. This equality between people is the necessary pre-condition for love to flourish.

How We Choose an Intimate Other

We choose to form intimate relationships with others on the twofold basis of the perception of the others as knowing and happily giving us our target positive strokes; and the hope and expectation that they will not give us our target negative strokes.

In the context of a committed, loving sexual relationship with a single chosen other, we are also seeking the fulfillment of achieving our personal dream of happiness in intimacy based on the sexual-emotional experiences we had in our relationships to our parents in the Oedipal stage of our development. The exception is people who are overwhelmingly Hurry Up, for whom the goal of intimacy is essentially the fulfillment of the pre-genital need to be given the unconditional, non-reciprocal love that ensures their survival. For each of us it is only possible to fall in love with another who is perceived as having core characteristics relevant to our personal dream. Our personal dreams are a fantasied perfectibility of our Oedipal experiences, in which the wounds that were inflicted on us then will be healed by recapitulating that experience, with a difference. That 'difference' is the secret yearning in each of us, whose fulfillment — which would be our ecstasy — is implicitly promised by any other person with whom we are capable of falling in love.

> In life, we do not just experience people objectively as individuals but also as role players in our own lives, returning again and again in different guises.
>
> *Tindall*

The ecstasy of being in love is the anticipation or the realization of our core secret longing to rectify wrongs done to us in our Oedipal relationships to our parents.

While our dreams of ecstatic happiness in intimate relationships are focused on the essential 'difference' from our original Oedipal experience, they also contain an essential sameness, without which the 'difference' would not be significant. A child brought up in a small house without a garden, and who longed for a garden that he could not then have, may be made very happy as a grown-up if he lives in a house with a garden. He is unlikely to be happy in a large house without a garden, or in a farmhouse surrounded by a hundred acres. And he would probably not be as happy in a large house with a garden as in a small house with a garden. He has nothing against the 'small house' of his childhood, only the absence of a garden. So, similarly, in his choice of an ideal mate for himself, he wants to find the characteristics that his conditioning has made him comfortable with, together with slight and singular variations that will transform the blighted happiness of his childhood into the perfect happiness of his dreams.

Our dreams of loving sexual intimacy are about our own relationship to one other person, but our Oedipal experience contained three protagonists, ourselves and both our parents. Thus our personal dreams of love with one other may be a complex mixture of the original components of our experience: ourselves as love object in relationship to our opposite-sexed parent; ourselves as rival to our same-sexed parent; and our perception of our parents' relationship to each other. We all want to perfect all these components, although we differ in the emphasis we place on each of them concerning what most needs modifying to make our happiness complete. The general picture of our overall dream is accessible through asking ourselves the following questions: If your father had been the way he was, but better than he was in some important respect, how would he have been? How would your mother have been happier for this difference in your father? How would you have been happier for this difference? If your mother had been the way she was, but better than she was in some important respect, how would she have been? How would your father have been happier for this difference in your mother? How would you have been happier for this difference? In this way an individual's dream of happiness in love can be made fully conscious and articulate, with him- or herself as the idealized version of his or her same-sexed parent in relation to an idealized version of his or her opposite-sexed parent, including the relation of each to their children. And thus we make ourselves the creative artists who, within the genre of the 'school of painting' to which we necessarily belong, and with a few highly relevant and dextrous brush strokes, transform the flawed picture of our lives into a masterpiece of its kind. In our ambitions in the world at large, as well as in our bid for ideal love, we each have a vague but omnipresent consciousness of continuing the path to perfection from where our parents left off. Call this source of our desires 'karma', 'genetics', 'conditioning' or what you will.

Re-forming Ourselves and Our Partners

At the time we begin an intimate, loving relationship with another, our dream of love is still potential rather than actual. If we are in love with our partner, we are so because he or she is seen by us as the one who will be the idealized version of our opposite-sexed parent. 'Love begins with a metaphor. Which is to say, love begins at the point when a woman enters her first word into our poetic memory' (Kundera, 1986 (2)). We love the people we love as much for the enhancement of ourselves, in enabling us to be 'better than' our same-sexed parent, as for the 'better' love they offer us, compared with what our opposite-sexed parent gave us.

> If I love someone, he must deserve it in some way. . .
> He deserves it if he is so like me in important ways that
> I can love myself in him; and he deserves it if he is so
> much more perfect than myself that I can love my ideal

> of my own self in him.
>
> *Freud*

If our partner is in love with us, he or she reciprocally perceives us as ready and willing to play the roles that will fulfil his or her dream. This is the wonder and joyous miracle of two people being in love with each other; each is amazed that the singular, beloved other who fits his or her unique dream, independently avows the reciprocity of this fulfillment.

> We are often unaware of ourselves, of our own energy, until we are 'in love', when we begin *resonating* to another, at which time the resonance may so fill us that to everyone around us we hum with an unexpected radiance.
>
> *Blair*

The dreams themselves that are being fulfilled by each partner for the other may be quite dissimilar, and each individual may be quite ignorant of the other's dream. But a wise lover wants to know the other's dream and so be able to enflame the other's love for him or her and keep it burning brightly.

Narcissistically basking in the other's love without pliantly and artfully reinforcing the idealized image of oneself in the other's mind jeopardizes the fulfillment of the promise. Without knowledge of our partner's dream our fulfillment of that dream becomes a largely fortuitous matter; and the bitter accusations of selfishness that partners hurl at each other when their dreams are dashed are the consequence of one or both of them failing to diagnoze and be the subtle healer of the other's Oedipal wounds. When healing has been the hope and expectation and is not fulfilled, the relationship is experienced as the reiteration of the original Oedipal experience without the 'difference' that is love's longing. The original wound is re-opened and deepened, which is experienced as poignant disillusionment at best and an agonizing nightmare at worst. To the romantic idealist, when heaven is the expectation its absence is hell. The fulfillment of love takes effort and artistry. Many people unimaginatively and falsely presume the sameness of their own and their partner's dreams, out of which so many intimate relationships deteriorate into two people each living in solipsistic pain and loneliness.

Our partners are meant to be for us an improved version of our opposite-sexed parent. While there is happiness in finding this ideal 'ready-made', some temperaments seek relationships that give them the opportunity to make the other into their ideal. The people who make this choice are, I think, more than averagely passionate; and part of their achieved happiness resides in the revenge they take against their parents for the wounds their parents inflicted on them. 'Revenge is necessary to re-establish equilibrium in the emotional life. It rules us, deep down. It is at the root of Greek tragedies' (Nin). To achieve such revenge adds an extra dimension of triumph to the realization of our dreams. 'To have thoughts of revenge without the strength or courage to execute them means to endure a chronic suffering, a poisoning of body and soul' (Nietzsche).

To this end, some people choose to fall in love with a partner who presently has the very short-comings of their own opposite-sexed parent, but is perceived as having the potential and willingness to grow beyond that parent in his or her capacity to love and be loved. The child longed, but failed, to 'improve' the opposite-sexed parent; now he or she has the opportunity to succeed. And if he or she does now succeed — usually over a period of years of courageous and passionate commitment to this cause in relationship to the chosen other — his or her happiness is very great. He is now able to say to his parents, 'Here is another who loves me and receives my love in the ways you never would. You made me believe I did not merit the love I wanted from you. See how wrong you were.' The parents are perceived to be appropriately humbled, the child has his revenge, and the umbilical cord is, finally, fully severed. Paradoxically, only when we have thus expressed the residual hatred of our parents often suppressed from consciousness, can we love them again, with the same a-sexual affection we felt for them and they for us before we were three.

Keeping Love Alive

Great as is the achieved happiness of experiencing our loving relationships as the healers of our Oedipal wounds, once this primary purpose is established and secured, love must renew itself through new purposes. Life is not static; post-orgasmic happy lassitude is short-lived; biologically and psychologically we need constantly to be engaged in the pursuit of the fulfillment of desire, if we are to feel fully alive. New purposes must be found from time to time in loving relationships that serve the continued growth of the individual partners; or else the relationship will deteriorate into stagnant lassitude or resentful insecurity.

The happier a couple has been in the process of achieving mutual healing of each other's Oedipal wounds, the more natural resistance there is to expanding the boundaries of the relationship when the time is ripe. When a phase in our lives has been unhappy, the future, however unknown, can be looked forward to with optimistic hope; but when a phase of our life has been happy, the prospect of change is inevitably interpreted as foreboding a diminishment of happiness. The prototype of the fear of natural and inevitable transition from one phase to another in our lives is the crisis faced by most mothers when their children are ready to leave home. For most women, the rearing of their children is a happy and profoundly rewarding twenty-year period in their lives, and the signs of imminent psychological independence of their children prompt them into feeling that a precious relationship is being taken away from them. Yet it is common knowledge that a truly loving mother fully allows and, indeed, insistently encourages her children to leave her, psychologically and physically, when the time is ripe, even though she feels the poignancy of the transition and she has no real idea of what equal fulfillment may be found in new structures in her life in the future. However, it is also common knowledge that mothers who lovingly and healthily make this transition, quickly begin to create new, independent and deeply rewarding structures for themselves and, within a few years, often amaze themselves by feeling less than delighted when their grown-up children, at regressive moments, want to 'come home to Mum'.

The obverse is, of course, also true. The relationships of overtly or covertly clinging mothers to their grown-up children inevitably deteriorate into pathological symbioses, full of resentment and acrimony; and, if and when the break is finally made, the children can only heal themselves by keeping physically and/or psychologically at a very safe distance from their toxic mothers. The mothers are left sighing at what they perceive as the injustice of their 'selfless love' for their children being so unrewarded, especially when they compare themselves to the 'selfish' mothers they know whose grown-up children are so good to them! But, of course, justice has been done; we all get exactly what we really deserve.

And so it is in loving sexual relationships, which also have phases. While the first essential phase for all successful loving sexual relationships is, I believe, the phase which serves the purpose of healing each partner's Oedipal wounds, that phase is very unlikely to last for a lifetime. For love to stay alive, a relationship must develop new purposes, consciously articulated and creatively struggled for by both partners in the interests of the individual development of each of them and the continuance of erotic desire and love between them. While the risk of failure has to be accepted, as in any purposeful, creative undertaking, failure of a new purpose does not necessarily spell doom for the continuance of the relationship. Other purposes can be created, with the advantages of maturity and loving gratitude that each partner by now feels for the basic healing done him or her in the past by the other. But refusal to move forward from the happy past into the uncertain future can only stagnate, and in due course poison with resentment and hate, the happiest of intimate relationships. This was epitomized in a marriage concerning which the wife first consulted me a couple of years ago.

This woman had, as a child, been emotionally neglected by both her parents and explicitly unloved by her father. She grew up to feel herself helplessly lacking in self-esteem and incapable of self-sufficiency. At nineteen she met a man who, as a child had been an impotent witness to his father's chronic physical violence towards his mother, and he felt profoundly guilty and ashamed that he could do nothing to protect his mother from his father. They fell mutually in love.

They married, and for the next twenty years, were very happy in their relationship. He told her every day how much he loved her, showered her with material gifts, and she always sat on his knee and was cuddled by him while they watched television together. She was a stay-at-home housewife.

After they had been married for about twenty years — interestingly, the time span in which a child typically is closely cared for by his or her parents — the wife began to feel she would like to develop her individual self-esteem by training for and getting a job away from home. Her husband overtly encouraged her, and she acquired a suburban shop and began to run it effectively and with much pleasure. But the more her self-esteem developed, the more her husband began to complain and discourage her; not, as might be supposed, for neglecting her housewifely duties, but on the grounds that she looked tired and ill and was making herself neurotic, quite the opposite of the actual case. She was torn in two between her desire to please her husband by giving up her new-found independence and her desire to grow herself into a self-confident woman in the world at large. (Such opportunities occur for all of us in our early forties in response to the many challenging astrological transits that confront us at that period of our lives (see Chapter 2).)

She joined a therapy group of mine, once again with, at first, the explicit encouragement of her husband, who agreed she was 'neurotic' and needed help. In a very short time her self-confidence grew enormously, and her appearance, demeanour and even her voice changed. From being a 'helpless little girl' she began to blossom as a sexy woman, and she became aware that her husband's paternalistic love of her for twenty years had filled the void where her father's love should have been but never was. Now she was ready, belatedly, to become a woman and to enlarge her relationship to her husband. She wanted now to become his equal and also, through her now emerging Parent ego state, to redress the former imbalance of their relationship and begin to nurture the needy little boy in him, which all his life had been masked by the strictly Nurturing Parent role he had cast himself in: to be so much 'better than' his father and to expiate his guilt towards his mother.

But the more mature and self-confident his wife became, the more he insisted on her helplessness. He even began cooking their meals, saying she wasn't competent to do so. And he insisted that her psychotherapy was making her 'worse and worse'; he demanded that she gave it up. Bravely facing her choice with full consciousness, she left the therapy group.

That was a couple of years ago. She has been in touch with me sporadically since then and is poignantly becoming ever more resignedly unhappy. She still loves her husband and has decided to play her relationship with him in accordance with his clear, but actually quite unfounded, terror that she will only stay with him as long as she is helplessly dependent on him. That is, he is profoundly convinced of his own essential unloveworthiness and cannot believe that any woman would freely love him. When I last saw the wife, she told me she feels, 'dead inside'. Her husband goes on insisting that they are wonderfully happily married. The price he is now paying for his self-deception and cowardice is impotence — his original most hateful perception of himself in his childhood — the present significance and pain of which he discounts on the grounds of his 'overwork'.

Astrologically, Pluto, by transit, will be forming a square aspect to the Sun-Saturn conjunction in his natal horoscope in a couple of years time. The enormity of the power of this transit, combined with my contextual knowledge of this man's life, enables me to predict with virtual certainty that it will be impossible for him to continue burying his head in the sand. As an astrologer, I can know with the utmost confidence that in his life, in a couple of years time, there will be an upheaval of the very roots of his being. Whether he willingly 'goes with' this transit and chooses bravely to strip bare his deepest fears and exorcise them vehemently in the name of a new future, or whether he vainly struggles to resist and so is forced to do so, by 'a nervous breakdown', his wife leaving him or some other drastic 'happening', is up to him. This is his present combination of free-will and necessity.

Thus loving intimacy is an evolutionary creative process, the maintenance of which involves the acceptance of new challenges and risks that occur along the way. Loving and living entail movement, the only alternative to which is stagnation and death. Maintaining loving, erotic intimacy with a chosen other for a lifetime involves moving forward with courage when a given purpose has been accomplished, through the pain and fear of transition, to a new purpose that rekindles desire and creative struggle. The same applies to our engagement with our work and all else that gives meaning to life. Courage, I believe, is the only irreducible virtue there is. In every aspect of life there are only two choices: creatively and courageously to live or fearfully and resentfully to stagnate and die.

Loving intimacy with another is special amongst all our creative endeavours inasmuch as it entails the growth of another as well as of ourselves. As M. Scott Peck defines love in his excellent book, *The Road Less Travelled*, it is 'the will to extend oneself for the purpose of nurturing one's own or another's spiritual growth.'

Staying fully alive, including keeping love alive, means having the courage to risk change. Confrontation with our partners of the need for change as often as this need naturally arises in any given relationship involves the risk that, having served its essential purpose for either or both partners, the relationship no longer has meaning and should be dissolved.

This realization is always poignant and painful, but avoidance of full consciousness is a cowardly evasion of this possibility and always exacts a heavy price. 'The obvious is frequently the last thing we are willing to see, especially when it carries an unwelcome message. . . . We often poison ourselves with this avoidance' (Greenwald). The truth always expresses itself, no matter how successfully we suppress it out of full consciousness.

Matching Metaphors

Whether we know it or not, by and large we fall in love at first sight.

> In certain cases the sex function can perceive everything that can be known about a person in a single instant.
> *Collin*

The quest for loving sexual intimacy is so central a pursuit in our lives at any time that we do not have it that, consciously or otherwise, we are constantly on the *qui vive* for a suitable other.

Probably about ninety percent of the criteria that determine whether or not another is even a possible intimate partner for ourselves are obvious and conscious to us.

Individuals vary somewhat in the 'necessary but not sufficient' criteria by which they limit their choices but, very generally speaking, communality in such factors as race, religion, education, class, colouring, physique, height and age are sought by most people as providing the basic compatibilities needed as a backdrop to the idiosyncratic details on the basis of which they make their final choice. Thus, for most people, a large majority of available others whom they encounter in their lives are automatically rejected very assuredly, since half a glance is sufficient to establish that some necessary characteristic is obviously missing.

What our minds are actually concentrating on, largely unconsciously, are the deep, irrational and special characteristics that we are seeking above and beyond the general conscious criteria of basic communalities that are so easily recognized. And because our concentration is so focused we can, and usually do, know with the unerring precision that only our uncensored unconscious minds are capable of, that another person is relevant to our heroic dream of intimacy. We can, indeed, see a stranger across a crowded room. . .

> Who meets him, or who meets her in the street, see that they are ripe to be each other's victim. . . Some people . . . meet . . . and a hundred signs apprise them of what is about to befall. *Emerson*

The conscious communalities that we seek between ourselves and others are the friendship components of our relationships, because friendship is the interaction of like-to-like; the deep, largely unconscious oppositenesses that we seek between ourselves and others are the love components of our relationships, because love is the interaction of opposites and begins with the most fundamental oppositeness of the two genders which categorize all mankind. Friendship is comfortable and pleasant because the samenesses between friends reassure each of them that at least some of their ways of being and doing are valid. 'Friendship is almost always the union of a part of one mind with a part of another; people are friends in spots' (Santayana). Love is uncomfortable and exciting, because the dynamic tension of oppositeness between lovers demands of each of them that they acknowledge the validity of ways of being and doing unlike their own. Components of both friendship and love are needed in a happy intimate relationship, although we may not like the people we love, just as much as we by no means love all the people we like. We like people 'because' . . .; they simply reflect back to us and endorse aspects of ourselves. We love people 'in spite of' . . .; in their differences from us they complexly both irritate our narcissism and, by complementing core aspects of our individuality, reinstate the 'wholeness' we lost in our Fall from paradise, which is the central theme of the Creation Myth in all cultures. Our perception of a loved other is that he or she removes our doubts about the value of ourselves, as contrasted with the acceptability of ourselves that we find in friendship. As Freud put it, we fall in love with our 'ego ideal'.

We fall in love with people who are relevant to our personal dreams; but they are also relevant to our personal nightmares because, by definition, our dreams and nightmares are the poles of single core dimensions of our being. In love, it is much easier to find and bond with somebody who will facilitate us in fulfilling our nightmares than our dreams, because we experienced our nightmares in our childhood Oedipal pains, and the repetition compulsion rules our lives. Our unfulfilled dreams have no precedent in our childhood experience, so we have no unconscious compulsion to fulfil them. Except for those people whose Oedipal experiences have been so essentially happy that a simple reiteration of those experiences is all they ask, trusting ourselves in our choices of people with whom we fall in love requires conscious determination and a powerful will to resist the temptation to fulfil our nightmares. As I have stressed so often, the quest for pain 'doesn't make sense' to our conscious minds, so only those people who have the depth of insight to admit to their personal painful compulsions can enable themselves willfully to overpower these compulsions in favour of the fulfillment of their dreams. We are at least as excited by and prompted to fall in love with those people who will fulfil our nightmares as our dreams. It takes courageous self-consciousness and self-control to turn away from the immediate gratification of falling in love with somebody who will bring us essential pain in favour of waiting for somebody who will bring us essential joy. The repetition compulsion aids and abets us constantly to find, with great ease, those who will cause us our familiar pains; we have only our self-conscious will to help us in finding those who will cause us essential joy. 'At no time is an ounce of prevention better than a pound of cure than at the beginning of a relationship' (Greenwald). Joy is harder and takes longer to find than pain.

While, for each individual, the deep characteristics in another that offer the potential for the fulfillment of his or her dream of love are largely idiosyncratic, in my experience there are some reliable rules of thumb that can be a conscious guide.

Above all else, it seems to be the case that love can only flourish between people whose childhood pains are experienced by each of them with approximately equal intensity. There can be no profound compatibility between somebody who had an essentially happy childhood and somebody who had an essentially miserable one. The quantities of childhood unhappiness need to be matched in a couple for long-term compatibility between them to be possible. The more the experienced quantities of unhappiness match, the more compatible a couple will be. This is a function of the Child to Child relationship between them.

Next in importance are the overt, immediately recognized Parent to Parent compatibilities of race, culture, religion, class, etc.; criteria so emphasized by parents to their children, and the importance of which children so often disavow. In early adulthood children are still in their antiscript stage of development and may pointedly choose to rebel against all that their parents most value; at other times, people in love at a Child to Child level may hopefully disavow the importance of their Parent to Parent incompatibilities while knowing, in their hearts, that they are taking a grave risk. The older we get the more pertinent do our Parent ego states become to our overall roles in life. Certainly, once we become actual parents our Parent values predominate in our domestic transactions, Parent to Parent with our spouses and Parent to Child with our children; and even for people who do not become actual parents, in the normal course of adult development as we become more and more 'established' in the world, we concomitantly acquire authority, which is what the Parent ego state is all about. Parent ego state incompatibilities between a couple that seem trivial at first will be greatly increased in their significance as time goes by.

The next most important clue to the potential for long-term compatibility between a couple is gender symmetry in their original Oedipal pains. If one partner's significant pains were experienced through his or her opposite-sexed parent, so must the other partner's; if one partner's significant pains were experienced through her or his same-sexed parent, so must the other's. So, for example, if a man's experience of his essential Oedipal pain was in his relationship to his mother, he needs a woman whose experience of her essential Oedipal pain was in relationship to her father. Where there is gender asymmetry, although equal degrees of pain were experienced by each of the individuals which may make for immediate attraction between them, at the deeper levels of their being their 'wires are crossed' and any developed intimate relationship between them is likely to be fraught with many non-verbal misunderstandings.

If degrees of experienced pain, Parent ego state values and attitudes, and gender symmetry in their personal Oedipal myths are well-matched between a couple they have, in principle, the basis for long-term happiness with each other. However, there is one further general factor that is a significant determinant of the overall quality of an intimate loving relationship, namely whether it is, at core, like-to-like or complementary. So, for example, if each was orphaned in early childhood, this like-to-likeness gives the relationship the potential for the rare empathic profundity that shared suffering can bring. An example of a complementary relationship is where one partner was suffocatingly 'smother-loved' and the other was the oldest of a large family and was never allowed to be a 'real' child.

Complementary relationships are easier than empathic ones. In complementary relationships the partners can immediately fall into their long-practised, familiar roles with each other; although if they are self-conscious people, both seeking to expand their boundaries, a complementary relationship also offers the potential for a co-operative learning experience through which each partner, in due course, extends his or her options to experience the roles they were each not allowed in childhood. The basic fulfillment for each partner is being appreciated by the other for the goodness in them that only got them negative strokes from their parents in childhood.

Empathic relationships are based on the identification of each individual with the other's profound pains; they suffer together, rather than alone, and are inclined to a self-sufficient exclusiveness in their relationship, rather like the intimacy that can often be observed between twins. But in order for an empathic relationship to have long-term viability, the individuals have to meet the challenge of developing together those personality characteristics that make for wholeness, which neither of the partners in the beginning possesses. Two playful children soon realize that somebody has to pay the gas bill, although each will implicitly want the other to be the one to do so. Conversely, two ultra-responsible people, who have so adapted to the lack of love they were given in childhood, have no models in each other upon which to base and develop the capacity for irresponsible, joyous expressiveness that they both so need. Nevertheless, if the challenges of an empathic relationship are faced and worked through, the eventual outcome is likely to be a love of rare depth and permanency.

Another method of applying conscious deliberation to whether or not a given relationship has potential for long-term happiness is by assessing the significance of the best aspects of the relationship to each of the individuals.

Each human being has needs for sexual, emotional, intellectual and spiritual dialogue with intimate others. Statistically, it is very unlikely that only one other can be a fully satisfactory partner for all of these needs. So it is important for each of us to be clear about the hierarchical order of these needs in ourselves. A couple may wholly agree with each other about what it is between them that makes them most attractive to each other and yet disagree about the significance of this basic aspect of their relationship. So, for example, a couple may have a wonderful sexual and intellectual relationship, but emotionally and spiritually they do not satisfy each other's needs and wants. This is fine so long as sexual and intellectual dialogue are top of the list for both of them. If emotional and spiritual dialogue are top of the list for both of them they will soon be very dissatisfied with their relationship. If sex and intellect are top of the list for one, and emotion and spirituality are top of the list for the other, the first will be happy with the relationship and want to maintain it, but the other will be very unhappy and unfulfilled in the relationship, whether or not he or she, for whatever reasons, maintains or breaks up the partnership.

> A man whose centre of gravity lies in one function, may find a woman who is his complement in that, and who thus arouses his keenest excitement. But she, although truly his companion in that function, may have her own centre of gravity in quite a different function where he can give her nothing and where her instinctive needs are met by somebody else. *Collin*

Happy, loving intimacy consists of the effective blending of the love metaphors of two people. Each needs to provide the other with core fulfillment of his or her longing, but there can never be a total fit between their dreams. Indeed, total congruence would mean total lack of stimulation and consequent lack of sexual desire, as was the case for a woman who consulted me. She was married to her virtual twin, she and her husband being born within a few hours of each other. She confessed to me that though she felt 'closer to her husband than she could imagine ever feeling towards any other person', she also felt terribly bored by him and had not been sexually aroused by him except before they were married, when sex between them was exciting by virtue of being illicit and furtive. All intimate relationships need a balance of stability and challenge, and a combination of Parent samenesses and Child oppositenesses between the partners for love to flourish. Love is not easy. Loving entails probing to the core of another's being and really listening to the answers given by the other. Love means metaphors have been offered, understood and received by each from the other. Each knows the other's greatest joys and greatest pains and lovingly enhances the former and avoids the latter. This takes attention and effort. We are not born sensitive to others' needs; only when we are at least moderately self-satisfied do we have enough energy left over after attending to ourselves to attend to others and their needs. Love is indubitably present when, even in his or her own distress, a person remains sensitive to and avoids causing another his or her core pain.

An ideal marriage is one where, through well-matched metaphors, each of the partners is enabled, projectively, through the other, to exorcise the ghosts of his or her childhood: to fulfil their respective Oedipal dreams. In the realm of intimate relationships the greatest triumph and joy for each of us is found when we revenge ourselves on our parents by being better than the parent we most blame; and we make happier, through displacement onto our chosen mate, our other parent who, we believe, was most sadly deprived. Thus our intimate relationships can incorporate ourselves role-playing an idealized version of our opposite-sexed parent in relation to our partner's idealized version of our same-sexed parent, as well as the prototypical roles of ourselves as idealized version of our same-sexed parent and our partner as idealized version of our opposite-sexed parent. For individuals who make up a couple, their separate myths may be utterly disparate. What matters is that each of the individuals is subjectively perceived by the other to be like and different from their respective parents in just the ways that matter.

We are all inventions of each other. *Roth*

Chapter 7

The Enemies of Love

Beneath the surface, most intimate relationships pivot on fear.

Ferguson

Fear and Righteousness

Every aspect of our being and doing in the world is monitored by the universal human constructs of good and evil, blame and responsibility and reward and punishment, irrespective of whether or not we are consciously preoccupied with these matters. In relating to other people we all want to gain the most for ourselves for the lowest possible price of consideration for others that we can get away with, while still keeping our consciences clear.

At birth we are utterly dependent on the goodwill of others for our survival but are unaware of this fact. In childhood we become increasingly aware of our inability to be self-sufficient, and the necessity for us overwhelmingly to submit to the demands of our parents and other grown-ups; we dream of the time when we will be utterly free to eat as many biscuits as we like and watch any television programme at any time, according only to our desires of the moment. In adolescence, we express vehement anger concerning the power of others to hold us in obeisance to the fulfillment of their 'large' desires in order for them to grant us the fulfillment of our 'small' desires. In adulthood, our self-sufficient capacity to fulfil our narcissistic desires is constrained only by the amount of money we are able and willing to earn; now we hold the purse-strings and the power and, in the normal course of events, we find ourselves increasingly able to have what we want for ourselves for less and less necessary consideration of others. In middle-age, we begin to lose the desires themselves, the fulfillment of which has been the mainstay of our energetic motivation. We become poignantly aware that all the power in the world cannot reverse the process of the decay of our bodies, and ultimately of our minds, on whose vigor all our desires and their fulfillment depend. Until, in decrepit old age, the only power left to us is that of any accumulated money we may have that can buy us a degree of physical comfort as we come full circle to the helplessness of infancy and the single essential desire to go on being alive.

However, probably few people live out their lives in such unqualified crudity. To a greater or lesser extent, all human beings want to read and write and talk and interact with the world and other people in countless ways that have little if any relevance to their self-preservation or narcissistic desires. The innate curiosity with which we are endowed that, initially, prompts us to better our understanding of the world and other people in the interests of our self-preservation, very quickly becomes also the source of its own intrinsic satisfactions. To a greater or lesser extent, we are all encouraged to, and do, become interested in people and things other than ourselves; the bare bones of our fundamental entirely selfish motives are fleshed out with non-instinctual aims, from so early a stage in our lives as to make these aims second nature.

Furthermore, and more crucially, we deeply know that at

no time in our lives can we be fully assured of the even short-term continuance of our self-sufficiency. Our bodies are frail and subject to the vicissitudes of their internal functioning and external assault at any time. We hope and expect that we will not become helpless before old age, which in the arrogance of youth we may presume to be an eternity away; but we all know and fear the possibility that disease or injury could, at any time, render us as helpless as new-born babies and wholly dependent on the goodwill of others for our continued survival. In such a state we would be no use to anybody, but we expect that we would be kept alive by others out of their love for us, which is the name we give to our own and others' motives that transcend narcissism. Love is what makes the world go round, because it is the currency of the most basic contract each human being makes with the rest of the world: I will look after you, even if you can be no use at all to me, if you will look after me likewise. The comparative rarity of infanticide and granny-bashing rests wholly on the construct of 'love' which, like finding intrinsic interest in things and people outside ourselves, is taught by permission and precept so early in life as to become second nature.

But despite the profoundly inculcated motives to be interested in the world and to love other people, self-preservation and self-gratification come first. Interest in anything and love for anybody can only be expressed with energy that we have left-over after our own survival needs are met. While a good case can be made from testimonial evidence that in some instances love may supersede self-preservation, most often in the love of a mother for her children, the vast majority of people, and the law, condone as healthy and natural the grossest atrocities one human being may inflict on another in the name of self-preservation.

Now human beings are psychological as well as physical beings, and our concept of 'self' includes our minds as well as our bodies. Self-esteem refers to a lot more than our positive assessment of our bodily attractiveness; indeed, it probably refers principally to the qualities of our minds and hearts, which are the intangible, symbolic containers of the intangible, symbolic attributes which are unique to human beings as a species. We value and protect our narcissistic concepts of ourselves as intelligent, kind, generous, compassionate, etc., every bit as much as we value our bodies, because these concepts of our self-esteem are the currencies we use in bartering with others to persuade them that we are of use to them and so deserving of them extending consideration to us. The positive psychological attributes we believe ourselves to possess are the ways in which we define ourselves as 'good' and, therefore, deserving of positive strokes from others.

In an ideal world, we would all be assuredly confident of the overwhelming 'goodness' of our psychological attributes and thus assuredly confident of our intrinsic loveworthiness. This loveworthiness would reliably invoke the love of others no matter how biologically powerless we became, because the psychological attributes of our self-esteem are understood to withstand the ravages to our mere physical potency and attractiveness. But, of course, we are not assuredly confident of our overwhelming 'goodness' and associated loveworthiness. To a greater or lesser extent, we all have doubts about our own 'goodness' based on the negative strokes we received as children. People have negative as well as positive self-esteem and attribute to themselves a whole range of 'bad' characteristics such as stupidity, incompetence, selfishness, greed, etc., by which they fear they are unworthy of love. If people don't find us loveworthy, our survival is at stake; so struggling to change our 'badness' into 'goodness', at least in others' eyes, if not in our own, has first priority in our transactions with others and most especially in our most intimate interactions, where 'being loved' is the core *raison d'être* of the relationship.

The cosmos is probably a-moral, but in the context of human life we are all both 'good' and 'bad'. The 'good' in us is the value we are to others' well-being; the 'bad' in us is our unwillingness to be valuable to others, while using their value for our own narcissistic aims. The bad in us frightens us; we fear that we will be found out and punished, ultimately by death. We want to be good but cannot help but believe we are bad, to the extent that our parents told us we were when we were very young. We are good to the extent that we believe we are good; we are bad to the extent that we believe we are bad. The defensive structures of the five personality types are the devices we deploy in our struggles to turn our 'badness' into 'goodness'. The Drivers — Be Perfect, Hurry Up, Please, Try Hard and Be Strong — are the 'virtues' we deploy to convince ourselves that we are 'good' and not responsible for the punishments of our most painful payoffs.

Thus we are all a mixture of genuine goodness, based on our positive self-esteem, and righteousness which is the camouflage for our negative self-esteem. In our intimate relationships, there is more or less continuous dialogue between the goodness and righteousness in ourselves and the goodness and righteousness in the other. When the goodness in ourselves and our partners predominates over righteousness, love can be made and maintained; when the righteousness of ourselves and our partners predominates over good, love will be killed, or is already dead. Unlike the authentic goodness in us, which is secure and welcomes the equal goodness of another, the righteousness in us is insecure and is threatened by the righteousness of another. The maintenance of righteousness within a relationship necessitates a continuous battle for 'virtuous' supremacy over the other because righteousness is inauthentic, based on the lies we tell ourselves.

> People lie to themselves, to relatives and friends, to spouse or lover, and often, even to their God. They often see themselves as well as the relationship they are in, through the muddled haze of dreams and expectations. They want a particular partnership or marriage to work or not work. They read into it whatever their imagination will tolerate. . .
> *Schulman*

Our inauthentic righteousness is constantly in need of reinforcement to maintain the very tenuous belief in our 'goodness' that it gives us.

> Many promising reconciliations have broken down, because both parties come prepared to forgive, neither party came prepared to be forgiven. *Williams*

'I am holier than thou' is the belief we seek to protect ourselves from our fears, which is the antithesis of the equality which is the only medium in which love thrives.

So, in the final analysis, all our feelings can be boiled down to love versus righteousness, which are immediately derived from positive self-esteem versus fear. While none of us is ever free of fear and its cloak of righteousness, the greater our authentic, positive self-esteem, the greater our ability to love. The greater an individual's positive self-esteem, the greater is his or her ability to love and desire another freely rather than, in the name of love, using the 'badness' in another for the purpose of maintaining his or her own specious righteousness, to keep fear at bay.

> Two people love each other only when they are quite capable of living without each other but choose to live with each other. *Peck*

Love is the root of all goodness; fear is the root of all evil. Fear makes us keep our partners locked in their fears, so as to maintain the roles they play in allowing us to mask our own fear with righteousness.

> Evil is the use of power to destroy the spiritual growth of others for the purpose of defending and preserving the integrity of our own sick selves... In short it is scapegoating. *Peck*

Fear and its attendant, righteousness, are the cancerous enemies of love and desire.

The five personality types between them contain all that is in our Adapted Child. All that is most 'bad' in us and all that is potentially most 'good' is in our Adapted Child. Our negative self-esteem and our irrational fears are the bad in our Adapted Child, and Be Perfect, Hurry Up, Please, Try Hard and Be Strong each have their characteristic ways of expressing righteousness to mask our negative self-esteem and fear in our intimate relationships. Each form of righteousness bears allegiance to one or two of the stereotypical roles of Persecutor, Rescuer and Victim. The five forms of righteousness associated with the five personality types are the archetypal enemies of love. No relationship, however loving, can be entirely free of them but, unfettered, they murder love.

Duty

'A sense of duty is useful in work but offensive in personal relations' (Russell). 'Duty' is the righteousness component in Be Perfect. It is the most righteous of all the righteousnesses. It plays the role of Persecutor. It humiliates and implicitly reduces to zero the value of the other. It effectively says, 'You are a deep disappointment to me and are not worthy of love. However, I married you, or otherwise committed myself to you, so I will not let you down. You will find me faultless in the fulfillment of my obligations, but that is all you are entitled to. Loving you is not part of my obligation to you, and I don't love you because you have failed in your obligations to me and have killed my love.'

'Duty' holds itself superior to all lesser morals who 'imperfectly' may dissolve their contractual commitments when love has died. Its guilt, self-hatred and depression are so great that only supreme righteousness is enough to hold them at bay. 'Duty' has probably itself been similarly treated in childhood, dutifully cared for but without tenderness, and has grown up longing for the tender love it never got. But so idealized is its notion of love that it is bound to be disappointed. Behind its intimidating, arrogant, hard façade its experience of life is agonizing. Its terror is of change because it knows that any change, however slight, would diminish its absolute control over itself and its environment, which is its only safeguard against the suicidal risk of its excruciating pain. 'Really to live is an act of unceasing rebirth. . . At the limit, the alternative to transformation is death' (Rudhyar). Be Perfect knows what love is, and longs to give and receive it, but chooses a partner unable or unwilling to give love. It recapitulates the nightmare of its childhood, with itself now in the role of the autocratic, dominating parent. Its denial of love for the other is the only outlet for the rage which is actually felt towards its own dominating parent.

Through another whose equally high moral standards it respects and who treats it with gentle tenderness, Duty can gain its needed permission to see duty to itself as its first entitlement and, indeed, its first obligation.

Need

'Need' is the righteousness component in Hurry Up. It is the least righteous of all the righeousnesses because it is stuck at a pre-Oedipal developmental stage, before the concepts of 'goodness' and 'love' are really known. Its interest in the world and other people is very slight, and it animates people as if they were 'transitional objects', teddy bears who are not real but can be fantasized as real according to its own needs, and who retain their comforting sewn-on smiles no matter how much it bashes them. It plays the role of Victim. It effectively says, 'You have got to give me everything I want. I am your baby and you are my Mummy/Daddy. In return, I will sometimes be nice to you and play Koochi-koochi-koo (sex) with you. If you don't do everything I want you to do for me, I'll scream and I'll scream and I'll scream . . . until you do.'

'Need' is overwhelmed by fear and desperate to be safely contained by another who will relieve it of all responsibilities. It is so unknowing and inept in maintaining its own basic survival that it is utterly self-centred and insatiably greedy. 'Need' was powerfully traumatized by some form of abandonment before the age of three and has not developed its self-sufficiency beyond that age. Its terror is of being alone, because being alone reduces it to the helplessness of an abandoned infant. It does not know what love is, although it will claim it has 'fallen in love' instantaneously with anybody who is willing to take care of it, and it immediately offers itself sexually in its bid to secure the other's love. In the sexual embrace it manages, for a moment, to believe it is unconditionally and timelessly bonded to the other; but the other's subsequent expression of separate individuality justifies it in feeling abandoned and desperate, which it expresses as hatefulness and hostility. It destroys love before it even begins.

Only if and when 'Need' is willing to forgo the repeated anxious excitement of the chase after its dream of the one who will give it the unconditional, timeless love of a mother to a baby, and becomes willing to look after itself adequately, will it ever be capable of the giving as well as taking, on which the experience of love depends.

Symbiosis is not relating. Babies do not relate to their mothers; their smiles and clinging are designed by nature to invoke the willing fulfillment of their needs by their mothers. The one-way love of a mother for her baby is the only one-sided love that can be maintained. All other loves are between two fundamentally separate, self-sufficient individuals who come together in wonder and desire, making I, Thou and Us.

Expediency

'Expediency' is the righteousness component in Please. It is supremely manipulative and makes itself unconscious of what it is doing so as to remain 'innocent'. It plays the roles of Rescuer and Victim. It effectively says, 'You are more powerful than I am and make me do as you want. I know you will always win in open battle, but I will get my revenge on your domination of me by obeying 'the letter of your law' while hurting you in ways that you cannot quite put your finger on. This will be my autonomous triumph. I will help you (Rescuer) or be obedient to you (Victim), but I'll never give you any genuine feeling. This will hurt you deeply, but you will have no right to complain, because you won't be able to fault what I do.'

'Expediency' cannot afford to be fully conscious of what it is doing because it would then be obliged to accept equal responsibility with the other for the pain between them; and in repressing this knowledge it inevitably represses much other knowledge as well. It is replaying with its present partner its incomplete separation from its opposite-sexed parent, on whom it is resentfully dependent. Behind its 'niceness', it is a nervous wreck, because its terror is of the truth. Emotional depth and complexity are dangers to be avoided at all cost, because they threaten to expose the guilty secret of its incestuous desires. 'Expediency' blushes more than any other enemy of love. It wants to live life lazily and comfortably on the 'nice' surface. Its blinkered, tunnel vision keeps out the shadows and the sunshine of life.

Through another who has the strength of love for it to force it to moral responsibility by denying it any instructions to which it can be manipulatively 'obedient', 'Expediency' can gain its needed permission to accept and relish the pain and the joy of passionate intimacy.

Togetherness

'Togetherness' is the righeousness component in Try Hard. It is supremely aggressive which gets it into a lot of trouble, so it periodically retreats into pathetic helplessness in a bid for pity rather than the anger it usually invokes in others. It plays the roles of Persecutor and Victim. It effectively says, 'I know I am a failure, but I can't bear to know this. You have to be my ally in blaming the unfairness of the world for my lack of success. If you don't, I'll make you a worse failure than I am and so make myself feel a success by constantly comparing myself to you.'

'Togetherness' hates and envies self-confident others and looks for and clings to another who is at least as unself-confident as itself in a bid to wall itself off from the rest of the world through the enclosed self-sufficiency of its symbiosis with its partner. It is replaying with its present partner its incomplete separation from its same-sexed parent, towards whom it feels inferior and impotently angry. Its terror is of autonomy, because it then would have to face its cowardice towards honestly competing with others and, consequently, realistically acknowledging the limits of its own abilities. Only by experiencing itself as potentially the most powerful person can it keep at bay the fear that it may never be as powerful as its same-sexed parent. It oscillates between playing the role of its aggressively humiliating same-sexed parent and being the frightened, helpless child in its relationship to its partner. It wears itself out in the aggressive role and is likely to 'mellow' into cynical bitterness and sexual as well as general impotence in its relationship to the world.

Through another who is willing and able to give it the 'tough love' of pitilessly pushing it relentlessly to work for the fulfillment of its ambitions 'Togetherness' can gain its needed permission to fulfil its potential and gain its rightful, sexy, self-esteem.

Sex

'Sex' is the righteousness component in Be Strong. It uses sex as a way of righteously avoiding acknowledging its cold unwillingness to be touched by another. It plays the role of Rescuer. It effectively says, 'I know you would reject me if I asked for anything from you, because I am unloveworthy, so I'll never show you my feelings and you'll never be able to hurt me. I'll hold you in my power by your need of me and my knowledge of your vulnerabilities, but you'll never catch me saying "I love you".'

'Sex' avoids intimacy under the camouflage of 'intimacy'. As the more salacious Sunday newspapers put it, 'Intimacy then took place'. It is reiterating its defence against the pain it felt in childhood in response to its valuelessness to its parents. Its parents, happily or unhappily, were self-sufficient in their symbiosis with each other and the child withdrew, wounded, from its failed bid to have a significant emotional impact on their relationship. 'Sex's' terror is of vulnerability because it believes vulnerability must inevitably lead to rejection, so it avoids intimacy by choosing a partner who either, like itself, fears vulnerability and so maintains a reciprocal emotional distance, or one who is so 'Needy' as to be incapable of true intimacy. 'Sex' pays the price of deep loneliness, its only gratification being the smug, false strokes it gives itself or gets from others for its 'altruistic' self-denial. 'Regardless of our caring for others, we cannot do their growing for them. . . Helpfulness usually turns out to be a toxic intrusion' (Greenwald).

Through another who sees beneath 'Sex's' invulnerable façade and is willing, very gently and repeatedly, to affirm its loveworthiness, 'Sex' can be enabled to gain its needed permission to reveal its wounded heart and be rewarded with the ecstasy of the experience of sex as the expression of love, rather than the 'enjoyable', mechanical satisfaction of a physiological need which is all 'Sex' knows.

> In the technocratic West we are still children in the area of the supernatural, versed only in the physiology of love, consuming textbooks on the ABC to orgasm; and barely aware of interior energies, we nevertheless pine after their sanctity, trying to crush from the body, from the cunts and tits of pornography, the essence of what it is that really moves us. But from oriental and esoteric legend drifts the knowledge that to sleep with someone means actually to become aetherically mingled with them, to begin to fuse into what may become, after years of conscious love, a single aetheric being. No woman who has tested some of this extraordinary sanctity can remain a tigress of female liberation, and no man a chauvinist pig.   *Blair*

In my psychotherapeutic practice I am saddened to meet many young men and women to whom nobody has ever mentioned that sex is meant to be reserved for the expression of love; and not to be indulged in uninhibitedly as a 'natural appetite' to be freely appeased. Now young people are free to 'have sex' without prior testing of their emotional compatibility. While it is, of course, the case that in every age and culture men and women have flouted the normative sexual taboos imposed on them, I think it has made a very important difference in the past thirty years that young people are no longer required to pay even lip-service to the ideal of sex being limited to the expression of committed love between a couple. Thus many couples seem to drift into marriage on the basis of an established sexual relationship but no deep knowledge of each other. And I hold the unfashionable conviction that this is a significant contributing cause of the present explicit failure of a third of all marriages.

> Inhibition is the price of entry into every real satisfaction. . . Shamelessness is the idealized state of things in late modernity. . . Nervous illnesses are inju-

ries of resistance to sacred order returning in those who wish not to mind it. *Rieff*

A summary of the not-OKnesses and needed antidotes to the five faces of righteousness is given in the table below.

THE FIVE FACES OF RIGHTEOUSNESS

Face	Underlying Terror of	Core Not-OKness	Not-OK Role(s)	Needed Antidote
Duty	Change	Criticality	Persecutor	Tenderness
Need	Being alone	Greed	Victim	Self-sufficiency
Expediency	Emotional truth	Dishonesty	Rescuer and/or Victim	Moral responsibility
Togetherness	Autonomy	Envy	Persecutor and/or Victim	Self-esteem through accomplishment
Sex	Vulnerability	Coldness	Rescuer	Emotional involvement

Chapter 8
The Five Personality Types in Intimate Relationships

> The key to every man is his thought... He can only be reformed by showing him a new idea which commands his own.
> *Emerson*

Life and Love as a Game of Cards

The two most fascinating considerations concerning people are the samenesses and the differences between them. We are all alike and all different. Compatibility and incompatibility may be observed in samenesses between any two people; and compatibility and incompatibility may be observed in differences between any two people.

We are all alike in wanting strokes from others and in seeking repeated validation of the profound, largely unconscious, existential decisions we formulated in early childhood. We are all different in the particularity of the strokes we seek and the particularity of the existential decisions we seek continuously to validate by reaffirmation.

The first requirement for us to function effectively in any

transaction with any other human being is a minimum knowledge of 'human nature', through which we recognize the communality of all people everywhere in their general needs and frailties. People who interact with others with an implicit consciousness of the primary samenesses rather than the differences between all people exude a modest warmth that never fails to attract people to their presence. In my opinion, this is the *sine qua non* of all lovingness; but it is not sufficient for intimacy.

Without any knowledge of the differences between ourselves and any other, our essential narcissism impels us to treat the other as if he or she were identical with ourselves; so whether or not we please him or her is bound to be fortuitous. 'Good manners' facilitate us in pleasing all people, at least within the bounds of the culture to which our particular 'good manners' apply, at a minimal superficial level; but to achieve any degree of intimacy with another, some acquired knowledge of our own and the other's idiosyncratic natures is needed.

> The normal man is, by definition, influenced as much from within as from without... Although there are doubtless individuals whose type can be recognized at first glance, this is by no means always the case. As a rule, only careful observation and weighing of the evidence permit a sure classification... because every individual is an exception to the rule. Hence one can never give a description of a type, no matter how complete, that would apply to more than one individual, despite the fact that in some ways it aptly characterizes thousands of others. Conformity is one side of a man, uniqueness is the other.
>
> *Jung*

The metaphor that I find provides the most precise image of the samenesses and the differences between us is that of a pack of cards, the games that can be played with it and the hands that can be dealt. God holds the pack which contains the totality of all that is possible; each of us is dealt a hand which is one of a virtually limitless number of possible hands. Each hand may be likened to and contrasted with any other hand in a large number of ways, the ways chosen being determined by relevance to the game being played at any particular time.

We have no choice in the hands we are dealt; but we are free to choose which game or games we will play; and we are free to play our chosen games lightly or seriously, with desultoriness or enthusiasm, with attention or absent-mindedness, with good or bad grace, with clumsiness or artistry. No hand is intrinsically 'better' or 'worse' than any other; playing out a grand slam with a fistful of court cards and trumps can be as boring as playing an adroitly skilful game with no trumps or court cards can be joyful.

Shall we only play the games where our own hand grants us a head-start towards winning? Or sometimes chose to play games where the below-average value of our hand grants us the pleasure of challenging us to stretch to boundaries of our innate limitations? Shall we learn to play one game supremely well? Or enjoy the variety of learning and playing a number of games with limited skill in each? Shall we play for high stakes or low? Shall we play games of high chance, or high skill? In all these matters we are free to choose and are responsible for the consequences of our choices.

Seated across the table from our partners, what must we do to make the game as pleasurable as possible for both of us? Explicitly establish with our partners the conventions by which we will covertly communicate to each other the contents of our respective hands. Sort our cards and categorize them in a way that makes most sense within the rules of the game. Make sure we have all our cards in our hand and none is hidden behind another. Ascertain the strengths and weaknesses of our hand and communicate them to our partner, within the bounds of the rules of the game. Attend carefully to our partner's communications to us, sorting out the components of his communication into responses to us and the independent information he is also giving us about his own strengths and weaknesses. Arrive at a mutually agreed, explicit contract. Play the game co-operatively, attentively and with finesse and pleasure. Apologize for any errors we make, and happily forgive our partner for his or her errors, with the good sportsmanship derived from our knowledge that we are 'only human' and it is 'only a game'.

The game I have devised is a variation of the game originally created by the genius of Freud. My pack has five suits. In my five-suit pack, Be Perfect is trumps, except if its value in a given hand is excessive, when it is demoted to worthlessness. Hurry Up has the lowest value, and Hurry Up cards must be discarded or cancelled out by Be Perfect cards before the Please, Try Hard and Be Strong cards of middling value can be played. Points are scored for making tricks for ourselves or our partners; and bonus points are scored for making tricks for ourselves and our partners simultaneously. We may choose moves of low risk and low potential gain or high risk and high potential gain. Low numbered cards are Child cards, which have greatest freedom and least power; Jacks are Adolescent cards, which have limited freedom and limited power; Kings and Queens are Parent cards, which have least freedom and most power; Aces can be used in any of the Child, Adolescent, or Parent modes. The aim of the game is life-affirming happiness. The Joker can be optionally used in the game; in combination with some Be Perfect cards it has the power to bestow mystical transcendence on a player, making him or her the outright winner.

Be Perfect

A man too good for the world is no good for his wife.
Yiddish proverb

Man The Be Perfect man, in his intimate relationships, is indisputably the boss. He is totally responsible and abrogates all the power. He is unerringly moralistic and dutiful. He demands that his standards and precision be maintained in everything that is important to him, and he is intimidatingly persecutory concerning the short-comings of others which he interprets as lack of moral fibre. As long as he deems his partner 'worthy' he loves her passionately, but if and when he is disillusioned by her his hatred of her, and of himself for his error in having loved her, is enormous. The passion of his loves and hates are the orgasmic outcome of the counterforce to the rigid control by which he lives his life.

He works very hard and productively and is rarely found in a subordinate position; he is the boss, respected and loved or respected and hated. If he is satisfied by his work and contented with his loves, he is a benevolent patriarch; dissatisfied with his lot, he is a cynical and unforgiving Persecutor.

He is not mean and can be bounteously generous to people or causes he deems 'worthy'; but he can be pettily stingy about 'unnecessary', frivolous or 'wasteful' spending. He writes the cheques and holds the purse strings for 'the little woman'.

A moderate Be Perfect is the best of men, and the woman he loves has cause to appreciate the steadfast security and care he bestows on her. An extremely Be Perfect man is the worst of men, and the woman he loves and hates is amongst the most psychologically and/or physically battered of women. A pinch of tenderness keeps Be Perfect on the side of the angels.

Woman The Be Perfect woman's domain is typically her home, in which her order and/or cleanliness are dictatorially imposed on all those who share a roof with her. Usually she is very house-proud and hard-working, and you can set your watch and your calendar by the stringency of her timetabling of her daily, weekly, monthly and annual tasks. Sometimes, in response to the rigidity of Be Perfect imposed on her as a child, she may live in antiscript, in which case her home and her daily activities are utterly chaotic and disorganized; but she will constantly worry and Try Hard — ineffectively,, of course — to catch up with an enormous pile of ironing, dirty dishes etc., that forever surround her. Woe betide anybody who uses an ashtray she has just washed or interferes with the chaos only she understands! In principle, she wants a partner who, independently, has exactly her standards about how life should be lived, but so precisely idiosyncratic are her 'absolute necessities' that such a partner is an impossible dream, so she sighingly accepts a lesser mortal who is willing to obey her. She is the wife of the 'hen-pecked husband'.

On the credit side, those she cares for are the happy beneficiaries of her utterly responsible attitude to her duties and her meticulous attention to detail. Her household never runs out of milk or toilet paper!

Sexually, like her male counterpart, she is capable of great orgasmic passion and she has a secret, or not so secret, desire to be raped by the man she loves. But if love has died or everything is not 'just right', her frigidity is as icy as her passion is hot.

Parent Be Perfect parents demand and get obedience and respect from their children. In return, they care for their children, physically and morally, with unflagging and utterly reliable devotion. No child of a Be Perfect parent ever has cause to doubt that his or her gym clothes will be washed and ironed for school tomorrow, or that his or her material and educational needs will be securely provided for until he or she is well and truly grown-up.

In so far as Be Perfect parents will tolerate no falling short of their moral and other values, they may seriously fail their adolescent children. Unless they transcend the rigidity of their demands for obedience and respect, out of the wisdom that knows that adolescents must be somewhat rude, rebellious and disobedient to their parents in order to complete their maturation healthily, Be Perfect parents may pay the price of their grown-up children hating them. Their children will never cease to respect them, but for that respect to be compounded with love rather than fear and hate, they must bend a little and admit to themselves and to their children that they have feet of clay.

How to get the best out of Be Perfect people Reassure them that there is nothing to worry about. When things go wrong, reassure them that it is not their fault. Be prompt in your responses to them and arrive at appointments with them on time. Tease them playfully as, for example, one of my children, catching me anxiously trying to line up a bedspread exactly parallel to the edge of the bed, said, 'Would you like me to get you a set-square?'

Never discount their worries. Instead, listen and let them know that you understand them; and do whatever you are willing and able to do to help them overcome their anxiety.

In an intimate relationship, if you believe your partner's Be Perfect goes too far and sabotages his or her overall well-being, you need to bring a great deal of Parent confidence and conviction to bear to confront him or her effectively; otherwise your partner will simply discount what you say. Whether his or her autocratic intolerance is moral or intellectual, it needs to be confronted gently but firmly, calmly and rationally.

> . . . the choice is between accepting a narrow range of permitted thought and behaviour or, alternatively, acknowledging being delinquent or mentally, ill whenever one goes beyond the scheduled boundaries.

> There is a need to create a third system in which one can accept approximate meaning, approximate virtue, approximate satisfaction, and approximate justice.
>
> *Kahn*

Express your own, different values clearly and with conviction to your Be Perfect partner. Remind him or her that we all have to die, regardless of how carefully we live. 'Imperfection is a natural quality of the mortal, a law a compulsive neurotic refuses to accept' (Stekel). Give examples of how a certain degree of risk-taking is necessary for creative achievement. Suggest how other people hate his or her closed-minded dogmatism and bigotry, and that kindness is a greater virtue than right-ness.

A Be Perfect person, minus his or her intolerance, bigotry and autocratic self-righteousness, is as wise, steadfast, warm and good a person as you will ever know.

Hurry Up

> The demand to be loved is the greatest kind of arrogance.
>
> *Nietzsche*

Man The Hurry Up man is notably unreliable in his intimate relationships. He is physically and psychologically unrelaxed, unpredictable and extremely self-centred. He needs a partner whose maturity and stability will provide him with a secure structure in his life to mitigate his deep sense of futility, and who will controllingly keep his self-destructive impulses within safe bounds. He demands that his variable whims be unhesitatingly indulged, and he tyrannizes others with his Victim neediness. 'The worst form of tyranny the world has ever known: the tyranny of the weak over the strong. It is the only tyranny that lasts' (Wilde).

Taken at face value, he may appear to be a raunchy, potent man, but his sexual activity is actually a device to get himself held and reassured. He relates to the woman in his life as a frightened toddler to a reassuring mother. Developmentally he is fixated at a pre-Oedipal stage and is actually incapable of relating as equal to equal in mature eroticism. He may well be sexually promiscuous, in which case many a woman will be flattered into bed with him by his apparent overwhelming desire for her which he may blithely call 'love', only to find when she wakes up in the morning that he has already gone. If he has the deep good sense to realize, as he usually does eventually, that he desperately needs the security of one good, mature woman, he will cling to her and yet constantly test her love for him by his narcissistic, infantile temper tantrums and rebellion against the controlling structures she imposes on him that he so desperately needs.

In his work, the Hurry Up man tends to be a ne'er-do-well, due mainly to his unreliability and irresponsibility. If he is the breadwinner, in order to maintain himself and his family adequately, he needs to be in employment that keeps him on the move, physically and psychologically, for he cannot bear to be still.

A mildly Hurry Up man can be a stimulating companion in the hectic spontaneity he brings to his relationships. An extremely Hurry Up man can only sustain a relationship with a woman whose need to be a martyr is quite extreme.

Woman The Hurry Up woman is a whining little girl in her intimate relationships. She is generally disorganized and is inclined to 'have a headache' or otherwise 'feel unwell' whenever her daily responsibilities are greater than she is willing to meet. She expects her partner to be a constant 'good Daddy' to her and she uses extreme emotional blackmail, if necessary, to keep him constantly at her beck and call.

She is often quite open about her distaste for sex but she is willing to tolerate it with her partner for the 'cuddles' that come with it which give her the reassurance they imply, that she is safely loved and contained. In her quest for a man to love her unconditionally and forever, she is inclined to mask her distaste for sex with very ready and explicit 'come-ons' to men and elaborately contrived fantasy in the sexual act itself. Thus she plays the role of a sexy woman to bind her partner to her but, like her male counterpart, because she is essentially fixated at a pre-Oedipal level, she actually has no understanding of sex as the expression of mature love.

A mildly Hurry Up woman may entice and enthral her partner by keeping him on his toes. An extremely Hurry Up woman can only sustain a relationship with a man whose self-esteem is very low, which he masks by the strokes he gives himself for being loyal and continuously indulgent to his needy partner.

Parent Hurry Up parents demand that their children love them. Hurry Up mothers are usually very happy in the first year of motherhood, interpreting their infant's overwhelming neediness as an expression of love for them; but as soon as the baby becomes 'wilful' they become less and less enamoured of parenthood. Children are usually frightened of Hurry Up parents, especially their volatile unpredictability, and grow to have little expectation of any emotional security to be derived from them.

Hurry Up parents are glad of every intimation that their children are growing less dependent on them and are inclined happily to acquiesce to the first adolescent demands their children make to leave home and live their own lives. When their children have left home, they expect their children regularly to ring them up to see how they, the parents, are but show little interest in finding out how their children are managing their lives and what help they might be to them. The children may remain tied to a continuing relationship with Hurry Up parents by a sense of obligation or pity but they know they have to look elsewhere for any reliable nurturance for themselves.

How to get the best out of Hurry Up people Praise them for their efficiency. Enjoy their hectic spontaneity. Reassure them there is plenty of time.

Never be intimidated by their hysterical outbursts and demands. Instead, tell them quietly but firmly that you are leaving them for a short time but will be back soon and willing to listen when they are willing to talk calmly and rationally.

If you are in an intimate relationship with a Hurry Up person you probably love most of all his or her neediness of you. Beware of needing to keep him or her in a state of neediness for your own emotional security. Be brave enough to be truly loving by setting firm limits to indulging his or her greedy demands and also make some demands for yourself. Your rewards will eventually be the greater satisfaction of love given to you freely, rather than desperately; and, through the necessary effort you need to make to convince him or her of the intrinsic value of life, your own spirituality will be greatly enhanced. It is not loving to indulge every whim of a greedy, demanding person; real love sets limits that enable the other person to grow in autonomy and self-reliance.

Please

The real aim of the man who represses himself in the guise of civility is to repress others without seeming to do so. In this way the forms of civility may promote the very barbarism to which they are supposed to be the antidote.
Mount

Man The Please man is 'Mummy's darling boy', with all the gratification and resentment that that role relationship implies.

If, as is usual, the gratification is greater than the resentment, he probably replaces his mother with a wife who is a close replica of her, in early adult life: he presumes himself to be entitled to be continuously waited on by a woman who 'naturally' is delighted to cater to all the details of his physical and emotional needs. In return, he sees himself as 'a good provider'. He is the archetypal male chauvinist pig. In his work, he is usually a contented employee who can be relied on to do what is required of him, although rarely more, and he enjoys working for hierarchical organizations in which he has bosses to whom he can defer and subordinates to whom he can give orders.

Sexually, he is affectionate rather than randy, and is delighted to be seduced and 'mothered' in the sexual act. He sees sex principally as a way in which partners are 'nice to each other'. He lacks passion, and is singularly inept in erotic artfulness. He is generally content to maintain the security of a lifelong symbiotic attachment to his chosen mate, so long as she is willing to be satisfied with an emotionally bland relationship and she doesn't 'rock the boat' by wanting to delve into the unsafe depths of her own or his psyche.

If the Please man is more conscious of his resentment than his gratification in his symbiotic attachment to his mother, he may live out his antiscript by refusing artfully ever to be intimately committed to any woman. This type of Please man is likely to have a succession of affairs with women, in each of which he manages to maintain a 'no promises' contract. 'If there were a devil it would not be one who decided against God, but who, in eternity, came to no decision' (Buber). By this means he also may justify himself in keeping two affairs going contemporaneously, as an emotional insurance policy against the deep expectation he has that, sooner or later, any woman will deem him a 'naughty boy' and leave him. Indeed, sooner or later, nearly every woman realizes he is never going to be truly committed, and his fears of abandonment are thus well-founded.

Meanwhile, despite the fact that he never gives love wholeheartedly, the Please man maintains an infuriating little-boy, innocent righteousness in the face of the criticism by the woman in his life that he is ungiving. Doesn't he always 'do the right thing', he reassures himself. 'The last temptation is the greatest treason: to do the right deed for the wrong reason' (Eliot). He is the kind of man who wines and dines a woman expensively, has sex with her, and sends her a bunch of roses the next day; then she may never hear from him again!

Irrespective of whether he marries young and maintains a symbiotic relationship with his wife, or resentfully avoids a commitment to any woman in order to avoid the 'suffocation' that is his definition of intimacy, each Please man manifests both a clinging dependency and a covert, artfully evasive, vengeful lack of consideration towards the women in his life. He lies to himself first in order to be able to lie to others with a clear conscience. Relatively speaking, he is emotionally illiterate; expediency is his chief rule of thumb.

A mildly Please man is everybody's idea of 'a nice bloke'; an extremely Please man is a smarmy cheat.

Woman The Please woman is 'Daddy's little girl' and expects to be treated as a princess by the men in her life. In principle, she believes she is entitled to spend, spend, spend, without any need to worry or even think about where the money comes from. In return she sees herself as a well-dressed, well-coiffured, well-manicured asset to her man's image in the world at large. She always does and says the diplomatically 'right thing' and makes an excellent 'company wife'. She likes to have and to keep 'a nice home', and is willing to put in the necessary work to entertain, for both business and social purposes, in accordance with conventional norms. She is proud of being abreast of current fashion in her clothing, possessions, habits and attitudes. She gossips and bitches with her female friends but she also does her bit for charity. She is the archetypal 'nice, suburban, middle-class housewife'.

Sexually she is compliant and affectionate; and it never occurs to her that her partner could ever want anything different or more than she gives him. She is petulantly outraged if she is faced with the reality of her partner showing any interest in another woman; her outrage often being justified on the grounds of the insult to her implied in the other woman's dowdy clothes or unattractive physical attributes compared with her own.

A minority of Please women, like their male counterparts, never achieve any sustained intimate relationship with any man. For them, no man shows himself as willing and/or able to indulge them continuously, as their fathers did, so they settle for brief sexual affairs with men who are willing, temporarily, 'to give them a good time': taking them out in lavish style and giving them all the accoutrements, roses, perfume, etc., that betoken 'love'.

A mildly Please woman is everybody's idea of 'an attractive woman'; an extremely Please woman is a vapid dolly-bird, without a real feeling or thought in her heart or head.

Parent Please parents are overwhelmingly concerned that their children are well-scrubbed, 'nicely' dressed, well-spoken and well-behaved enough to call forth credit to themselves from family, friends, neighbours and their children's teachers. They fear being disliked by their children and so indulge them materially as much as they can possibly afford. They presume that this is a measure of their great love for their children, for which the children are expected to be duly appreciative and, as they grow up, increasingly to reciprocate their parents' gifts and favours.

Please parents are committed to the closely-guarded and insistent presumption that theirs is an unequivocally 'happy family'. They are profoundly hurt and shocked by their adolescent children's recalcitrance, rudeness and lack of consideration for them, and they loudly bemoan, 'After all we've done for you. . .' Eventually, they are likely to get from their children just what they deserve: respectful consideration in outer action which pays lip service to love, without any of the authentic feeling that they, the parents, crave. 'A spoiled child never loves its mother' (Taylor). They feel hurt by their children, but never realize that they are getting back from them exactly what they have given. And these parents usually go on, throughout their lives, giving material things to their children in the name of love.

How to get the best out of Please people Thank them politely for what they do for you. Stay near the surface of things in your communications with them. If you embarrass them with too gutsy words or feelings, they will blush and not know how to respond, and will resent you for it.

Never lose your own temper in response to their bad temper or rudeness. It is their covert aim to make you respond in a socially unacceptable way so that they can slither out of awareness that they behaved badly and focus only on your bad behaviour. Instead, express your anger in a seething but controlled, polite way. They may still refuse to accept responsibility for what they have done, by deciding they have been misunderstood, but they will be forced to awareness that something they did or said made you angry. If they have told you an outright lie, and you know that they know they have done so, don't fall into the trap of accusing them of it verbally; they will slither out of responsibility for it with the adroitness of Houdini. Instead, accuse them with a stony silence, while staring them straight in the eye; there is no escape from this.

In an intimate relationship, confronting a Please person effectively requires the patience of Job. Their repression is very deep and even potent psychotherapists may require years to break down their armour. The approach that works best is to give them no strokes at all, positive or negative, for their clichés and platitudes, so that they are forced to fill in the vacuum exposed by your silence with something real. Stroke them abundantly for any, however small, behaviour or remark that is clearly authentic and autonomous. Let them see your hurt feelings in response to their failure to give a feeling response to your feelings and thank them when they express authentic aggression because this is what they are most frightened of doing.

If, out of your patient love, you eventually succeed in making a Please person emotionally responsible and grown-up, you will have gained not only true intimacy with him or her, but deep wisdom and power for your dealings with other people.

Try Hard

> We have cause to fear him who hates himself, for we shall be the victims if we cannot seduce him into loving himself.
> *Nietzsche*

Man In his intimate relationships, the Try Hard man looks down on or up to his partner, or a mixture of both. He is incapable of relating to people as equal to equal. However, he chooses his partner on the basis that he can rely on her to be his staunchly committed equal in one respect: blaming other people or 'circumstances outside his control' for his failure to fulfil his ambitions in the world. He feels battered by the world, and he expects his partner to compensate for this and his large inferiority complex by her unflagging expression of her pity for his bruises and admiration for the outstanding abilities she knows he has, even if nobody else seems to appreciate them. In return, he treats his partner likewise and explicitly praises her abilities in public, out of his projective presumption that her value is also unappreciated by the world at large. But woe betide his partner if she dares ever to suggest that he may be responsible for his failures; then he turns very nasty indeed, and aggressively derides and humiliates her at every opportunity, both privately and publicly.

Sexually he is very unsure of his basic masculinity, which he tends to compensate for by macho-aggressive behaviour. However, this rarely achieves the delirious submission of his partner that he supposes it should; so he often resorts to 'humbly adoring' the animus of a professionally successful 'liberated' woman, who is happy to take the sexual initiative and seduce him. This is very flattering to his ego in the short-term, but at a deep level he feels he has been cheated of his masculine prerogative and tends, often quite unconsciously, to revenge himself on his 'superior' partner by becoming increasingly impotent as soon as the first flush of the affair has subsided. As in the rest of his life, sexually he quickly corners himself into a 'no-win' position.

A mildly Try Hard man, in his wistful Little Boy Lost role, can be seductively charming to the maternal instinct of a confident woman; an extremely Try Hard man is a snarlingly aggressive bully who invokes an immediately hostile aggressive response from men and women alike.

Woman Because the core unhappy preoccupation of Try Hard is potency, a Try Hard woman may be less obviously handicapped than her male counterpart. A Try Hard man, when he chooses to adapt to his lack of self-esteem by passive humility, inevitably remains deeply bitter that he is paying the price of not manifesting his biological, assertive masculinity; whereas a Try Hard woman may choose the passive, submissive option quite compatibly with the biological norms of her femininity. But there is a masculine as well as a feminine component in the psyches of all human beings, notwithstanding that masculinity is naturally dominant in males and femininity in females. So the Try hard woman feels and expresses the same angry, hostile, competitive, bitter resentment for her essential lack of self-esteem as a Try

Hard man, even though typically to a lesser degree. Just as the Try Hard man is expressing his 'unfinished business' concerning rivalry with his father, so the Try Hard woman is expressing her 'unfinished business' concerning rivalry with her mother. The Try Hard man is deeply intimidated by the power of other men who are all stand-ins for his father, and the Try Hard woman is deeply intimidated by the power of other women who are all stand-ins for her mother. A man's power is stereotypically measured in his success in his work, and a woman's power is stereotypically measured in her attractiveness to men; so Try Hard men are enviously hostile towards successful men, and Try Hard women are enviously hostile towards attractive women.

Sexually the Try Hard woman is, because of her lack of self-esteem, notably jealous and possessive of her partner. She is very fearful of losing him to another woman and, if her jealous possessiveness is great enough, she may eventually drive him into the arms of another woman.

A mildly Try Hard woman may be charming in her modesty to a paternalistic, often older, man; an extremely Try Hard woman is as off-putting in her aggressive malcontent as her male counterpart, to men and women like.

Parent Try Hard parents are very fond of telling their children how lucky they are to have the material and other privileges and opportunities denied them, the parents, in their childhoods. While the parents insist, from their Parent ego states, how glad they are that their children have so many advantages they never had, the children hear the much louder and truer message of envious discontent with their lot communicated from their parents' Adapted Childs. In response, the children pity their parents and are loath to make them envious which they know their parents would be if they, the children, dared to achieve the worldly success or happiness they believe their parents were so unfairly denied. Furthermore, if the children do succeed, in whatever way their parents did not, the children feel they are not entitled to take any credit for getting what they want in life; it is all due to the 'luck' of the advantages they were given by their 'unlucky' parents.

It is from adolescence onwards, when children seek to establish their full adult self-esteem, that Try Hard parents communicate most potently their punitive envy of their children. Try Hard is most potently communicated by the Try Hard parent to his or her same-sexed children, by virtue of children modelling their basic self-esteem on identification with their same-sexed parent. Thus Try Hard parents generally prefer, and have a better relationship with, their opposite-sexed children. The grown-up children of Try Hard parents continue to pity their parents and defend them to the world at large, but they also hate their parents for their crippling of them, and their hatred is expressed as regular outbursts of aggressive and hostile quarrels with them.

The greatest gift all parents can give their children is their own satisfaction with their lives. 'Where the parent's needs are reasonably satisfied, the children have a better chance of being content, since they might then see some possible future pattern of integration into a reasonable adult world' (Woods).

The obverse is Satanic. The Try Hard parent is one who, feeling him- or herself cast out of Paradise, seeks to gain some compensatory happiness by making others, especially his own children, unhappy also. As I remarked earlier, Try Hard parents more than any other bear witness to 'the sins of the fathers being visited upon the children even unto the third and fourth generation'.

How to get the best out of Try Hard people Ignore the competitiveness implicit in the remarks they make. For example, to 'Have you only got a 17-inch television? Mine's a 26-inch', respond, 'That sounds nice', implying, 'I'm glad you've got what you want. I've got what I want, too. I don't envy you or expect you to envy me'. Or in response to their obsessive concern with being superior by virtue of having the right answer, such as, 'I knew it was going to rain today. You said it wouldn't. I was right', reply blandly, 'Yes you were'. Try Hard people are so frightened of their experienced humiliation if they turn out to be wrong in factual matters that they often do not make open predictions at all but only after the event say, 'I knew it would rain ages before you said it would'.

Never let them off what they have committed themselves to do; doing so implies that you have as low expectations of them as they have of themselves. Instead, express anger towards them for not getting on with whatever it is; this powerfully implies that you have no doubt about their capability. This is the essence of what is required in an intimate relationship with a Try Hard person to facilitate him or her in moving through the barrier to success. The person will complain that you are tyrannical and heartless, but your willingness to do this thankless task will be the mark of your love. This is also what is required of all loving parents in their relationships with their adolescent children who are in a natural Try Hard stage of their development. Parents who let their children off in response to protestations of incapacity are not being kind but are cruelly expressing a deep desire for their children not to succeed.

Since sexual self-esteem is inevitably an issue in Try Hard, the way to best help someone overcome Try Hard varies according to whether he or she is the same or opposite gender to ourselves. When the person is the same gender, the essential message we need to transmit is, 'You're as OK as I am; if I can do it, so can you'; and this message can be transmitted by explicit Parent exhortation as well as covertly. When the person is of the opposite gender the task is more difficult and must be accomplished more subtly, by invoking an archetypal Parent sexual response to us, because explicit Parent exhortation to a Try Harder of opposite gender to ourself only makes their Try Hard worse. Thus a woman wanting to help a man transcend his Try Hard needs persistently to be helpless at the task the man lacks confident maleness in; and a man wanting to help a woman transcend her Try Hard needs persistently to be helpless at the tasks the woman lacks confident femaleness in. In an intimate adult relationship, probably the biggest reward for lovingly forcing your partner to transcend Try Hard will be his or her transformation into a fully desiring and lusty sexual partner.

Be Strong

> The knowledge that he never mentioned
> His love for her, or heard her say,
> That she loved him — his well-intentioned
> Design to keep all pain at bay,
> To shield him from the agitation
> Of passion with the insulation
> Of casual conduct, light and bland —
> Hurts like a nail torn from his hand.   *Seth*

Man   The Be Strong man is epitomized in the idea of the gentleman. He stands up when women enter the room, holds doors open for them and generally acknowledges and defers to the traditional conventions concerning role differences between the sexes. His clean, well-groomed appearance and manners (sometimes including the accessory of a moustache which is a thoroughly reliable indicator that he is Be Strong) make him a very welcome addition to any dinner table. A Be Strong bachelor — and the bachelor class is overwhelmingly comprised of Be Strong men — is never short of social invitations. He is a Barbara Cartland hero and women fantasize the glory of being the one for whom he will finally shed his good manners and his clothes in the unbridled sexual passion that they are singularly capable of arousing in him. They are usually profoundly frustrated. His armour of cold detachment, which is his protection against his conviction that he is intrinsically unloveworthy, is very thick and derived usually from a lack of warmth in his relationship to his mother and an unhappy relationship between his mother and father. He is competent in his work but he expects to be unappreciated in his work as well as in his personal relationships, so he is often happiest self-employed.

A woman in love with a Be Strong man in her desperation to elicit an emotional response from him, is likely, eventually, to take the sexual initiative as a last-ditch attempt to make him lose control of himself with her. If he is extremely Be Strong he will resist even this and the woman will give him up as a lost cause. This may jolt him into awareness of the price he is paying for the pride of his self-sufficiency and may or may not prompt him, at last, to express his need of the woman. 'Only my near-absence guarantees his near-presence, and it is an exhausting game to play' (O'Brien).

More typically, when a woman has compromised herself sufficiently to make it impossible for him to disbelieve that she desires him, the Be Strong man will 'perform' considerately and adequately, but without the 'I love you' that the woman longs for. Still the gentleman, he will probably then 'do the right thing' and marry her. She will go on hoping that, in due course, as he becomes secure in her love for him, he will feel and declare his love for her. He may or may not.

I recently heard a joke about Be Strong that says it all. Two men friends meet in the street.
1st gentleman: Hello, old chap, How are you?
2nd gentleman: Not too bad. Actually, I've been getting these terrible headaches lately and my doctor sent me to this Harley Street psychiatrist fellow.
1st gentleman: What did he say?
2nd gentleman: He said I'm in love with my umbrella. In love with my umbrella?! It's absurd. I mean to say, I'm very fond of it...

The woman he marries may be like himself, in which case they will live together amicably with an absence of true intimacy that neither of them bemoans, because they don't know what they are missing. Or else he marries a desperately needy and/or greedy woman whom he Rescues in a bid to 'earn' the love he believes he does not deserve; in which case he quickly becomes the Victim of her Persecutory complaints against the insufficiency of what he gives her; and he is confirmed in his deep conviction that reaching out for love can only bring him pain.

A mildly Be Strong man is a considerate and reliable gentleman; an extremely Be Strong man is a profoundly lonely and alienated block of ice, whose coldness breaks the heart of any woman who approaches him.

Woman Because a certain degree of reticence is a biologically natural component of female sexuality, a Be Strong woman is not as obviously handicapped in her intimate relationships as her male counterpart. She may call her Be Strong 'feminine modesty' and men may be charmed, at first, by her masquerade. But she quickly reveals herself as being terrified of intimacy, derived usually from a lack of warmth in her relationship to her father and an unhappy relationship between her mother and father. She is constantly on the look-out for indications that any man's expressed interest in her is inauthentic and she disdains most men as having nothing to offer that is of any value to her. 'Nothing is wrong except the refusal to play' (Brown). And even when she finds herself being drawn to a man, she cynically discounts the authenticity of her own feelings, on the grounds that if she 'really' loved him her feelings for him would be completely positive, rather than mixed with the dislike she feels for his shortcomings, shortcomings she homes in on with an eagle eye. She is more capable than any other woman of one night stands for the mere satisfaction of lust, after which she can immediately shrug off the encounter as meaningless and quickly forget the man, and even his name!

Like her male counterpart, she is competent in her work but expects to be under-appreciated, so she generally chooses a job such as social work or one of the 'helping professions' where she is granted the autonomy to bossily tell her 'inferiors' what is good for them and get their servile gratitude for what she does. She is quite comfortable amongst male colleagues because her professional role relationship to them legitimizes her need to keep her emotional distance.

She is a Rescuing busybody in the affairs of others and prides herself on the number of people who seek her good counsel concerning the pains and vicissitudes of their lives. She enjoys the vicarious thrill of other people's emotional experiences, and she especially relishes the 'bad endings' of the love affairs between other people which began with such high hopes and expectations. Thus she confirms the 'superiority' and 'wisdom' of her own abstention from love, which is her defence against the intimacy she longs for but is terrified of.

She usually marries a clingingly dependent, emotionally infantile man, from whom she derives the security of his neediness against her presumption that no emotionally mature man who can independently choose a woman out of his unneedy desire would ever choose her. For this security she almost inevitably pays the price of continuously feeding her partner's narcissistic neediness without any appreciation from him in return. Thus she confirms her conviction of her unloveworthiness. She is likelier to feel even lonelier when married than when single.

A mildly Be Strong woman is a woman whose competent reliability combined with her emotional reticence appeals to the wooing and winning impulses of a sexually confident man. An extremely Be Strong woman is a patronizingly interfering busybody, resented by women for the one-sided intimacy she exploitatively extracts from them, and feared and loathed by men for her psychological castration of them.

Parent Be Strong parents enjoy parenthood very much because it legitimizes their felt need to 'earn' love by giving and giving without any expectation of being given to in return. They are wise as parents because, by default, they know the truth that children are not really capable of loving in the mature sense of the word until they have been given love bounteously and without price until their twenty-odd year maturational process is complete. Be Strong parents are deeply gratified by the mere glad acceptance by their children of the love they give them, which acceptance they so doubt in their relationships with their grown-up peers. Be Strong parents often feel the deeply wounded loneliness of their own childhoods to be largely healed by the happiness of their relationships to their children.

The respect in which Be Strong's parents fail their children is in their unwillingness to allow their children to express emotional pain. Inasmuch as they have found it necessary to protect themselves against fully realizing the agony of their own stroke-deprived Childs by their puritanical 'let's-get-on-with-things' resilience, by projective identification, they cannot bear any emotional pain experienced by their children. It is as if they say desperately to their children, 'Just don't feel pain. I'll do anything you like, so long as you are always happy'. As for other parents, it is when their children become adolescents that Be Strong parents are most likely to fail their children. In adolescence, children quite naturally have to experience large emotional swings consonant with their hormones, and in response to their knowledge of their Be Strong parent's inability to cope with their pains, they are forced unnaturally to protect their parent's vulnerability by pretending, as far as possible, that they are constantly optimistic and ebullient. Be Strong parents can learn from their children, if they are willing, that to feel pain and express it makes people 'human' and is not 'unmanageable' as they falsely presume it to be. Rescuing people from their needed experiences of pain is as selfish as denying them the right to any of their happier experiences.

How to get the best out of Be Strong people Praise them for their consideration and kindness. Praise them for their reliability. When they invite you to dinner or for a treat that will cost them money or effort, tell them that you would like, for a change, to treat them instead. Hold back from effusiveness toward them and respect their occasional need for privacy and aloneness. Give them strokes through irony. For example, 'I must say you're the most unreliable person I know' which they can accept, with a smile, more easily than a straightforward positive stroke. Be warmly appreciative of any presents they give you.

Never try to force them to directly express their sad or lonely feelings; they will only deny them and retreat from any intimacy you have achieved. Never shout or express your own emotions hysterically in their presence. If you do they will crumble inwardly and silently remove themselves from your presence wearing a stony mask and you will have achieved nothing. Nevertheless, they need to be told calmly and clearly that feelings, not reason, make the world go round, and there are times when being 'uninvolved' is not the proud virtue they claim but cruel inhumanity.

In an intimate relationship, be patient in seeking explicit verbal expressions of affection from them. Give them strokes that demonstrate in thoughtful deeds rather than words that you love them. More than anything else, Be Strong people long to be convinced that you feel loved by them and are glad of their love. Once they are so convinced they will shed their brittle armour for you alone, and be yours forever.

Chapter 9

Fifteen Couplings

> Domestic laws should be made according to temperaments, which should be classified. *Hardy*

Pain and Joy in Intimate Relationships

At a purely biological, Natural Child, level, the discriminations we make between people are very crude. Like other animals, our essential narcissism usually dictates that we prefer others who reflect back to us our own image, mostly in terms of colouring, shape and size. We are all probably also attracted to general robustness and other characteristics associated with the survival of the fittest.

But the turn-ons that excite us most — the psychological parts of our responses to others that overlay our basic animal nature — are all informed by our Adapted Child. Simple, physical orgasm is not a patch on 'the real thing', which is, uniquely for human beings, a physical response compounded with emotionality and consists of a huge variety of possibilities that Freud subsumed in the general dichotomy of sadism and masochism. There are pleasures in our pains and pains in our pleasures, and the compulsive nature of our Adapted Child testifies to this truth. While we are all capable of relating from and to the Parent, Adult, Natural Child and Little Professor in ourselves and others, the pragmatic reality in all our lives is that it is our Adapted Childs that generally call the tune. Our Parent expresses tenderness and loving control, and receives respect; our Adult expresses and receives information and ideas; our Natural Child and Little Professor express and receive the simple joys and pains associated with being bodily alive; and our Adapted Child feels and expresses our passionate involvement with the world and other people.

Our Natural Child and Little Professor unreflectively know only this moment of pain and joy. Our Adapted Child is poignantly aware, while wishing otherwise, that this present pain is but an instance of the pain, as well as joy, to which we committed ourselves in the childhood decisions we made in response to the injunctions we received. Our Adult mitigates the pains in our Adapted Child with a degree of detachment we achieve through rationalizing our feelings with 'objectivity'. Our Parent mitigates the pains in our Adapted Child with a degree of hope we achieve through justifying our feelings with 'morality', which promises future joy, in the next world if not in this one, for present 'goodness'.

The cosmos is I believe a-moral and gives not a damn for our constructs of 'good and evil', 'reward and punishment', nor even for our directly experienced pain and joy. Humanly speaking, it is a matter for each individual to choose for himself that point on the continuum between total narcissism and total sublimation which he judges maximizes joy and minimizes pain for himself. Empirically, though, the point chosen needs to be somewhere in-between the two extremes. Total embroilment in the Adapted Child is mindlessness and the pleasures of the mind are too good to miss. Total embroilment in the Adult and Parent is lovelessness and the pains and incomparable joy of love are too good to miss. 'There is not a woman in the world the possession of whom is as precious as that of the truth she reveals by causing us to suffer' (Proust). Falling in love is a manifestation of our willingness to experience the greatest vulnerability for those moments of ecstasy and 'meaning' that mock death. Two or three such experiences in a lifetime is a privilege. Never to have been in love is the saddest deprivation.

We decide in childhood the personal meanings we will give our own pains and joys; and the repetition compulsion rules that we will confirm these chosen meanings in every experience of pain and joy we have for the rest of our lives. Our childhood meanings are our life sentences. As in our interactions with the world at large, in our interactions with intimate others, the pains we experience neither 'happen' to us nor are imposed on us by others. Like it or not, we fall in love with a chosen other for the immediate, albeit usually unconscious, knowledge we have that that other, in his or her way of being, will willingly co-operate with us in confirming the validity of our childhood decisions concerning the pains as well as the joys that will be our lot in life. We know, in a non-articulated way, every potential between ourselves and any person we meet in a matter of minutes, if not seconds. And our intimate others are deeply and knowingly chosen for the particular pains and joys that relating to them bring us. Notwithstanding the superficial and facile observations and judgements people may make about any couple, all intimate relationships are, by definition, between colluding equals. We are never truly misled. In every 'bad' that is done us by our intimate partners, we have colluded. A needed person has as much need to be needed as a needy one needs; a Victim has as much desire to be Victimized as a Rescuer or Persecutor has to Rescue or Persecute. The only genuine mistake we make in seeking an intimate relationship with another occurs when we infer from some false evidence that another is a character in our personal myth when he or she is not. A mild, short-lived disappointment is the worst consequence of this error. But in every touch between one person and another that binds them, the touching surfaces, by definition, adhere equally to each other. If and when this equality no longer applies, a couple becomes unstuck and parts; as long as they are together they are equal in their attachment, whether the attachment be essentially based on creative loving joy, the agonies of purgatory or hell or something in-between. ' "Why does this always happen to me?" may lead to serious and constructive thinking and to personal growth in the best sense, if it takes the form of "What did I really do to deserve this?" ' (Berne)

Pain which stretches the boundaries of our egos, and joy which is the fulfillment of our ego ideal in the other and the other's ego ideal in us, both exist in all intimate relationships. 'What we cannot face in ourselves we see in people we dislike; what we cannot find in ourselves we see in those we love' (Freeman). The only alternative is deadly stasis. Nevertheless, on balance, any particular relationship is sooner or later revealed as essentially enriching or essentially destructive. Each of the five personality types emphasizes some criteria in relating to others that cause it comfort and some that cause it agony. Bravely facing the knowledge of our own and our potential partner's personalities gives us the freedom to choose, knowing and accepting the inevitable prices of our choice. There are antipathies between some of the types that no amount of tolerance can overcome for the purpose of maintaining an intimate relationship. But intellectual awareness is nonetheless very worthwhile, both for parting amicably from an unworkable intimate relationship and for getting on tolerably well with people of antipathetic types to our own in more superficial relationships.

> No work of the mind and no deed of the heart can have a decisive success with one class of men without incurring the condemnation of the other. This antagonism is, without doubt, as old as the beginning of culture, . . . because no party can be brought to admit either a deficiency on his own side or a reality on the other's, yet there is always profit enough in following up such an important antagonism to its final source, thus

> at least reducing the actual point at issue to a simpler formulation.
> *Jung*

There are fifteen possible relationships between the Adapted Child of one person and the Adapted Child of another: five relationships between like types and ten relationships between different types. Since most people have two types at the core of their personalities, the Adapted Child to Adapted Child relationship of any two people is typically made up of four discrete ways of relating, each of which has its own discrete pleasures and pains. For example, if one person's Adapted Child is, at core, Be Perfect and Hurry Up, and another's Be Perfect and Please, there will be a Be Perfect to Be Perfect aspect to their relationship, a Be Perfect to Please aspect, a Hurry Up to Be Perfect aspect and a Hurry Up to Please aspect; and the couple will experience these aspects as very distinct parts of their relationship. Given that there is no escaping the predominance of our Adapted Childs in our relationships, it can be very useful to a couple to analyze the Adapted Child to Adapted Child part of their relationship into its separate components. By this means the couple are able self-consciously to prefer the pleasanter aspects of their relationship and avoid the nastier aspects, while still realistically acknowledging the inevitable centrality of Adapted Child to Adapted Child transactions in their total relationship.

Out of many years experience, my diagnoses of the fifteen possible couplings between the five personality types can be taken as very reliable, although the descriptions are inevitably exaggerated stereotypes when applied to the reality of a particular relationship. It is merely my intention to communicate the general flavour of what to expect from each of the pairings; the usefulness of my descriptions will depend on the reader's willingness to translate my comments imaginatively into the realm of his or her own experience. My generalizations are derived from analyzing the meanings of the Adapted Child relationships of many people, but they are in no way intended to be dogmatic statements of fact. Nevertheless, I hope that my comments reflect sufficiently commonplace experience that the reader will, in many cases, readily match his or her own observations to mine.

A summary table of the advantages and disadvantages of each of the fifteen pairings, given at the end of this chapter, may be used in combination with the summary table of the individual types at the end of Chapter 5 as a quick and reliable guide to knowing other people, and the ways and means of getting the most and the best rather than the worst and the least out of them and ourselves in our relationships with them.

Inter-personal Relationships

In this section, where I designate one of a pair as 'he' and the other as 'she' I do so for the sake of verbal simplicity. Men and women are intrinsically equally able to adopt either role in all of the possible pairings.

Be Perfect and Be Perfect Like most couplings of like-to-like, this pair usually get on well with each other. They are apt to be united by their common beliefs, and so long as they do not disagree fundamentally about what is and is not important in life, they give each other the security of feeling right about things. Their life together tends to be ritualistic, extremely well-organized and ordered. However, if they do disagree fundamentally about their values in life, they will bicker and criticize each other interminably and probably end up feeling intransigent mutual hatred. A negative Be Perfect to Be Perfect relationship is epitomized in the internecine war in Northern Ireland, the Israel-Arab conflict and in all religious wars that have ever been fought.

Be Perfect and Hurry Up At the profoundest levels of their personalities the individuals who form this couple are supremely well matched. When referred to the deepest psychological level, Be Perfect and Hurry Up are expressions of the fear of death and the temptation of death respectively. To this extent Be Perfect is a cowardly stick-in-the-mud and Hurry Up is a brazen daredevil. They are able to cancel out the unhealthy extreme that each on its own stands for and to create instead an optimally healthy balance in their relationship between organization and efficiency, thrift and extravagance, caution and daring, structure and spontaneity ... and many other adaptive compromises between a wide range of polarities in life. Transactionally, Be Perfect tends to play the role of the sometimes indulgent and sometimes controlling Parent to the sometimes charming and sometimes exasperating Child of Hurry Up. The only possibility of serious harm in this relationship arises when one or both express their Adapted Child at a very high pitch. When this occurs, the two Adapted Child ego states may escalate each other in a vicious spiral until they lose their separate identities and collide in murderous/suicidal insanity.

Be Perfect and Please This is often a very stable and contented relationship based on agreed dominance and submission roles. Be Perfect is the boss and Please is happily obedient. Be Perfect's quest for having things be and be done exactly the way he wants is fulfilled and, complementarily, Please is profoundly reassured in knowing she is doing the right and good thing. 'You have done well', given by Be Perfect is usually happily received by Please as a positive stroke, even though others might resent the patronage implied. However, because of their contented equilibrium, Be Perfect tends to lack any stimulating challenge to his rigidity of outlook and Please gains no permission to live outside the bounds of her repressive conventionality. Such couples sometimes find expression of the suppressed side of the Adapted Child in each of them through episodes in which Please expresses some fleeting defiant rebelliousness and Be Perfect responds with angry criticism. But Be Perfect quickly controls the outburst of Please and things usually return rapidly to their normal peace and calm.

Be Perfect and Try Hard This is often an obviously unhappy relationship based on open warfare. Both are very critical of each other; but Be Perfect, who tends to be the more intelligent in this partnership, is usually the one who in arguments consistently ends up being the victorious Persecutor while Try Hard ends up being the humiliated Victim. Be Perfect is using Try Hard to project her own feeling of worthlessness out of herself, while Try Hard is continually reinforced in his fundamental belief that 'No matter how hard I try, I'll never be successful enough'. Be Perfect often threatens to leave Try Hard, but she knows secretly that she is dependent on Try Hard for her needed feeling of superiority. Both know their relationship is likely to continue in its often violent unhappiness for a long time.

Be Perfect and Be Strong This couple is usually united by a puritanical attitude to life. Often they are both ambitious and work very hard to achieve their goals. Be Perfect easily accommodates to Be Strong's view that 'reliability is the better part of love'; and Be Strong pleases Be Perfect by being willing to get on with things without complaining. They are likely to enjoy conversations with each other that are serious, playfully critical and sophisticatedly ironical. They are unlikely to cause each other pain, but they tend to reinforce rather than positively modify each other's essential over-dutifulness at the expense of Natural Child spontaneity and pleasure.

Hurry Up and Hurry Up Since the deep intention of Hurry Up in relation to others is 'I'll reject you before you can reject me', a relationship between two people who are principally Hurry Up is so unstable that it is unlikely to be formed at all. However, in contradiction of the deep but usually consciously denied aim of not maintaining intimacy, Hurry Up is phenomenally obsessed with finding lasting love. So when two Hurry Up's meet they are likely to experience themselves as falling overwhelmingly in love at first sight; and they often fall straight into bed with each other at their first meeting. The relationship ends with a bang rather than a whimper, a short time later, when one of them simply doesn't turn up to an arranged meeting, or in some way expresses as much hateful lack of regard for the other as he or she expressed loving commitment at their first meeting. When Hurry Up to Hurry Up is a minor component of a couple's relationship it will probably find expression in either or both of them slamming out of the house without saying where they are going or for how long. Sometimes they get drunk or 'stoned out of their minds' in each other's company, but the isolation each of them then feels is as great as it would be if they were each alone.

Hurry Up and Please From the point of view of Hurry Up, this relationship can be nearly as good for him as a relationship with Be Perfect. Although Be Perfect is more capable than Please of providing Hurry Up with the profound existential control he so desperately needs, Please can offer Hurry Up a great deal of reassurance. It is as if Hurry Up is saying, 'It's no good expecting love to last. People give it to you for a little while, but then they inevitably withdraw it and you are left alone.' To which Please replies, 'I know exactly how you feel, how frightening it is to think of being left alone. But, you know, it's not inevitable. So long as you are good, the people who love you will stay with you forever. Here, let me show you how to be good.' Through this implicit dialogue between them, Hurry Up learns how to be Please and so achieves protection from the much more frightening Hurry Up in him. The satisfaction to Please in this relationship derives mainly from the reassurance of security she gets from knowing that her partner's emotional dependence on their relationship is even greater than her own.

Hurry Up and Try Hard   This relationship is full of tension and aggression. Try Hard is 'driven crazy' by Hurry Up, and Hurry Up is made wildly impatient by Try Hard. Each justifies his or her own Adapted Child inadequacies in terms of the provocation of the other. Hurry Up says, 'If only he weren't so damn slow I could be calm'; Try Hard says, 'If only she'd give me some peace I could finish this.' Neither of them achieves anything positive by this dishonest projection of responsibility for their hang-ups, but they may eventually succeed in provoking violence or serious bodily illness in each other.

Hurry Up and Be Strong   This is probably the most painful relationship of all. Each of the partners is fundamentally seeking to prove the inevitability of profound loneliness, and they powerfully support each other in fulfilling this quest. The relationship often begins with Be Strong acting as Rescuer of Hurry Up's Victim, but these roles are quickly succeeded by Hurry Up Persecuting and rejecting Be Strong who then becomes the Victim. Hurry Up confirms, 'It's futile forming a relationship. Other people never give me what I need, so it's best to refuse what they offer me, because it won't be enough and it won't last long anyway.' Be Strong confirms, 'No matter how much love and caring I offer another person, I am unappreciated. The only reason that makes sense is that I am intrinsically unloveworthy.' Hurry Up deeply knows that her insatiable quest to be unconditionally and overwhelmingly loved is an unrealizable dream; from her all-or-nothing frame of reference, she invariably ends up with nothing. At the deepest level of his being, Be Strong is so unused to receiving love that he doesn't dare form a relationship with somebody who would love him for fear that he would not know how to react. Hurry Up asks for everything and gets nothing; Be Strong asks for nothing and gets nothing. When Hurry Up and Ffer' describes the principal Adapted Child relationship between a couple, it may be very reliably inferred that they will assure each other of extreme pain and unhappiness, which will be a reflection of the profound emotional neglect and/or traumatization that each of them suffered in childhood.

Please and Please This couple is usually united in a very stable relationship of mutual dependence. Each of the partners is terrified of being left alone, and so they are both rigidly obedient to their unspoken agreement that they will each be and behave towards the other in accordance with conventional, respectable propriety in general, and in the ways each other asks in particular. Thus they achieve the emotional security they crave above all else. The price they pay for this is the stiflement of spontaneity and authentic expression of emotion. Neither risks offending the other and so disturbing the safe equilibrium of the relationship, but to an outsider the covert resentment between this couple is often palpable. Sometimes this relationship continues on a conventional and even keel for a lifetime; sometimes such a couple punctuates the essential politeness of the relationship with periodic angry quarrels which release (though often unconsciously) the built-up resentment each feels for his or her symbiotic dependence on the other.

Please and Try Hard This is most likely to be an amicable but dreary relationship. That is, neither is likely to hurt the other, but neither will they stimulate the other to reach beyond the narrowly unambitious and respectable limits they impose on their lives. In England it is a prototypical lower-middle-class marriage in which the wife is the Please and the husband the Try Hard partner. Please is nice to Try

Hard in not pressing him to achieve anything, and Try Hard conforms in his behaviour to Please's need to be respectable. The worst they are likely to do to each other from time to time is for Try Hard to think, but rarely say aloud, that Please is affected and pretentious, and for Please to think, but rarely say aloud, that Try Hard is a failure.

Please and Be Strong This is basically a deeply unhappy relationship, but one which often endures for a lifetime. It is very commonly the chief component of many English and especially middle-middle-class marriages, the husband usually being the Be Strong and the wife the Please partner. The trouble with this relationship is that it provides each of the partners with easy affirmation of his or her most painful feelings without providing any positive compensations. Please is dependent on another's instructions as to how to behave to please the other person; Be Strong longs to have his needs understood and met without his having to give voice to them. Please asks Be Strong to tell her what he wants her to be and to do; Be Strong replies, 'I want you to give to me in a spontaneous and authentic way, not according to instructions.' Thus they are locked in an impasse between their incompatible needs. Please accuses Be Strong of being cold, and Be Strong responds by crawling further and further into his shell. Be Strong 'proves' the impossibility of ever being loved for himself, and Please 'proves' she is a good person who is misunderstood and so vilified as bad.

Try Hard and Try Hard Of all the like-to-like relationships between Adapted Child ego states this is the one least likely to work for the benefit of both partners. Hurry Up and Hurry Up is equally unbeneficial to both partners but rarely endures for more than a few months anyhow. At best, this couple may be united in hostility and envy towards most other people which may, for example, find expression in their working together for a lost cause. However, it is more often the case that the envious hostility of each is projected onto the intimate other, with each chronically criticizing the other in order to boost his or her own very precarious self-esteem. In this relationship each partner will secretly sabotage the other's achievement of his or her ambitions; they are both constantly on tenderhooks lest the other win over them in some way or other. Life together for this couple is one long aggressive competition.

Try Hard and Be Strong This is a relationship between essentially incompatible types. They are so fundamentally incapable of gratifying each other that a long-term relationship is unlikely between them. Try Hard aims for what she wants materially in such a way as not to achieve it; Be Strong asks for what he wants emotionally in such a way as not to get it. They are on different wavelengths. When this Adapted Child interaction is a minor aspect of the total relationship between a couple, Try Hard will feel envious and aggressive towards Be Strong, and Be Strong will adopt a stance of cold and bored aloofness towards Try Hard. Try Hard envies Be Strong his cool, which Try Hard perceives herself as lacking because of insufficient luck or opportunity; and Be Strong finds Try Hard a bore for whining and for generally wearing her heart on her sleeve. In transacting with each other, Be Strong generally limits himself to peremptory brush-offs to Try Hard, and Try Hard is consumed with frustration and rage.

Be Strong and Be Strong This relationship is characterized by a great deal of mutual independence between the partners. Each is especially averse to what they would call emotional suffocation, so they support each other in mutual understanding of the other's need for privacy. So long as both have important interests outside as well as within their relationship they get on very well together, and they are grateful for their intimacy and commitment to each other which relieves them of the pain they each experienced as single people in reaching out for love. If one of them does not have an important interest outside the relationship he or she will become resentful of the lack of time given to the relationship by the other; one will feel neglected and the other suffocated.

TABLE OF INTER-PERSONAL COMPOUNDS

Compound	General Advantages	General Disadvantages	In Working Relationships
Be Perfect and Be Perfect	mutual respect and harmony if values shared	mutual disharmony in judgements if values disparate	good in an equal partnership or if subordinate fully respects boss
Be Perfect and Hurry Up	healthy complementarity in many areas of life	drive each other insane if intensity of either or both too great	enjoyably volatile relationship for both if Be Perfect boss; if Hurry Up boss, only works if Be Perfect given lots of autonomy
Be Perfect and Please	Be Perfect is permitted to express wish to dominate and Please finds reassurance in being confidently controlled	Be Perfect's rigidity and Please's inhibitions are not challenged; a narrow-minded relationship	very good if Be Perfect boss; very bad if Please boss
Be Perfect and Try Hard	outlet for aggression of each	the chronic unhappiness of open warfare	very humiliating for Try Hard if Be Perfect boss; short-lived relationship if Try Hard boss
Be Perfect and Be Strong	mutual respect and intellectual pleasure	reinforce each other's rigidity; neither's Free Child is encouraged	a generally good, 'get-on-with it' relationship
Hurry Up and Hurry Up	shared futility	provoke each other into escalating self-destructiveness	very unlikely to form a relationship of any duration
Hurry Up and Please	a safe harbour for Hurry Up; reassurrance of being needed by another for Please	a sense of suffocation for Hurry Up; some existential insecurity for Please	they like each other

Fifteen couplings

Hurry Up and Try Hard	mutual projection of responsibility onto the other	Hurry Up is made wildly impatient; Try Hard is 'driven crazy'	open warfare
Hurry Up and Be Strong	rationalizes isolation and loneliness of each	profound unhappiness for each only negative strokes given or received	are frightened of each other
Please and Please	emotional security for each	secret resentment of each towards the other; mutual inhibition of spontaneity	good mutual identification
Please and Try Hard	limited by stable security for Please; some unthreatened self-esteem for Try Hard	lack of stimulation for either; a dull, unchanging relationship	are kind to each other
Please and Be Strong	may do-good together	mutual unhappiness; Please feels misunderstood; Be Strong feels unappreciated	dislike each other
Try Hard and Try Hard	may be united in envy and hostility towards others	chronic mutual aggressive competitiveness	competitively aggressive; only good if they unite to fight 'authority'
Try Hard and Be Strong	outlet for resentment of each	mutual hatred; Try Hard is consumed with impotent rage; Be Strong is constantly aggravated	mutual resentment and misunderstanding
Be Strong and Be Strong	mutual independence and respect	lack of emotional warmth or	generally very good; confident reliance on each other

Chapter 10

Till Death Do Us Part?

> Some have been thought brave because they were
> afraid to run away. *Fuller*

Life as Faction

We create the world with our thoughts. Out of the amorphous clay of the universe in which we exist, we sculpt the forms that give our lives meaning: experiences, ideas, and 'other people' that are joyful and painful, beautiful and ugly, good and evil. We are all inventions of each other. Because we are human, we are glad to accept responsibility for the joy and beauty and good in our lives, but prefer to perceive the pain and ugliness and bad in our lives as fortuitously 'happening' to us or involuntarily imposed on us by other people. Denial and projection are the chief devices by which we preserve the inherent narcissism of our fragile egos, which I have observed recently in unadorned simplicity in my two-and-a-half-year old granddaughter. A few weeks ago, when she dropped and broke a cup, she simply said, 'I didn't'. A few days ago, sitting opposite me at the table, she accidentally knocked some food off her plate onto the floor and, without batting an eyelid, stared at me and said, 'I think you did that'. As grown-ups, our narcissism hides from itself in webs of camouflage that we sophisticatedly spin, but our primary aim in every instance of pain, ugliness or evil in which we participate is to maintain the perception of our own righteousness. A 'You did it' projection implies a developed concept of 'self' and equivalent 'selves' in others, which is the usual baseline on which we build the edifices of our ego. In extremis, when the ego attacks of others are more than our projective defences can withstand, we regress to the most primitive level of consciousness in which it is still possible to maintain a sense of self; 'other selves' cease to exist and we are left with our single self, distinct only from the rest of the universe, against which we flailingly deny our responsibility with 'I didn't do it'.

However we have orchestrated our themes in our earliest months and years of life, we are bound to them. We cannot escape the dimensions we created for ourselves in childhood, and the possibilities for our lives are tightly circumscribed by them.

> . . . human lives . . . are composed like music. Guided by his sense of beauty, an individual transforms a fortuitous occurrence . . . into a motif, which then assumes a permanent place in the composition of the individual life. . . Without realizing it, the individual composes his life according to the laws of beauty in times of greatest distress.
> *Kundera*

We are physically and psychologically bound by the limits of what we are, and it is as stupidly futile to waste our energy in wishing to be psychologically other than what we are as it is to wish to be the other gender, have different coloured eyes, or be a different height from the one we are. But for each of us, within the circumscription of that unknowable amalgam of nature and nurture that made us what we are, there is a unique heroic story wanting to be told. That story was vivid to each of us in the honesty of childhood, when we saw life in all its imaginative essence. Our grown-up lives are inevitably cluttered by pragmatic necessities that, if we let them, so overwhelm our consciousness that we simply plod through life as purgatory and cynically dismiss as 'romantic fiction' the passion and the heroism we have lazily renounced. We need to lift the veils of pragmatism and expediency that cloud our vision, to re-discover our dream of glory and 'selfishly' pursue the path to its fulfillment; to make ourselves artists and our lives the beautiful outcome of our artistry, to which satisfaction we are inherently entitled.

The heroic path is not the easy choice; it couldn't be heroic if it were. There are dragons to be slain, and our confrontations with our personal dragons are frighteningly frought with the possibilities of danger and pain. Most people prefer to live myopically, disdaining and discounting the dragons and heroes and heroines in their own Child as childish. This book has been written for those people who prefer passion, pain and joy to the sterility of filling their lives with 'grown-upness' and 'getting by'.

By and large, our myths contain two distinct, although often overlapping, themes: how we will 'succeed' in the world at large, broadly based on our 'unfinished business' with our same-sexed parent; and how we will be loved by our chosen sexual partner, broadly based on our 'unfinished business' with our opposite-sexed parent.

Our unfinished business with our same-sexed parent concerns the aggrandisement of our power, which, inasmuch as it refers to our self-esteem, involves our sense of worthiness in having our dream of love fulfilled; but it is principally focused on the achievement of our status in the world at large, through what we do. Our unfinished business with our opposite-sexed parent concerns the fulfillment of our dream to be loved for what we are.

'Doing' is the masculine principle in us all; 'being' is the feminine principle in us all. So, by and large, men feel themselves unready for the fulfillment of love until their masculine self-esteem is assured through some measure of worldly accomplishment; and, by and large, women feel themselves unready wholeheartedly to pursue careers until their feminine self-esteem is assured through loving and being loved by a man. In the long run, men need to 'be' as well as 'do' and women need to 'do' as well as 'be' in order to be wholesome human beings, and healthy intimacy, sexual or other, can only flourish between two distinctively whole people. 'A productive partnership cannot thrive on identification. Separateness, being over against the other, is prerequisite to true encounter' (Durkin).

It is in the development of spirituality associated with the quest for meaning in life that men and women can each reach successfully beyond the attractions and antipathies between the genders, to a higher level of living that encompasses masculinity and femininity and unites individual men and women in their common humanity. Broadly speaking, feeling and intuiting (the Child) is the femininity in us all, thinking and knowing-how (the Adult) is the masculinity in us all, and believing (Parent) is the humanity in us all. But the secularization of life has reduced morality (the Parent) to 'enlightened self-interest', and left us, collectively, on the brink of despairing nihilism.

As hero or heroine of our personal myth, the process of our lives is toward the triumph of fulfillment and the serenity at the end of our lives when, restrospectively, everything we have experienced can be seen, without sanctimonious piety, to have been an essential part of our life plan, neither good nor bad but simply the way things had to be for us. 'One remains young only on condition the soul does not relax, does not long for peace' (Nietzsche).

> We are a process. . . It requires a great deal of courage to face oneself and to be oneself. . . We may close our eyes, but the wheel still turns. . . Freedom exists in the ability to give crises either a meaning of growth and

> fulfillment or a meaning of frustration and helplessness.
> *Szanto*

The ideal conclusion of our lives is only arrived at by those who have faced and worked through the fears that stand in the way of the development of their egos, because the serene conclusion is arrived at from a vantage point that transcends the ego, and nobody has yet transcended his or her ego without having an ego to transcend.

So for each of us the heroic path is becoming an ever healthier version of our own authentic self.

> The real original sin is that of self-satisfaction with things as they are, the refusal to accept change and the always offered gifts of the spirit; the refusal to be transformed and to become more than one is now.
> *Rudhyar*

It is the courage and the struggle, not the outer achievement, that is the measure of a man's or woman's worth; and the private soul achievement cannot be directly known through the achievement that is visible to the world. Only in loving, sexual intimacy may we learn to know another and ourselves be known at the mythic centre of our beings.

> What is unique about the 'I' hides itself exactly in what is unimaginable about a person. . .
>
> Using numbers, we might say that there is one-millionth part dissimilarity to nine hundred ninety-nine thousand nine hundred ninety-nine millionths part similarity. . .
>
> Only in sexuality does the millionth part dissimilarity become precious, because, not accessible in public, it must be conquered. *Kundera*

Revenge is Sweet

Notwithstanding that, essentially, we create all we experience, phenomenally and pragmatically there is 'objective reality' in the world and in other people, which makes different people actually invoke different responses in us. No relationships, happy or unhappy, occur by chance, and we are willy-nilly drawn to people who offer us the pains of our unfinished business with our parents. Relationships serve purposes for each of the participants and are equally mutually symbiotic for as long as they last. No relationship is ever actually 'wasted' because it comes to an end, or for any other reason.

For example, relationships formed with the intention of intimacy between people who are irrelevant to each other's mythic needs soon dissolve because they contain no real joy and no real pain. Mild, short-lived disappointment in oneself for one's misperceived hope is the usual price paid, and the purpose of such relationships might be to teach the individuals the necessity for deeper discrimination in the choice of an intimate other.

And people who form intimate relationships out of the primary aim of finding a guaranteed antidote to loneliness, usually pay the price of agonizing loneliness within their relationships. The purpose of such relationships might be to teach the individuals that no relationship, whatever its potential, can be healthier than the individuals who comprise it. Relationships which are pre-emptively formed in a compulsive bid to 'be loved', evade the work we need to do to make ourselves healthily self-loving, and capable of loving another. Such relationships are doomed to failure.

The ending of a relationship signifies that its purpose has been fulfilled for one or both of the partners. Acrimonious endings are, of course, commoner when the purpose of the relationship has been fulfilled for one partner but not for the other. The one for whom the purpose has not been fulfilled will be forced to experience the agony of learning that love is not necessarily forever and cannot be contractually guaranteed. The one for whom the purpose has been fulfilled will be forced to experience the greater, I think, agony of his or her guilt and the humiliation of acknowledging his or her essential unrighteousness.

In time, all such learnings make for wisdom, but our immediate responses to the pains of the crises we are involved in are naturally all the primitive, malevolent emotions of jealousy, rage, resentment, bitterness, despair, etc., which are the authentic reactions of our wounded egos. 'Terrible are the wounds of a murdered dream' (Kundera). Adult understanding and Parent benevolence at such times are hypocritical and self-deceptive; our Child must have its full say first. And anybody who can authentically claim to feel no hostile aggressive emotions in response to the ending of an intimate relationship must also be admitting that he or she never knew any positive passion in that relationship either. The contemporary propensity of separated couples piously to avow their unremitting goodwill and friendship for their previous partners is powerful inferential evidence for the loveless basis of their relationships in the first place.

Blaming and hating are the healthy catharsis of mourning lost love, the pain of which is the basis for the ego growth we need to make at that time, and without which the next partner we choose will almost certainly cause us the same unhappiness as our previous one, no matter how 'different' we delude ourselves he or she is at the beginning of the relationship.

> Perhaps if you can accept the pain that almost kills you, you can use it, you can become better. . . Otherwise, you just get stopped with whatever it was that ruined you and you made it happen over and over again and your life has — ceased really — because you can't move or change or love any more. *Baldwin*

Love and hate, blame and guilt are existentially inseparable dimensions of our passion for life at the deep irrational core of our being. People who make a proud claim to rationality in response to emotional confrontations with others are actually making a shameful admission of their inhumanity, although their repressed emotions will bitterly contaminate their outlook for the rest of their lives. Only the authentic expression of our powerful feelings makes it possible that, in due course, we need 'not burden our remembrances/With a heaviness that's gone' (Shakespeare).

The general purpose of all our intimate relationships, however unconscious we may be of it, is the fulfillment of our revenge on our parents for the pains they inflicted on us in the eternal triangle of our Oedipal relationship to them. In intimate relationships, we are required, by our own design, to work through unfinished business with our parents by projectively dealing with the relevant aspects of our parents that we see in our partners. In the simplest relationships which are formed by people who had the simplest relationships to their parents, we see a very close match for our opposite-sexed parent in our partner, and ourselves identify closely with our same-sexed parent. But in most intimate relationships people more complexly see aspects of each of their parents in their partners and correspondingly respond with an admixture of aspects of each of their own parents in themselves. There are bound to be some elements of pain in all intimate relationships by virtue of the fact that everybody experienced some degree of pain in his or her childhood relationships to his or her parents. The more pain a child experienced, the more pain will he inevitably need to experience in his grown-up relationships, in order to triumph over the dragons in his personal myth. So the more pain an individual has experienced in his childhood relationships to his parents, the more likely it is that he will need more than one intimate relationship in his adult life to slay all the dragons on the path to his heroic fulfillment.

Truth wounds in order to cure; we all have to deserve our ideal mate, through the redemption of the unexorcised evil in ourselves passed on to us by our parents.

> A man, according to the Zohar, may only find his other half by walking in the way of truth. Only then may he have a chance at completion... But there are no guarantees in this regard, for a man may become 'perverted in his ways', and if he does his true mate is transferred to another. He may never know her in this life unless he, by his own efforts, rectifies his way...
>
> *Poncé*

Pauline Stone's *Relationships, Astrology and Karma* delineates, in astrological terms, the essential purposeful meanings of many of the most common, dynamic pains between couples.

There are three kinds of dragons, any or all of which may need to be slain by an individual on his or her path to happiness in general and long-term loving intimacy in particular. They are unexpiated guilt towards one or both of our parents, that is, a sense of wrongdoing in ourselves for which we have to make recompense; anger towards one or both of our parents, whom we experienced as having failed in their duty towards us; and impotence in ourselves in response to our parents' claims to have been permanently handicapped by pains inflicted on them, that is, a sense that we have been 'luckier' than our parents and will only be entitled to the fulfillment of our potential if and when we have first suffered equivalent handicapping circumstances in our own life.

Thus the man who, as a child, impotently witnessed his father's brutality to his mother, could not experience himself as sexually potent until he had expiated his guilt towards his mother through protectively nurturing a 'helpless little girl' wife for twenty years.

A woman whose parents separated when she was an infant and whose father then emigrated to America and made no contact with her until she was grown-up, experienced her father as avoiding the 'nuisance' that she might be to him.

When she grew up, she was unable to form a contented, long-lasting relationship with a man until she had punished her father through making a nuisance of herself, as she saw it, in several relationships with men who refused to form a committed relationship with her and kept her at arm's length, while erratically seeking her company and her intimacy when it suited them.

A man was forced to leave school at fourteen to support his widowed mother and a younger brother and sister. At twenty-four, he felt able to leave home and then, with iron determination, caught up on his schooling, went to university and, in due course, became an eminently successful scientist. His son went to a fee-paying school and completed a science degree but thereafter restlessly moved from job to job, Try Hard-ly and resentfully 'getting nowhere' in his career ambitions. At twenty-eight he married a severely disturbed woman whose unpredictable volatility and profligacy caused him great pain and material hardship. At thirty-eight — note the ten years that matched the duration of his father's bondage! — he was divorced and married a woman with whom he has established a very successful business.

Having chosen a relevant, intimate other, the essential meaning of the relationship will turn out to be either the pain we need at this point on our life path, readying us for joy with a different partner after we have served our appropriate sentence; or the joy of the fulfillment of our earned and achieved dream. While at the deepest level of our being I think we anticipatorily know exactly what we are letting ourselves in for, being human, we are all inclined consciously to the wishful thinking that assures us, at the time of entering into it, that this relationship will be the final fulfillment of our dream.

What are we to infer when pain escalates and joy diminishes in a particular relationship? Is it time to part? The authentic answer for any individual within a couple is to be found by asking and answering the further questions: What is the purpose of this pain for me, and have I truly assimilated the learning I needed through the pain of this relationship? What 'unfinished business' with either or both of my parents am I completing with this other? What penance am I paying for my wrongdoing to one or both of my parents? What vengeance for what wrongs that were done to me by either or both of my parents am I now passionately expressing? What suffering am I purposely inflicting on myself to match the suffering of one or both of my parents in order to be entitled to fulfil the joyful potential of my life? Or am I merely recapitulating, without purpose, the deepest pains of my relationship to my parents in a cul-de-sac from which there is no going forward, and my only exit is by reversal?

When, for one or both of the partners in an intimate relationship, pain has outstripped joy, and the purpose of the pain is known to have been served, whether or not the relationship still has life-enhancing meaning depends on what is left between the couple once the sado-masochistic gratifications of the Adapted Child to Adapted Child interactions are removed. When one or both partners no longer needs to play out with the other the painful Adapted Child functions of the relationship, and decisively desists from instigating or reacting to invitations to mutual pain, what remains between the couple's Parent, Adult, Natural Child and Little Professor ego states is seen with clarity. Sometimes there is a lot left that happily justifies the continuance of the relationship. New dimensions can then be added to the relationship to replace the old, new purposes consciously articulated between the couple that serve the continued unfoldment of the myth of each of them; and they may become more deeply united in appreciation of the growth that each of them has achieved by living through and transcending the now outmoded painful structures of the past.

Sometimes, when the Adapted Child to Adapted Child pain between a couple has served its purpose, and one or both decisively desist from instigating or reacting to further invitations to pain, there is little or no compatible joy between the other ego states to be seen, and the only authentic thing to do is to part.

> A loving relationship is nothing more nor less than an agreement between two individuals to fulfill specific conditions for that relationship to survive. It is a contract to service the deep desires and needs of each other as long as each desires. When either party wishes to terminate that contract, nothing should prevent it.
> *Hauck*

It takes courage to stop being a Persecutor, Rescuer or Victim and deprive ourselves of the security of the strokes, however negative, that these roles so comfortably provide. It takes more courage to risk finding there is nothing of value left in an intimate relationship once the painful Adapted Child interactions are removed. It takes more courage to hurt a partner who is content to perpetuate the status quo, by depriving him or her of the strokes, however negative, on which he or she has come to depend, and to demand a new authentic, non-symbiotic equality in the relationships. The courage to grow ourselves in our intimate relationships and to insist on the growth of the other as a condition of the continuance of the relationship is tough love, which forgoes the comfort and security of established equilibrium in favour of passionate aliveness. 'True love does not shield others from understanding the consequences of their acions' (Friedlander). When we choose 'tough love', the end of the relationship is the risk we take and, consequently, the loss of the gratification and security we got from it. This can be a very high price; but fearfully clinging to the compulsive, symbiotic games between the Adapted Childs of ourselves and another, with new sticking plaster intermittently applied to the festering wounds of each of us, because we want the secure comfort of 'a relationship' at any price, is a deadly lie.

The crucially enhancing quality in effective relating is alert, open-minded response to the unanticipated meaning of present communication. The crucially destructive quality in unhappy relating is compulsive, pre-emptive reaction to a presumed unchanging, ever-repeated communication; and there are couples who morbidly repeat an invariable few, never-mind-the-meaning-feel-the-pain transactions between them, for fifty years of purgatory together.

We cannot do others' growing for them, and when, despite our earnest desire for mutual growth, our partner is unwilling, our only authentic response is to leave the relationship. Mourning is a stabbing pain of finite duration; staying in a relationship to avoid this pain is a lifelong ache. Our first duty is to the heroic fulfillment of our own myth, and cowardly clinging to the security of a relationship which has become essentially destructive to one or both partners costs us a creeping and painful paralysis of our souls. 'Upon those who sacrifice the future to the present the future will, in time, exact a terrible revenge' (Barker). In intimate relationships, as in life itself, when the fear of death becomes an obsession, the safeguarding 'certainties' by which we seek to delude ourselves that we may hold death indefinitely at bay, turn our lives into a living death. Death and certainty are synonymous, life and uncertainty are synonymous.

> All he knew about old age was that it was a time when a person had passed his maturity; when fate had ended; when there was no longer any need to fear that terrible mystery called the future; when every love that came along was certain and final. *Kundera*

Life and relationships are paradoxically made most joyful when we relish them because they are finite in duration and there is no knowing how soon the end may be.

> A man's growth is seen in the successive choice of his friends, for every friend whom he loses for truth, he gains a better. . . Nothing is secure but life, transition, the energizing spirit. *Emerson*

Laughter and Forgetting — In appreciation of Milan Kundera

Life is movement towards the wholeness of the picture we want to see in the end. When the picture is complete, we are ready to die. If we merely allow our picture to put itself together, our lives are safe and dull and passionless; if we create our pictures as artists, we are never sure what exactly our completed picture will look like, and our lives are uncertain and exciting. Life is the opposite of certainty; but so is chaotic uncertainty the opposite of art. Striving for the optimum balance between Be Perfect and Hurry Up — order and chaos, the fear of death and the desire for excitement, discipline and spontaneity — is the volatile, unremitting quest of the whole of our lives, whether we are conscious of it or not.

We create our lives retrospectively, when a certain distance enables us to see episodes of the past as distinct pieces of the jigsaw puzzle we are putting together to make the picture of our lives.

> The past is full of life, eager to irritate us, provoke and insult us, tempt us to destroy or repaint it. The only reason people want to be masters of the future is to change the past. *Kundera*

A completed patch of our jigsaw puzzle may give us enough to guess, by extrapolation, what the whole picture is about, but we may have to change our minds as we proceed. We make mistakes when we try to squeeze the wrong piece of experience, or the wrong person, into a particular place, and the artist in us is then ashamed and seeks to negate our folly.

> . . . he was in love with his fate, not with himself. Those are two very different things. . . He felt responsible for

his fate, but his fate felt no responsibility for him. He had the same attitude to his life as a sculptor to his statue or a novelist to his novel. . . Zdena insisted on remaining part of the opening pages of the novel. She refused to be crossed out. . . The reason he wanted to remove her picture from the album of his life was not that he hadn't loved her, but that he had.

Kundera

The 'permissive society' of the past twenty years has been the enemy of love in denying the need for pain or shame in intimate relationships. Many people have, of late, chosen meaningless mere physical sexuality, without pain or joy, moving from one lifeless bodily contact to another. They have read the testimonies of previous generations concerning the supreme joy of loving sexual intimacy and have presumed this joy to be intrinsic to the act of sex, rather than in sex as the supreme expression of earned love. Cynical nihilism is the sad price that has been paid by very many young people who are not protected against this misunderstanding as previous generations were by the moral imperatives associated with a religious education.

Milan Kundera (*The Book of Laughter and Forgetting*, 1986) convincingly posits that we seek to undo the follies of our lives by two devices, laughter and forgetting.

> We laugh through what we can't dispel,
> While apathy and terror hound us
> On well-intentioned paths to hell. *Seth*

Laughter distances us from our ego's pains by mocking the seriousness of what it purveys; forgetting kills off that which does not fit the picture we want to make. And, in between, we gloss over our deep incompatibilities with other people to compromise between the unattainable ideal and the despair of the knowledge of our ultimate solipsism.

Laughter and forgetting must both count as the enemies of love because they respectively negate its passionate seriousness and its authentic existence.

> A joke is the enemy of love and poetry. . . Love can't be laughable. . . Love has nothing in common with laughter. . .
>
> Forgetting is a form of death ever present within life.
>
> *Kundera*

Yet laughter is also the expression of those moments when we are blessed with an appreciation of the collision and reconciliation of opposites in a unity that is truer and happier than mundane duality.

> Laughing deeply is living deeply . . . serious laughter, laughter beyond joking. . . Whereas the Devil's laughter pointed up the meaninglessness of things, the angel's shout rejoiced in how rationally organized, well conceived, beautiful, good, and sensible everything on earth was. . . There are two kinds of laughter, and we lack the words to distinguish them.
>
> *Kundera*

We need love, laughter, and forgetting in our lives, and there is time for all of them.

Bibliography

Introduction

Berne, E. *Transactional Analysis in Psychotherapy*, Grove Press, 1961.
Berne, E. *Games People Play*, Andre Deutsch, 1966.
Freud, S. *Civilization and Its Discontents*, The Hogarth Press, 1963.
Kahler, T. (with Caper, H.) 'The miniscript', *Transactional Analysis Journal*, 4, **1**, 1974, pp. 26–42.
Klein, M. 'Is Astrology True?', *The Astrological Journal*, Jan-Feb 1988.
Lewi, G. *Astrology for the Millions*, Bantam, 1980.
Mayo, J. *Teach Yourself Astrology*, Hodder & Stoughton, 1964.
Mayo, J. *The Planets and Human Behaviour*, Fowler, 1972.
Nietzsche, F. *The Gay Science*, Vintage Books, 1974.
Seymour, P. *Astrology: The Evidence of Science*, Lennard Publishing, 1988.
Skinner, B. *About Behaviourism*, Jonathan Cape, 1974.
West, J. *The Case for Astrology*, Viking Arkana, 1991.

Chapter 1

Aristotle, quoted by Brentano, *Aristotle and His World View*, University of California Press, 1978.
Barker, G. *The Dead Seagull*, Macgibbon & Kee, 1965.

Douglas, M. *Purity and Danger*, Routledge & Kegan Paul, 1966.
Emerson, R. *Selected Essays*, Penguin, 1982.
Fowles, J. *The Aristos (1964–80)*, Granada, 1981.
Fox, R. 'Of human nature and unnatural rights', *Encounter*, April 1982.
Freud, S. *Civilization and Its Discontents*, The Hogarth Press, 1963.
Gibran, K. *Sand and Foam*, Heinemann, 1974.
Huxley, T. in Mackay, A. & Ebison, M. (Eds) *The Harvest of a Quiet Eye — A Selection of Scientific Quotations*, Institute of Physics, Bristol, 1977.
Jung, C. *Psychological Types*, Princeton University Press, 1976.
Nietzsche, F. *Human, All Too Human*, University of Nebraska Press, 1984.
Peck, M. *The Road Less Travelled*, Simon & Schuster, 1978.
Roth, P. *The Anatomy Lesson*, Jonathan Cape, 1983.
Segal, H. *Klein*, Fontana, 1979.
Tolstoy, L. *War and Peace*, Penguin, 1972.
Wren-Lewis, J. in Rycroft, C. (Ed.) *Psychoanalysis Observed*, Constable, 1966.

Chapter 2

Coren, A. in *The Times*, April 20, 1988.
Erikson, E. *Childhood and Society*, Penguin, 1965.
Freud, S. *Civilization and Its Discontents*, The Hogarth Press, 1963.
Hand, R. *Planets in Transit*, Para Research Inc., 1976.
Lowen, A. *Bioenergetics*, Coventure, 1976.
Malcolm, J. *Psychoanalysis — The Impossible Profession*, Pan, 1982.
Ortega y Gasset, J. in Auden, W. & Kronenberger, L. (Eds) *The Faber Book of Aphorisms*, Faber & Faber, 1962.
Pascal, B. in Auden, W. & Kronenberger, L. (Eds) *The Faber Book of Aphorisms*, Faber & Faber, 1962.

Ray, S. *Loving Relationships*, Celestial Arts, 1980.
Robertson, M. *Critical Ages in Adult Life*, American Federation of Astrologers Inc., 1976.
Rodden, L. *Modern Transits*, American Federation of Astrologers Inc., 1978.
Sheehy, G. *Passages*, Bantam, 1977.
Skinner, B. *Science and Human Behaviour*, Macmillan, 1960.

Chapter 3

Bandler, R. and Grinder, J. *The Structure of Magic*, Science and Behaviour Books, 1975.
Blair, L. *Rhythms of Vision*, Paladin, 1976.
Campbell, J. *The Hero With a Thousand Faces*, Princeton University Press, 1973.
Cohen, D. *Psychologists on Psychology*, Routledge & Kegan Paul, 1977.
Collin, R. *The Theory of Celestial Influence*, Shambhala Publications Inc., 1984.
Connolly, C. *The Unquiet Grave*, Arrow, 1961.
Eco, U. 'Reflections on "The Name of the Rose" ', *Encounter*, April 1985.
Emerson, R. *Selected Essays*, Penguin, 1982.
Emerson, R. in Auden, W. & Kronenberger, L. (Eds) *The Faber Book of Aphorisms*, Faber & Faber, 1962.
Fichte, X. quoted by Wilson, C. in *Frankenstein's Castle*, Ashgrove Press, 1980.
Hesse, H. *The Glass Bead Game*, Penguin, 1972.
Lakoff, G. and Johnson, M. *Metaphors We Live By*, The University of Chicago Press, 1980.
Levi, P. *If Not Now When?*, Michael Joseph, 1986.
Lewi, G. *Astrology for the Millions*, Doubleday, Doran & Co., 1940.
Lewis, C. *Mere Christianity*, Fontana, 1955.
Naipaul, S. *An Unfinished Journey*, Hamish Hamilton, 1986.
Nietzsche, F. in Auden, W. & Kronenberger, L. (Eds) *The Faber Book of Aphorisms*, Faber & Faber, 1962.

Nietzsche, F. *The Will to Power*, Random House, 1968.
Nietzsche, F. *Beyond Good and Evil*, Penguin, 1973.
Nietzsche, F. *Daybreak — Thoughts on the Prejudices of Morality*, Cambridge University Press, 1982.
Peck, M. *The Road Less Travelled*, Simon & Schuster, 1978.
Peck, M. *People of the Lie: the hope for healing human evil*, Simon & Schuster, 1983.
Powell, A. quoted by May, D. 'Heroic curiosity', *Encounter*, March 1971.
Prather, H. *Notes on Love and Courage*, Doubleday, 1977.
Radhakrishnan, S. *An Idealist View of Life*, Bradford & Dickens, 1947.
Roth, P. *The Counterlife*, Jonathan Cape, 1986.
Rudhyar, D. *The Astrological Houses*, Doubleday, 1972.
Rudhyar, D. *An Astrological Triptych*, ASI Publishers, 1978.
Sachs, O. *The Man Who Mistook His Wife for a Hat*, Duckworth, 1985.
Santayana, G. in Auden, W. & Kronenberger, L. (Eds) *The Faber Book of Aphorisms*, Faber & Faber, 1962.
Shakespeare, W. 'Henry the Fourth Part I', *The Complete Works of Shakespeare*, Oxford University Press, 1935.
Shaw, G. 'Maxims for Revolutionists', *Man and Superman*, Penguin, 1951.
Shaw, G. (Preface to) *Saint Joan*, Macmillan, 1986.
Silva, J. and Miele, P. *The Silva Mind Control Method*, Souvenir Press, 1978.
Strausz-Hupé, R. 'Maxims (II)' *Encounter*, March 1976.
Thoreau, H. in Auden, W. & Kronenberger, L. (Eds) *The Faber Book of Aphorisms*, Faber & Faber, 1962.

Chapter 4

Arnold, M. *Culture and Anarchy*, Cambridge University Press, 1979.
Bates, G. *Mind and Nature*, Dutton, 1979.
Beckett, S. *Waiting for Godot*, Faber & Faber, 1965.
Berne, E. *Games People Play*, Andre Deutsch, 1966.

Cloud, P. *Cosmos, Earth and Man*, Yale University Press, 1978.
Dickens, C. *Great Expectations*, Penguin, 1965.
Dickens, C. *Hard Times*, Penguin, 1969.
Douglas, M. *Purity and Danger*, Routledge & Kegan Paul, 1966.
Einstein, A. *Ideas & Opinions*, Souvenir Press, 1973.
Forster, E. *Howards End*, Penguin, 1953.
Freud, S. *Civilization and Its Discontents*, The Hogarth Press, 1963.
Heller, J. *Something Happened*, Corgi, 1974.
Kahler, T. 'The miniscript', *Transactional Analysis Journal*, 4, **1**, 1974, pp. 26–42.
Kundera, M. *The Unbearable Lightness of Being*, Faber & Faber, 1986.
Lowen, A. *Bioenergetics*, Coventure, 1976.
Nicholson, J. *Habits — Why do you do what you do?* Macmillan, 1977.
Nietzsche, F. *Daybreak — Thoughts on the Prejudices of Morality*, Cambridge University Press, 1982.
Nietzsche, F. *The Will to Power*, Random House, 1968.
Pareto, V. in Mackay, A. & Ebison, M. (Eds) *The Harvest of a Quiet Eye — A Collection of Scientific Quotations*, Institute of Physics, Bristol, 1977.
Pascal, B. in Auden, W. & Kronenberger, L. (Eds) *The Faber Book of Aphorisms*, Faber & Faber, 1962.
Peters, J. in *The Sunday Times*, February 17, 1985.
Peyre, H. *Marcel Proust*, Columbia University Press, 1970.
Robbins, T. *Jitterbug Perfume*, Bantam, 1985.
Rossel, S. *When A Jew Seeks Wisdom: The Sayings of the Fathers*, Behrman House, 1975.
Rudhyar, D. *An Astrological Study of Psychological Complexes*, Shambhala Publications, 1976.
Sartre, J. quoted by Bondy, F. in 'European diary', *Encounter*, July 1981.
Shakespeare, W. 'Hamlet', *The Complete Works of Shakespeare*, Oxford University Press, 1935.
Socrates, quoted in Brownson, C. *Socrates*, Heinemann, 1922.

Sterne, L. *Tristram Shandy*, Penguin, 1967.
Wilde, O. in Auden, W. & Kronenberger, L. (Eds) *The Faber Book of Aphorisms*, Faber & Faber, 1962.
Wilson, C. *The Outsider*, Picador, 1978.

Chapter 5

Freud, S. in Auden, W. & Kronenberger, L. (Eds) *The Faber Book of Aphorisms*, Faber & Faber, 1962.
Nietzsche, F. *Ecce Homo*, Penguin, 1979.
Nietzsche, F. *The Gay Science*, Vintage Books, 1974.
Shakespeare, W. 'Hamlet', *The Complete Works of Shakespeare*, Oxford University Press, 1935.
Tennyson, A. in *The Oxford Dictionary of Quotations*, Oxford University Press, 1977.

Chapter 6

Bandler, R. and Grinder, J. *Frogs into Princes — Neuro-Linguistic Programming*, Real People Press, 1979.
Berne, E. *Intuition and Ego States*, TA Press, 1977.
Blair, L. *Rhythms of Vision*, Paladin, 1976.
Collin, R. *The Theory of Celestial Influence*, Shambhala Publications Inc., 1984.
Emerson, R. *Selected Essays*, Penguin, 1982.
Freud, S. *Civilization and Its Discontents*, The Hogarth Press, 1963.
Greenwald, J. *Creative Intimacy*, Simon & Schuster, 1975.
Kovel, J. *A Complete Guide to Therapy*, The Harvester Press, 1977.
Kundera, M. *The Book of Laughter and Forgetting*, Penguin, 1986.
Kundera, M. *The Unbearable Lightness of Being*, Faber & Faber, 1986.
Nietzsche, F. *Human, All Too Human*, University of Nebraska Press, 1984.

Nin, A. *The Diary of Anais Nin (Vol. I 1931–4)*, Swallow Press, 1966.
Peck, M. *The Road Less Travelled*, Simon & Schuster, 1978.
Roth, P. *The Counterlife*, Jonathan Cape, 1986.
Santayana, G. in Auden, W. & Kronenberger, L. (Eds) *The Faber Book of Aphorisms*, Faber & Faber, 1962.
Shakespeare, W. 'A Midsummer Night's Dream' *The Complete Works of Shakespeare*, Oxford University Press, 1935.
Spinoza, B. de *On the Improvement of the Human Understanding/ The Ethics/Selected Letters*, Dover Publications, 1951.
Tindall, G. *Rosamond Lehmann — An Appreciation*, Chatto & Windus, 1985.

Chapter 7

Blair, L. *Rhythms of Vision*, Paladin, 1976.
Ferguson, M. *The Aquarian Conspiracy*, Routledge & Kegan Paul, 1981.
Greenwald, J. *Creative Intimacy*, Simon & Schuster, 1975.
Peck, M. *The Road Less Travelled*, Simon & Schuster, 1978.
Peck, M. *People of the Lie: the hope for healing human evil*, Simon & Schuster, 1983.
Rieff, P. *Freud: The Mind of the Moralist*, University of Chicago Press, 1959.
Rudhyar, D. *The Astrological Houses*, Doubleday, 1972.
Russell, B. in Auden, W. & Kronenberger, L. (Eds) *The Faber Book of Aphorisms*, Faber & Faber, 1962.
Schulman, M. *Karmic Relationships*, Samuel Weiser, 1984.
Williams, C. in Auden, W. & Kronenberger, L. (Eds) *The Faber Book of Aphorisms*, Faber & Faber, 1962.

Chapter 8

Brown, N. *Love's Body*, Random House, 1966.
Buber, M. *I and Thou*, T & T Clark, 1937.

Eliot, T. quoted in Kenton, W. *The Way of Kabbalah*, Rider, 1976.
Emerson, R. *Selected Essays*, Penguin, 1982.
Jung, C. *Psychological Types*, Princeton University Press, 1976.
Kahn, J. *Job's Illness — Loss, Grief, and Integration*, Pergamon, 1986.
Mount, F. in 'The Recovery of Civility' *Encounter*, July 1973.
Nietzsche, F. *Human, All Too Human*, University of Nebraska Press, 1984.
Nietzsche, F. *Daybreak — Thoughts on the Prejudices of Morality*, Cambridge University Press, 1982.
O'Brien, E. *A Fanatic Heart*, Penguin, 1984.
Seth, V. *The Golden Gate*, Faber & Faber, 1986.
Stekel, W. *Compulsion and Doubt* (trans. by Emil A. Gutheil), Liveright Publishing Corp, NY, 1949.
Taylor, H. in Auden, W. & Kronenberger, L. (Eds) *The Faber Book of Aphorisms*, Faber & Faber, 1962.
Wilde, O. in Auden, W. & Kronenberger, L. (Eds) *The Faber Book of Aphorisms*, Faber & Faber, 1962.
Woods, S. *The Man in the Street*, Pelican, 1975.

Chapter 9

Berne, E. *Games People Play*, Andre Deutsch, 1966.
Freeman, M. *Forecasting by Astrology*, The Aquarian Press, 1982.
Hardy, T. *Jude the Obscure*, Macmillan & Co., 1903.
Jung, C. *Psychological Types*, Princeton University Press, 1976.
Proust, M. in Auden, W. & Kronenberger, L. (Eds) *The Faber Book of Aphorisms*, Faber & Faber, 1962.
Seth, V. *The Golden Gate*, Faber & Faber, 1986.

Chapter 10

Baldwin, J. *Another Country*, Michael Joseph, 1963.
Barker, G. *The Dead Seagull*, Macgibbon & Kee, 1965.
Carotenuto, A. *Eros and Pathos* (trans. by Charles Nopar), Inner City Books, Canada, 1989.
Durkin, H. *The Group in Depth*, International Universities Press, 1973.
Emerson, *Selected Essays*, Penguin, 1982.
Friedlander, A. in a letter to *The Times*, June 22, 1985.
Fuller, T. in Auden, W. & Kronenberger, L. (Eds) *The Faber Book of Aphorisms*, Faber & Faber, 1962.
Hauck, P. *Jealousy — Why It Happens and How to Overcome It*, Sheldon Press, 1982.
Kundera, M. *The Book of Laughter and Forgetting*, Penguin, 1986.
Kundera, M. *The Unbearable Lightness of Being*, Faber & Faber, 1986.
Kundera, M. *Life is Elsewhere*, Faber & Faber, 1987.
Nietzsche, F. *A Nietzsche Reader*, Penguin, 1977.
Poncé, C. *Kabbalah*, The Theosophical Publishing House, 1978.
Rudhyar, D. *An Astrological Triptych*, ASI Publishers, 1978.
Seth, V. *The Golden Gate*, Faber & Faber, 1986.
Shakespeare, W. 'The Tempest', *The Complete Works of Shakespeare*, Oxford University Press, 1935.
Stone, P. *Relationships, Astrology and Karma*, The Aquarian Press, 1991.
Szanto, G. *The Marriage of Heaven and Earth — The Philosophy of Astrology*, Routledge & Kegan Paul, 1985.

Glossary

Cross-references are italicized

ADAPTED CHILD That part of the *Child ego state* which is learned, as contrasted with the *Natural Child*, which is innate. The Adapted Child is the precursor of the *Parent* ego state and is acquired mostly between the ages of about one and three, in the form of rigid rules restricting expression of the Natural Child. At this stage of development, such rigid restrictions are necessary for the socialization and safety of the child, because his *Adult* ego state is not yet sufficiently developed for him to be reasonable, and his Parent ego state, which will later express care for himself and others, does not exist. Along with all the necessary rules that parents transmit to the Adapted Child ego states of their children, they also transmit some unnecessary constraints based on their own maladaptive *decisions* about life which, in turn, are likely to become their children's decisions and their children's children's decisions . . . until such time as the vicious cycle is broken by awareness and objective readjustment of the personality.

ADULT The *ego state* that contains objective knowledge and skills. It first appears in the ego at about one year of age and grows most rapidly from then until about three years of age and again between the ages of about six and twelve, although it is capable of continued growth throughout life. Its function in the ego is to store and assess objectively information it receives from the environment, and to make sense of life by reconciling its own information with the values of the *Parent* ego state and the feelings of the *Child* ego state.

ANTISCRIPT An unstable part of the *Adapted Child*, which seeks to evade *script payoffs* by overt rebellion, but which inevitably achieves what it seeks to evade. Antiscript also describes temporary adolescent rebellion against Parent values.

ASPECT The angular distance measured along the ecliptic in degrees and minutes of celestial longitude between two points, as viewed from Earth. Astrologically, the most significant aspects between points are the conjunction (0°), the opposition (180°), the square (90°), the trine (120°), and the sextile (60°).

BLAMER An optional position in the *miniscript* process, in which the individual experiences and expresses *antiscript* feelings, thoughts and behaviour.

CHILD The *ego state* that contains feelings and impulses. It is the only congenital ego state. At first, it is only capable of the instinctive experiences of overall satisfaction or overall distress, but it develops, both naturally and by conditioning, the capacity to experience and express a wide range of differentiated feelings and impulses. Its most rapid development takes place in the first three years of life. See also *Adapted Child, Natural Child, Little Professor.*

CONTAMINATION A pathological mixture of the impulses and perceptions of two *ego states*, by which means an individual seeks, ineffectively, to resolve contrary impulses and perceptions of those two ego states in herself.

COUNTER INJUNCTION A *message* transmitted by a Parent *ego state*, usually of the mother or father, into the developing Parent ego state of a child.

DECISION A commitment made by the *Little Professor* or by

the *Adult ego state* in childhood to incorporate a given existential dimension or frame of reference or life plan into the *script*. Decisions reconcile and synthesize relevant *messages* received by *Parent*, *Adult* and *Child* ego states. Decisions fulfil the innate need of all human beings to experience life as ordered and predictable rather than arbitrary and chaotic so, once a decision is made by an individual, she has a powerful vested interest in abiding by it. In so far as our fundamental decisions about life are made before the age of six, at a time when the Adult ego state's reasoning capacity is still very immature and the data it has at its disposal is very limited, we all have, amongst our decisions, some that are no longer appropriate in our grown-up lives. Nevertheless, we cling tenaciously, though often unconsciously, to our decisions, and changing a decision is a very difficult task indeed. However, once an individual is aware of his decisions, he has the choice of channelling even the more difficult ones into a healthy and adaptive rather than unhealthy and maladaptive expression. Although they are made by the Little Professor and the Adult, decisions are expressed through the behaviours of the *Adapted Child*.

DESPAIRER The final position of the *miniscript* process, at which point a painful *decision* is reaffirmed.

DRIVER The beginning position of the *miniscript* process. There are five different drivers: Be Perfect, Hurry Up, Please, Try Hard and Be Strong.

EGO STATE A state of being of the ego manifesting a consistent pattern of thoughts and feelings related to a corresponding consistent pattern of behaviour. The three main ego states are the *Parent*, the *Adult* and the *Child*.

EXCLUSION A pathological dissociation of the impulses of an *ego state* from an individual's total functioning ego, by which means she seeks to avoid pain associated with that ego state.

FINAL MINISCRIPT PAYOFF The end of the *miniscript* process, at which point, a *script decision* is re-experienced and reinforced in the *Despairer* position of the miniscript diagram.

GAME A set series of ulterior *transactions* with a well-defined psychological *payoff* for each of the players.

INJUNCTION An inhibiting *message* transmitted by an *Adapted Child*, usually of the mother or father, into the developing Adapted Child of a child.

LITTLE PROFESSOR The exploratory, hypothesizing, creative part of the *Natural Child* which develops in the personality from about six months of age. The Little Professor is the precursor of the *Adult ego state*.

MALADAPTOR A position in the *miniscript* process, at which point the individual experiences a *racket* feeling.

MESSAGE An overt or covert *transaction*, usually from the mother or father, making a lasting imprint on the structure of the *ego states* of a growing child. Whereas ordinary communication is possible between any ego state of one person and any ego state of another person, a message is understood to be communicated only between the same ego states of the people involved. Thus our growing *Parent* ego state is fed by messages from our parents' Parent ego states, our *Adult* ego state receives messages from their Adults, and our *Child* ego state receives messages from their Child ego states.

MINISCRIPT A sequence of feelings, thoughts and behaviour, usually occurring in a matter of seconds or minutes, which culminates in the re-experiencing and reinforcement of a maladaptive *decision* in the *Adapted Child*.

NATURAL CHILD That part of the *Child ego state*, including the *Little Professor*, which contains and expresses spontaneously authentic feelings and impulses. It is basically innate but is also 'stroked up' by parents and other caretakers in our early months and years of life.

PARENT The *ego state* that contains values and beliefs, moral principles and generalizations about life. It is basically formed between the ages of about three and six, through explicit *messages* given by parents to their children concerning caring for ourselves and others. Its function in the ego is to enable the individual automatically to behave in ways which are conducive to his own and others' well-being, including the monitoring of the *Natural Child*, by granting indulgences or imposing constraints on it according to the Parent's own principles. In its constraining of the Natural Child the Parent often looks like the *Adapted Child*, but the Parent acts in accordance with general principles and is flexible, whereas the Adapted Child is utterly rule-bound and rigid.

PAYOFF The experience of a *racket* feeling and/or a *script decision*, in accordance with a formulation laid down in the *Adapted Child* in childhood. A payoff may consist of an oft-reiterated experience or a particular achievement in the individual's overall life plan.

PERMISSION A *message* transmitted by a *Natural Child*, usually the mother or father, into the Natural Child of a child, usually reinforcing some aspect of the Natural Child's innate capacity for pleasure or joy. Such messages may be directly transmitted as *strokes* given to the child when she exhibits certain behaviour or indirectly transmitted when the child observes her parents in their Natural Child *ego states*. Thus if a child sees her parents clearly enjoying such activities as reading, cooking, playing cards or being with friends, taking particular pleasure in these things will be included in the child's repertoire of permissions, together with the spontaneously expressed aspects of her own Natural Child for which her parents gave her *positive strokes*.

PERSECUTOR One of the compulsive, maladaptive roles through which the *Adapted Child* may express itself. The Persecutor role is associated with an inauthentic feeling of the kind, 'Now I've got you, you son-of-a-bitch!'

RACKET An habitually experienced bad feeling. Part of an

individual's *script*, which is expressed in the *Maladaptor* position of the *miniscript* process.

RESCUER One of the compulsive, maladaptive roles through which the *Adapted Child* may express itself. The Rescuer role is associated with an inauthentic feeling of self-righteousness.

SCRIPT The sum total of the *messages* and *decisions* made around them in the *Child ego state*. (See also *antiscript*)

STROKE Any act of recognition given by one person to another. Strokes may be positive or negative, conditional or unconditional. Our need for and quest for strokes is continuous and lifelong; when positive strokes, which make us feel good, are not available, we would rather receive negative strokes, which make us feel bad, than receive no strokes at all and be ignored. At birth we are only capable of appreciating the most fundamental strokes, that is, actual physical contact with another human being, but gradually we learn to value as strokes a wide variety of symbolic substitutes for actual physical contact, from the slightly valued nod of a passing acquaintance to the profoundly gratifying 'I love you'. The strokes, both positive and negative, that we were often given in childhood by our parents are the strokes that we are most likely to seek and get from other people for the rest of our lives. These are called our target strokes. We each have our own positive target strokes, which make us feel especially good about ourselves, and our own negative target strokes, which make us feel especially bad about ourselves. Nearly all strokes are conditional, but the most nourishing strokes are the unconditional positive ones, the most damaging the unconditional negative ones.

TRANSACTION What occurs, verbally and/or non-verbally, between two people when they meet. There may be overt and covert transactions occurring at the same time; and when this is so the covert transaction always contains the most important meaning of the transaction.

TRANSACTIONAL ANALYSIS A theory of child development,

personality, psychopathology and psychotherapy developed by the late Eric Berne in the 1960's. Most central to the theory are the concepts of *ego states* and *strokes*.

TRANSIT A significant *aspect* temporarily formed between the current longitudinal position of a planet and a sensitive point in the natal horoscope of an individual.

VICTIM One of the compulsive, maladaptive roles through which the *Adapted Child* may express itself. The Victim role is associated with an inauthentic feeling of helplessness.

Index of Names

Adler, A. 147
Aristotle 32
Arnold, M. 131

Baldwin, J. 278
Bandler, R. 115, 195
Barker, G. 35, 284
Bates, G. 141
Beckett, S. 134, 180
Beethoven, L. 171
Berkeley, Bishop 23
Berne, E. 10–11, 13, 14, 120, 155, 194, 259
Blair, L. 85, 104, 200, 228
Brown, N. 252
Buber, M. 241

Campbell, J. 113–4
Cartland, B. 250
Chamberlain, N. 146
Cloud, P. 140
Cohen, D. 93
Collin, R. 101, 207, 213
Connolly, C. 99
Coren, A. 77
Coveney, P. 140

Dickens, C. 123, 155
Douglas, M. 30, 140
Durkin, H. 275

Eco, U. 103

Einstein, A. 18, 135
Eliot, T. S. 242
Emerson, R. 24, 33, 84, 92, 113, 208, 230, 284
Erikson, E. 72–3

Ferguson, M. 216
Fichte, X. 112
Forster, E. M. 143
Fowles, J. 26
Fox, R. 33
Freeman, M. 259
Freud, S. 10, 11, 12, 13, 28, 30, 36, 67, 151, 154, 171, 199, 209, 233
Friedlander, A. 283

Gibran, K. 34
Goethe, J. 7
Greenwald, J. 207, 210, 227
Grinder, J. 115, 195

Hamlet 116
Hand, R. 80
Hardy, T. 256
Hauck, P. 283
Heisenberg, W. 18
Heller, J. 152
Huxley, T. 25

Johnson, M. 100
Jung, C. 34, 35, 231, 259–60

Index

Kahler, T. 10, 124, 125, 127
Kahn, J. 236–7
Klein, Melanie 28
Kovel, J. 193
Kundera, M. 142, 193–4, 199, 273, 276, 278, 284, 285, 286, 287

Lakoff, G. 100
Levi, P. 104
Lewi, G. 117
Lewis, C. 110
Lowen, A. 55, 134

Malcolm, J. 51
Mead, M. 79
Miele, P. 88
Monet, C. 171
Mount, F. 240

Naipaul, S. 93
Nicholson, J. 123
Nietzsche, F. 9, 29, 92, 102, 110, 112, 113, 116, 140, 151, 174–5, 201, 237, 245, 275
Nin, A. 194, 201

Oates, Captain 154
O'Brien, E. 251
Ortega y Gassett, J. 54

Pareto, V. 132
Pascal, B. 44, 145
Peck, M. 34, 101, 206, 221
Peters, J. 141
Peyre, H. 130
Pinter, H. 180
Plato 11
Poncé, C. 280
Portnoy 161
Potter, D. 99
Powell, A. 100
Prather, H. 116
Proust, M. 258

Radhakrishnan, S. 106

Ray, S. 70
Rieff, P. 228–9
Robbins, T. 134
Robertson, M. 73
Rodden, L. 80
Rossel, S. 145
Roth, P. 28, 87, 215
Rudhyar, D. 84, 116, 120, 223, 276
Russell, B. 222

Sachs, O. 88
Salters, D. 159
Santayana, G. 102, 208
Sartre, J. 147
Sasportas, H. 15
Schulman, M. 220
Scott, R. 154
Seth, V. 250, 286
Shakespeare, W. 112, 133, 139, 146, 161, 174, 193, 279
Shaw, G. B. 86, 108
Sheehy, G. 73
Silva, J. 88
Skinner, B. 12, 15, 41
Socrates 171
Spinoza, B. de 196
Spitz, R. 39
Stekel, W. 237
Sterne, L. 118
Stone, P. 280
Strausz-Hupé, R. 115
Szanto, G. 275–6

Taylor, H. 244
Tennyson, A. 188
Thoreau, H. 85
Tindall, G. 197

Wilde, O. 118, 237
Williams, C. 221
Wilson, C. 139
Woods, S. 248
Wren-Lewis, J. 29

Yiddish proverb 23, 234

Subject Index

Adapted Child 47–9, 53, 54, 57, 60, 63, 89, 102, 119, 120, 125, 127, 129, 157, 256–7, 297
adolescence 63–5, 94, 149, 217, 233
Adult ego state 43, 45, 49–50, 58, 63, 64–5, 66, 68, 69, 89, 112, 119, 153, 275, 297–8
aggression 16, 54–5, 56, 60, 97, 147, 165
alcoholism 134, 139, 158
alternatives 66, 67
angry outsider 165
anorexia nervosa 134, 158
antiscript 125, 162, 298
art, life as 99–102
astrology 12, 15–19, 73–4, 80–1, 89, 122–3, 204, 206, 280
autistic personality *see* Be Strong

baby, birth of 32–3
Be Perfect 124, 125–6, 130–4, 140, 177–8, 184, 222–3, 233, (man) 234, (woman) 235, (parent) 235–6, (getting best from) 236–7, 285
Be Perfect/Be Strong 162–3
Be Perfect/Hurry Up 158–160
Be Perfect/Please 160–1
Be Perfect/Try Hard 161–2
Be Strong 124, 126, 151–5, 187–9, 227–9, (man) 250–2, (woman) 252–3, (parent) 253–4, (getting best from) 254–5
birth to six months 42, 44–5
birth to three years 93, 94, 135
blame 28, 29, 31, 53, 104, 107, 108, 109, 111, 112, 214, 216, 278–9
Blamer 125–7, 298
boarding school 107, 137, 153, 166
brave individualist 167

cancer 145
categorizing people 121–3
character 57, 71, 92, 122
Child ego state 43, 49, 57, 64, 66, 69, 109, 112, 233, 298
cold intellectual 162–3
cold person 69
committed champion 162
complementary relationships 44, 212
compound personality types 156–170
compromise 55, 66, 67, 70, 104
conflict 53, 67, 102, 104, 128
confusion 62, 68, 71, 76, 102, 104, 108
consciousness 113
  limits of 31, 102, 104
contamination 67, 70, 70–1, 102,

103, 104, 129, 298
contented worker 168
control
  of environment 57–9, 134
  of people 52–3, 97, 141, 161, 168
counter-injunction 54, 64, 298
courage 116, 174–5, 206, 276, 283
creativity 34, 45, 66, 70

death 26, 30, 58, 80, 132, 134, 135, 166, 167, 258, 284
  denial of 30
  fear of 9, 29, 30, 38, 58, 59, 95–6, 219–20, 284
  of parent 56, 161, 162
decisions 42, 88–93, 94, 97, 114, 115, 119–121, 129, 173, 176, 298–9
defences of the ego 14
delusion 68
depression 59, 75, 76, 134 *see also* Be Perfect
desire
  fulfillment of 37, 38
Despairer 125–7, 299
destiny 35, 89, 172
determinism 16–7, 18, 25, 32, 122
development stages
  in adult life 19, 75–9
  in childhood 44–64
divorce of parents 58
do-gooder 168
'Don'ts' 47–8, 60, 119
dreams and nightmares 100
Drivers 124–7, 220, 299
drug abuse 139, 166, 167
duty 222–3

effort and thought 96
ego 14, 29–31, 38–9, 75, 80, 113, 129, 172, 276
ego states 14, 43–4, 56, 64, 119, 299

health and pathology in 65–71
eighty-four 79
emotional literacy 56
empathic relationships 212
energy 44, 56, 70
envy 147
Eskimos 17 evil 116, 135, 221 *see also* good and evil
excitement 25–6
exclusion 68, 69, 70, 299
expediency 225

fantasies
  fulfillment of 34
fate and free-will 31–5
fear
  in general 38, 79, 119, 128, 135, 139, 172, 173, 174–5, 221–2, 276
  of abandonment 46
  of being dropped 45
  of being undersirable 55
  of castration 55
  of death 29, 30, 38, 58, 59, 95–6, 284 *see also* Be Perfect
  of failure *see* Try Hard
  of life 95–6 *see also* Hurry Up
  of loud noises 45
  of pain 34
  of parents 120
  of rejection *see* Be Strong
  of responsibility *see* Please
  of retribution 47–8, 50
femininity 275
fifty-four 78
fifty-six to sixty 78
fighter of lost causes 161–2
Final Miniscript Payoff 299 *see also* Despairer
fixation 70, 72, 74
forgetting 286–7
forty-nine to fifty-one 77–8
forty-seven 77
free will 122, 232, 275–6 *see also* fate and free will

friendship 114, 208–9
frightened loner 165–7

games
   physical 66
   psychological 120–1, 124, 300
generous carer 68
genetics 32–3, 123
God 18, 23, 27, 110–1, 116, 133, 134, 231
good and bad/evil 27–31, 74, 94–5, 100, 102, 103, 106–12, 117, 140, 219–20, 221
'good enough' parents 94–5
guilt 28, 31, 53, 103, 106–8, 279

hang-ups 30, 48–9, 115, 119, 171–6
happiness 10, 28, 30, 36, 112, 116
harsh person 69
hate 108, 112, 147, 278–9
headaches 150
health and pathology
   in Be Perfect/Hurry Up 158–9
   in functioning of ego states 65–71
heart disease 134
horoscope *see* astrology
humble servant 167–8
humour
   sense of 134
Hurry Up 124, 125, 126, 135–40, 157, 173, 179–81, 187–8, 223–4, 233, (man) 237–8, (woman) 238–9, (parent) 239–40, (getting best from) 240, 285
Hurry Up/Be Strong 165–7
Hurry Up/Please 163–5
Hurry Up/Try Hard 165
hysterical personality *see* Please

id 14, 30
immaturity of men 52

impasse 66–7
imprinting 72, 84
incestuous impulses 50–2, 63–4
inconsistency 43
indecisiveness 66–7
independent thinker 163
indigestion 145
individual differences 121–3
infantile person 69
inferiority feelings *see* Try Hard
injunctions 48–9, 112, 113, 119, 300 *see also* messages
intelligence 132–3
interests 114, 115
irrationality 12

jealousy 147
joy 34, 35, 112, 113, 115, 116, 117, 120, 148, 210, 257, 258–9, 281
joyless person 69
judgement 66, 67, 70

'Kick me' 121
knowledge 42–3, 49, 57–8, 116, 122

language 17
latency 57–9, 62, 153
laughter 286–7
Little Professor 45–6, 47, 57, 88, 112, 173, 257, 300
lively conformist 165
love 10, 89, 96–8, 99, 147, 218, 221, 277–9
   falling in 207–15, 258
love between parents and children 62, 97, 101, 102, 103, 106, 109–112, 141, 146
loving 193–6, 231
luck 29, 148

magic 58–9, 132
Maladaptor 125–7, 300
manic-depressive personality 158–60

Index

manic personality *see* Hurry Up
marriage (ideal) 214, (failure) 228, (ideal) 280
masculinity 275
maturity 116, 141
meaning 18–9, 28, 29, 30, 34, 92–3, 99, 115, 116, 126, 135, 171, 173, 258, 272, 280 *see also* purpose of relationship
messages 54, 84–8, 94, 102, 108, 109, 110, 113, 114, 115, 119, 173, 176, 300
metaphor 99–102
miniscript 10, 124–130, 157–8, 300
money (and time) 96, 134, 139, 145, 150, 155
morality 49, 52–3, 64, 110, 119
mortality 28, 30, 58, 94, 99, 119, 131
mysticism 29–30, 31, 38, 79, 171–2

national stereotypes 169–70
Natural Child 44–5, 47, 57, 59, 88, 89, 112, 119, 143, 165, 256, 257, 300
necessity 32, 35, 119
need 223–4
'Now I've got you, you son-of-a-bitch' 121
nurturing 52–3

obsessive-compulsive personality *see* Be Perfect
Oedipus complex 16, 50–6, 63, 197–202, 203, 211, 279
one to six 143
one to three 47–50, 61, 94, 106
only children 143
operant conditioning 12–15

pain 8, 27–8, 29, 31, 35, 36, 37, 38, 42, 80, 85, 87, 95, 98, 102, 103, 104, 106, 109, 110, 111, 112–7, 119, 120, 124, 157, 171–5, 210, 258–60, 274, 279, 281–2
of love 10, 57–8, 97–8, 137
paranoic personality *see* Hurry Up
parent 47, 55, 58, 60–1, 63, 64, 94–5, 97, 102–3, 141, 146, 147, 149, 151, 161, 162, 169, 214, 274, 279
Parent ego state 43, 47, 50–6, 57, 58, 59, 63, 64, 66, 67, 68, 69, 71, 88, 89, 102, 103, 104, 109, 112, 119, 125, 142, 148, 152, 153, 161, 162, 165, 211, 233, 257, 275, 300–1
parental feelings 47, 60–1, 63–4
parental power 61, 94
parental responsibility 65
passionate philosopher 160
passive-aggressive personality *see* Please
passivity 34
payoff 120, 121, 124, 125, 126, 301
'peek-a-boo' 46
permissions 45, 46, 64, 119, 301
Persecutor 120–1, 153, 222, 226, 283, 301
Please 124, 125, 126, 140–5, 176, 181–3, 184, 225, 240, (man) 241–2, (woman) 242–3, (parent) 243–4, (getting best from) 244–5
Please/Be Strong 168
Please/Try Hard 167–8
pleasure 36–8, 85, 95, 115, 119, 256–7
prejudice 67, 71
proud loser 169
psychoanalysis 11, 13–4, 15, 17, 44, 70, 71, 72, 73, 81, 103, 132–3
psychotherapy 26, 41, 56, 60–1, 70, 80, 158, 159, 173, 228, 251, 256
puberty 58, 59–62, 138, 153

punishment 14, 29, 41, 47–8, 159, 161
purpose *see* meaning
purpose of relationship 203–7, 277–84

quiet achiever 169

racket 125, 301
rationality 12
reality 42–3, 89, 90–1
relationships between the types 258–269
religion 17–18, 94, 99, 131, 132
repetition compulsion 14, 92, 113, 120, 209, 258
Rescuer 120–1, 153, 154, 225, 283, 302
responsible leader 161
revenge 201, 214, 279
righteous blamer 160–1
righteousness 97, 220–2, (table) 229, 273
risk 26–7, 95
roles 120–1
roving adventurer 165

safety 25–6, 47, 48, 95
sanity 24, 90, 114
schizoid personality *see* Try Hard
schizophrenia *see* Hurry Up
scientific materialism 18
script 89, 94, 114, 115, 119, 125, 302
self 43, 45, 79, 126, 171, 273
self-esteem 29–30, 38, 39, 62, 63, 218–9, 274–5 *see also* sexual self-esteem
self-righteousness *see* righteousness
self-sufficiency 49, 52, 71, 218
selfishness 36–7, 97, 274
sense 39, 42, 87, 88, 116, 119, 121, 173, 230

separation of child from parents 136
separation of parents 58
seventy 79
sex and sexuality 16, 38, 53, 55, 58, 59, 62, 89, 131–2, 135, 152, 227–9, 276, 286
sex education 58
sexual
  desire and fulfillment 37, 38, 39, 55, 61, 62
  promiscuity 139, 166
  self-esteem 51–2, 62, 63–4
sharing 54
six to twelve 57–9, 88, 93, 132, 153
six to twelve months 45–6
six year old 56–7, 63
sixteen to twenty-one 63–5, 107
sixty-three 79
skills 49, 54, 72
smothering person 69
socialization 47–50, 53–4
sorry sinner 163–5
stroke (illness) 155
stroke balance 114
stroke currencies 85
stroke deprivation 39, 43, 70
strokes 14, 39–42, 49, 53, 84–8, 92, 108, 112–4, 173
sublimation 11, 257
superego 14
survival 39, 93–6, 119, 173
symbiosis 224
  between parents 97

talent 115, 171–6
target strokes 86–7, 114, 195, 197
temperament 44
tenderness 54–5, 234
theories 23–6
thirty-eight to forty-four 76–7, 89
thirty-five to thirty-six 76
thirty-four 76

Index

thought and effort 96
three to six 47, 50–6, 93, 94, 106–7
time and money 96, 134, 139, 145, 150, 155
timidity 116
transactions 120, 195–6, 302
Transactional Analysis (TA) 10, 13–15, 17, 19, 43–4, 57, 72, 80–1, 155, 302–3
transcendence of ego *see* mysticism
transits 73–4, 80–1, 89, 204–5, 206, 303
truth 23–7, 28, 89, 110, 116, 119
Try Hard 124, 126, 146–51, 160, 184–7, 188, 226, (man) 245–6, (woman) 246–7, (parent) 247–8, (getting best from) 248–50
Try Hard/Be Strong 169

turbulent person 69
twelve to sixteen 59–62, 107
twelve to twenty-one 93–4, 107
  see also puberty, adolescence
twenty-eight to thirty 75
twenty-four to twenty-five 75
twenty-one to twenty-two 75

ulcers 150
uncaring person 69
uncommitted doubter 158–60
unconscious 102–6, 113, 116

vanity 121
Victim 120–1, 153, 223, 225, 226, 283, 303
virtue 29, 116, 125

' "Why don't you?" "Yes, but . . ." ' 120–1, 155